FIELDWORK

The Human Experience

LIBRARY OF ANTHROPOLOGY

Editor: Anthony L. LaRuffa

Editorial Assistant: Phyllis Rafti

Advisory Board: Edward Bendix, Robert DiBennardo,
May Ebihara, Paul Grebinger, Bert Salwen, Joel Savishinsky

ISSN: 0141-1012
Other volumes in preparation

FIELDWORK   The Human Experience
Edited by Robert Lawless, Vinson H. Sutlive, Jr., and Mario D. Zamora

This book is part of a series. The publisher will accept continuation orders
which may be cancelled at any time and which provide for automatic
billing and shipping of each title in the series upon publication. Please
write for details.

FIELDWORK

The Human Experience

Edited by

Robert Lawless
University of Florida

Vinson H. Sutlive, Jr.
College of William and Mary

Mario D. Zamora
College of William and Mary

Gordon and Breach Science Publishers
New York   London   Paris

Gordon and Breach, Science Publishers, Inc.
One Park Avenue
New York, NY 10016

Gordon and Breach Science Publishers Ltd.
42 William IV Street
London WC2N 4DE

Gordon & Breach
58, rue Lhomond
75005 Paris

Library of Congress Cataloging in Publication Data
Main entry under title:

Fieldwork: the human experience.

(Library of anthropology, ISSN 0141-1012)
Bibliography: p.
1. Ethnology – Field work – Addresses, essays, lectures.
I. Lawless, Robert,   II. Sutlive, Vinson H.   III. Zamora, Mario D.
IV. Series.
GN346.F53 1982   306'.07'2   82-11955
ISBN 0-677-16460-2

Introduction to the Series

One of the notable objectives of the *Library of Anthropology* is to provide a vehicle for the expression in print of new, controversial, and seemingly "unorthodox" theoretical, methodological, and philosophical approaches to anthropological data. Another objective follows from the multidimensional or holistic approach in anthropology which is the discipline's unique contribution toward understanding human behavior. The books in the series will deal with such fields as archaeology, physical anthropology, linguistics, ethnology and social anthropology. Since no restrictions will be placed on the types of cultures included, a New York or New Delhi setting will be considered as relevant to anthropological theory and method as the highlands of New Guinea.

The *Library* is designed for a wide audience and, whenever possible, technical terminology will be kept to the minimum required. In some instances, however, a book may be unavoidably somewhat esoteric and consequently will appeal only to a small sector of the reading population — advanced undergraduate students and graduate students in addition to professional social scientists.

My hopes for the readers are twofold: first, that they will enjoy learning about people, second, and perhaps more important, that the readers will come to experience a feeling of oneness with humankind.

New York City   *Anthony L. LaRuffa*

Introduction to the Series

This volume

is

dedicated to Nathan Altshuler, Professor of Anthropology and Founder of the Department of Anthropology, The College of William and Mary in Virginia, for his significant contributions to American anthropology.

Contents

Introduction: Human Variations in Fieldwork

Until a little over two decades ago anthropological fieldwork was one of the greatest mysteries of all scientific and humanistic endeavors – to all, that is, except the appropriately initiated anthropologists. In the uniformed stereotype of the lay public these courageous (or foolhardy) souls – dressed most probably in pith helmet and knee socks – left the comforts of family, friends, and civilization to actually live, eat, and perhaps even hunt with unlettered savages for interminable periods of time under the hot sun, over the frozen tundra, through the dense, dangerous jungle. And anthropologists for the most part seemed content to let the public think what it wished and did little – until recently – to correct, augment, or deny the stereotype.

Such a situation reflected no particular intent on the part of anthropologists to fool the public; they simply were doing other things for other audiences – audiences composed for the most part of other anthropologists, various cross-culturally oriented behavioral and social scientists, and perhaps a sophisticated humanist or two. Many of the readers in this audience had already gone through some sort of fieldwork initiation, others had strong powers of empathy (or imagination), and still others – hopefully a small group – probably simply missed the inevitably unstated point of fieldwork. The point being of course that fieldwork cannot be stated but must be experienced.

In the 1960s when books on the experience of anthropological fieldwork began to appear, it became clear to all that the experience is both more and less than the stereotype suggested. It is less romantic because not all fieldworkers suffer the tundra, jungle, and sun, and few dress (or behave) like heroes out of a Tarzan movie; most are simply serious, hardworking professionals. It is more exciting than any stereotype could anticipate because the rewards are revolutionary – for example, the startling discovery of the psychosocial comforts and temporal affluence of preagricultural peoples. Nevertheless, personal accounts of the efforts involved in gathering the data that lead to these revelations were kept at a minimum throughout most of the history of anthropology. Until recently such accounts were even considered by many anthropologists to be unprofessional. Two anthropologists with an enormous amount and variety of fieldwork experience between them write of "the tradition — almost a code — of the third person: the anthropologist does not go to the field to discover or write of himself but to write of the subjects of his research" (Kimball and Watson, 1972: 2).

Indeed, the published accounts of the results of fieldwork, the ethnographies, conform to fairly well standardized reporting procedures. These procedures, from sophisticated research designs to simple categories of phenomena to be described, have been widely discussed, though there is a myth about research methods even among trained anthropologists; as one reports, "In anthropology we believe that there is not much literature on field methods. That's not quite true. There's an unbelievable amount of literature, but it's scattered widely through time and across many journals" (Agar, 1980: 11).

Despite the neatness suggested by most of these writings on methods, the personal experience of fieldwork encompasses enormously complex variations in personality, environment, customs, climates, beliefs, and so forth — all further complicated by the intercultural character of fieldwork with its explosive potential for interpersonal misunderstandings and conflicts. Nothing in the field is ever quite so clear as it was back home. And a lot of the unfamiliar experiences and strange events in the field somehow become understandable only when anthropologists return home to face the demands for a structured ethnography! One of the editors of this volume has, for example, addressed himself to the complicating variable of "accidents":

> As, I think, with most anthropological fieldwork, my experiences at the time seemed to be composed of an uncomfortably large number of half-understood events and apparently accidental happenings, which included going places I did not intend to go and hearing things I did not expect to hear. Most such "accidents" do not find their way into the standard academic literature for a variety of reasons, e.g., investigators may feel that confessing anything less than a smooth fieldwork experience may make them appear somewhat less than professional, most social paradigms emphasize final results and perhaps formal methods but not informal learning experiences. I suspect, however, that many of the data gathered in the field and much of their initial interpretation — which, I think, always begins in the field — result from lessons learned by accident, i.e. unexpected events unanticipated in the research design" (Lawless, 1979: 481).

In contrast to the actual experience, a formal definition of fieldwork presents it as a rather straightforward activity, a by-product of the investigative perspective of the natural sciences. Fieldwork is, then, "the act of inquiring into the nature of phenomena by studying them at first hand in the environments in which they naturally exist or occur" (Georges and Jones, 1981: 1). The expectation is that the inquiry will lead to understanding. Therefore it makes sense that "to understand a society, the anthropologist has traditionally immersed himself in it, learning, as far as possible, to think, see, feel, and sometimes act as a member of its culture and at the same time as a trained anthropologist from another culture" (Powdermaker, 1966: 9).

The paradox of fieldwork should now be obvious. Anthropologists are both observers and observees. In addition to the naturalistic methods of, let's say, botanists, who may study plants firsthand and indeed observe them in their natural environment, anthropological fieldworkers identify and empathize with the objects of their study, for they are studying members of their own species. Furthermore the "objects" that anthropologists study give their own explanations for their beliefs and behaviors − explanations that make more and more sense as the fieldworker comes more and more to think, see, feel, and act as a member of the target culture − even while the fieldworker-anthropologist is supposed to be striving toward or maintaining or even intensifying scientific objectivity. In fact, the reason for the stress on objectivity in gathering data and reporting the results of fieldwork (and for the commonly lamented sterility of ethnographies) springs from this bifurcated nature of fieldwork − anthropologist as friend and stranger, anthropologist as participant and observer, anthropologist and citizen and scientist, anthropologist as first person and third person, anthropologist as there but not there, present but unobtrusive, recording but not recorded. Precisely because of the personal presence of humanness, pure scientific objectivity is impossible to obtain. Disciplined subjectivity should be the goal − a goal made possible only through a clarification of the human variations in fieldwork.

These two aspects of fieldwork are so firmly entrenched that anthropologists who write about both the scientific results and their personal experiences usually find that they must write two books (see, e.g., Turnbull, 1961; and Turnbull, 1965). The ambiguity often noted in Claude Levi-Strauss's autobiographical account (see 1963) partially reflects the discomfort felt by many anthropologists with the mixture of personal feelings and abstract models in *Tristes Tropiques*.

Part of the reason for the paucity of writings on certain aspects of fieldwork may be simply due to its newness. Although the history of fieldwork is a sadly neglected area, at least one book gives a fairly substantial introduction, tracing it back to the spread of early empires such as the Greek and the Roman (see Wax, 1971: 21-41). But Franz Boas and Bronislaw Malinowski in the early part of this century were the first to

xiv   INTRODUCTION

live for acceptable lengths of time in alien societies and to systematically investigate and report alien beliefs and behaviors — both activities now regarded as hallmarks of modern anthropological fieldwork. For the most part anthropologists interested in improving these fieldwork activities concentrated their writings on the techniques of data gathering. A 1967 book, for example, carries an annotated bibliography of 348 items on fieldwork, and almost all of them are technical pieces scattered about in scholarly journals (see Jogmans and Gutkind, eds., 1967: 214-271). By 1980 we can discern a shift away from a focus on the technical side of methods to a growing concern with broader issues of ethics, rapport, and investigator set. A book published in that year carries about 300 items dealing specifically with the qualitative aspects of fieldwork (see Shaffir, Stebbins, and Turowetz, 1980).

The 1960s and 1970s witnessed the appearance of books that discuss the scientiific and epistemological issues surrounding fieldwork (see, e.g., Brim and Spain, 1974; and Pelto and Pelto, 1978), as well as readily available accounts of the technical side of their own fieldwork by anthropologists "who had been there" (see, e.g., Chagnon, 1974; and Beattie, 1965). In the 1970s and 1980s there even became available cookbook-type approaches for students wishing to do fieldwork (see, e.g., Crane and Angrosino, 1974; and Spradley, 1980). During these decades there were also personal accounts of a more emotional character (see, e.g., Maybury-Lewis, 1965; Read, 1965; Powdermaker, 1966; Alland, 1975; and Mitchell, 1978), generally written in addition to the ethnography — whence comes the anthropologists' professional prestige — reflecting the traditional split into objective and subjective. The most striking example of this split may be seen in the contrast between the highly technical writings of Malinowski (see, e.g., 1935) and his controversial diary (see 1967), a lightly edited field journal that the author never intended for publication.

Around the beginning of the 1970s collections of personal statements about fieldwork began appearing (see, e.g., Spindler, ed., 1970; and Kimball and Watson, eds., 1972). Many of the collections focus on rather narrow topics. At least one early collection, a well-known one, concerns the relationships of various fieldworkers with their key informants (see Casagrande, 1960). Another book concentrates on the interethnicity of fieldwork (see Kimball and Watson, eds., 1972). Some of these collections are indeed highly specialized. We have an entire book that deals only with one variation — the gender of the fieldworker (see Golde, ed., 1970). We have another entire book that deals only with Indian anthropologists and anthropologists working in India (see Beteille and Madan, eds., 1975). There is also a highly instructive and personal account of the relationships of the novice fieldworker to his mentor back at the university (see Kimball and Patridge, 1979). A new type of book on fieldwork differing from the collections and from the single-person accounts is one in which the authors comb the literature to give a flavor of fieldwork with the various quotations from anthropologists and with discussions of classic fieldwork situations (see, e.g., Georges and Jones, 1980).

After this recitation of books on fieldwork some readers might ask, "Why another one?" More careful readers will recognize that the relatively few books previously discussed only skim the surface of the variables involved in fieldwork. The most complex of the variations concerns humans — as individuals and in groups.

These human variations include not only the personality of the fieldworker and its compatibility with those of the informants but also the sociocultural background of the fieldworker and its often unforeseen influence on intercultural interactions. In addition there exists the tricky question of just what the indigenes make of the "face" the fieldworker puts on — an interpretation that may be entirely different from what the fieldworker anticipates. These variations also include such singularly important contrasts as whether the fieldworker is male or female, single or with a family, an indigene or a foreigner, or is in a hometown or in a new place. The influence of many of these variations are strikingly illustrated by several of the chapters in this volume. Some of the variations are not quite as clear cut as these contrasts suggests. More subtle variations include the initial identities of the fieldworker and how they change through interaction with the indigenes. The initial identities of the fieldworker may also change through events in fieldworkers' lives during intervals when they are away from the field. Still another variable concerns the prefield commitments of fieldworkers. The influences of many of these variations also are illustrated by several of the chapters in this volume.

This book, then, focuses on the important issue of fieldworker identity and on the development of this identity in traditional and modern types of fieldwork. Varieties of this theme include variations in the background and personality of the fieldworker and variations in the culture of the group studied and in the personalities of the informants. Among the messages of this book is that human variations can make a difference in how the identity of the fieldworker emerges. Another message is that most anthropologists seem to have found an acceptable role — or have forged an acceptable one — that allows fieldwork to get done.

It must be mentioned at this point that not all fieldwork has been successful; there have been failures. All anthropologists know about them through the cocktail circuit, but they are rarely written up. As editors we first wanted to do a book titled *Failed Fieldwork*, thinking that much could be learned from such a book, but we could not get anyone to contribute chapters.

Some of the chapters in this volume do illustrate extremely difficult field situations, and we think there is indeed much to learn from almost everything that happens in the field. We still do not know, for example, how to match fieldworker to culture. Certainly some anthropologists are better suited, by virtue of their personality, to work in certain cultures rather than in others. We really do not know enough, however, about these human variations to suggest which anthropologist should study what. A lot of grief might be avoided if we did. We hope there are some helpful lessons in the chapters that follow.

•   •   •

The opening chapter on "Learning Fieldwork" is by the dean of American anthropology, Charles Wagley and contains many lessons about fieldwork — lessons given to us as they were learned by Wagley during his first fieldwork experience as a graduate student in 1937 among the Indians of highland Guatemala. Wagley had the advice of the giants of second generation American anthropology — Alfred A. Kroeber, Margaret Mead, Ruth Benedict, Ruth Bunzel, A. Irving Hallowell, and others — but in the final analysis he had to learn his own lessons. One of these lessons is that fieldwork is a creative endeavor dependent on rather unpredictable accidents and human variations.

One lesson learned by "accident" was the value of the "returning fieldworker." Due to recurring illnesses Wagley took several weeks off to recuperate, and he returned to the field with his objectivity restored (as well as his health). In addition the warmth and openness of the indigenes was appreciably increased since they perceived Wagley's return as an indication that he sincerely wanted to live with them.

In another passage Wagley speaks of the physical awkwardness in attempting to participate in activities in which the indigenes are highly skilled through decades of practice. In this particular case the daily weeding of a maize field alongside his informants left Wagley too tired at the end of the day to record his experiences. He wisely suggests "passive participation and active observation."

The physical rigors of fieldwork are an important variable, and in the next chapter Robert Lawless emphasizes his conquest of the requirements for hiking in rugged mountains. Writing about events "On First Being an

Anthropologist" during his fieldwork in the highlands of Northern Luzon among a group of recently pacified headhunters, he implies that there is a close relationship between the physical adaptation with the habitat that every fieldworker must develop and the psychological identity that many anthropologists cultivate with the people among whom they live.

In the chapter by David Banks titled "From Structure to History in Malaya" we follow the fieldwork experiences of a black anthropologist working in an isolated region of western Malaysia. He feels that because of his identity as a non-white the indigenes were unable to fit him into the cultural slot reserved for the British — and by extension almost all other foreigners from First World nations. Because he was perceived as a non-white among non-whites in a world where whites ruled, he may have had an easier time establishing rapport. Banks takes each important category of informant and explains how rapport was established and what the advantages and obstacles were that stemmed from the human variations involved. These categories include the village headman, Banks's assistant, two teenage informants, the village shaman, and members of Banks's peer group in the village. Of specific professional interest is that the chapter details how field contact with specific groups caused Banks to shift the focus of his research from the description of structural systems to concern for historical problems of development. Banks also points out that his identity with one particular village faction lead to his anxiety that he was getting only one side of every story.

This problem of identification with a village faction and the resultant difficulty in establishing rapport with other factions is a recurring theme in the literature on anthropological fieldwork. In "Field Experiences in Three Societies" Enya P. Flores-Meiser describes how association with a faction hindered her fieldwork and then goes one step further in suggesting that fieldworkers' ability to establish penetrating rapport with differing socio-economic groups within the same society is probably rather limited. Flores-Meiser recounts and compares her experiences in three different fieldwork situations: as a Christian Filipino on a Moslem island, as a partially Westernized indigene studying her own natal community, and as a total outsider studying the Japanese in Brazil. In each of these variations she had to maintain a delicate insider-outsider balance.

Flores-Meiser also brings into play a little discussed factor: how anthropologists choose the peoples that they study. Such a choice is probably less rational than we like to pretend. Flores-Meiser tells of her childhood fascination about the Moslems derived from grade school textbooks. Fieldworkers often have a "preanthropological" personal curiosity about certain peoples, tribes, nations, groups that may have been nurtured from childhood fantasies, adolescent crushes, adult love affairs. Do anthropologists who start from such idiosyncratic premises operate differently in the field? An interesting question that needs further investigation.

In "The Conversion of a Missionary" Vinson H. Sutlive, Jr., thoroughly explores the topics of "missionary as anthropologist" and "anthropologist as missionary" — topics maligned by gossip, misinformed by stereotypes, and rarely approached with understanding. Sutlive went among the Iban of Sarawak holding one view of Christianity, and he returned with another. The conversion well illustrates the human experience of fieldwork.

Further developing an understanding of fieldwork and missionaries, Daniel Hughes writes of some uniquely "Contrasting Experiences in Fieldwork." During 11 months in Micronesia he was a Jesuit priest. Later, during his work in the Philippines, he was married and had a son. Hughes's graphic portrayal of his changing circumstances clearly shows how anthropologists' personal characteristics and situations affect fieldwork experiences and the data gathered. In Micronesia, for example, a detailed study of local sex practices would have been impossible for Hughes as a priest, but he could obtain delicate data on traditional and contemporary political systems by taking advantage of the positive image the indigenes have of priests. Hughes's wife in the Philippines was an indigene, and this proved to be both advantageous and disadvantageous.

Anthropologists have often married into the cultures they study, and the effect of having an indigene looking over your shoulder, so to speak, is again another human variation that needs further investigation. Indeed anthropology as a traditional Euroamerican activity now has professional indigenes looking over its shoulder. R. S. Khare, the author of "Between Being Near and Distant," is an Indian studying Indian culture. Introducing the term *native anthropologist*, Khare vividly illustrates the ambivalent burden for indigenous anthropologists of identifying with an essentially foreign profession and thereby becoming alienated from their own nativity. Khare goes on to discuss his identity and passage among three key informants and shows how each became a teacher and presented a process of learning in fieldwork.

As Khare and Flores-Meiser show us, anthropologists need not feel that they must travel thousands of miles from home to find a group exotic enough to deserve their attention. What is most fascinating may be right in our own backyards. Victor A. Liguori went only 20 miles from his university into the Guinea Marshes of southeastern Gloucester County, Virginia, and found an illiterate people whose 17th century English was beyond his comprehension. In "Come Ahead, If You Dare" he explains this language and how he got along with the locally feared Guineamen. Of particular interest is Liguori's discussion of the prejudice in the public schools against the children of these people. And again in terms of human variations, Liguori gives some well-founded warnings on knowing the intentions and propensities of your colleagues and acquaintances before introducing them as "friends" to the people you are working among.

Allan Burns' chapter "Feds and Locals" reviews the variations in fieldwork found in applied anthropology settings. Burns argues that traditional fieldwork and applied evaluation fieldwork are different in several dimensions. Applied work takes place in familiar contexts, usually in an ethnographer's own culture. Applied work exists in a shifting political environment where research is one of many resources that competing interest groups seek to use for their benefit. Because of these and other differences, Burns suggests that applied fieldwork socializes anthropologists away from the academy and toward the world of professional policy analysis. His own experience gained while working for a research company as an anthropologist is used to illustrate four stages of fieldwork as a socializing institution. For Burns the variety in fieldwork does not reside at the level of the fieldworker or local residents but in the interaction of fieldwork as research, a local community, and extra-local policy makers.

Mario D. Zamora stresses the significance of his "Initial Encounter, Choice, and Change in Field Research" in a Central Luzon village. Specifically he raises the question to what extent does the initial fieldwork experience determine career identity and choice. Zamora also underscores the need for an "anthropology of the anthropologists" to understand changing thoughts and experiences in fieldwork and to understand the emerging ethics of anthropologists from the Third World.

In the next to the last chapter, Patricia Snyder Weibust writes of fieldwork in an extended metaphor, comparing her experiences in a small village in the Philippines to the flood and ebb of the tides as she brings her world into contact with the rural Philippines. As she points out, "Filipinos Were My Teachers." Especially enlightening at a time of increasing numbers of female fieldworkers is the manner in which she handles the constantly amorous advances of the men of the village.

In the last chapter Charles Keyes essentially sums up the thrust of this volume by emphasizing the changing identities of the fieldworker in an alien culture. Using his work in a village in northeastern Thailand as an example, Keyes points out that the fieldworker does not simply gain an identity and then maintain the identity and accompanying role but instead the situation is more compex and always in flux. The fieldworker is plugged into the electricity of the social current producing static and sparks and causing the indigenes to reassert their own cultural assumptions, for, as Keyes explains, the social identities of his wife and himself "sprang not from our peculiar nature as undefinable aliens but from the cultural premises which the villagers employed in determining all social identities, their own included." The fieldworkers' understanding of their identities therefore aids in the understanding of the culture of the people they are working among.

This introduction has highlighted some of the features in the chapters that follow and has shown that all the chapters illustrate in one way or another the importance of human variations in fieldwork. One of the hallmarks of fieldwork and writings about it is that all investigators and readers learn their own lessons. There is much more in these chapters than we can cover in a brief introduction. Readers will discover this on their own. We do not want to delay them any longer.

The Editors

REFERENCES

Agar, Michael H., 1980, *The Professional Stranger: An Informal Introduction to Ethnography.* New York: Academic.

Alland, Alexander, Jr., 1975, *When the Spider Danced: Notes from an African Village.* Garden City, New York: Doubleday.

Beattie, John, 1965, *Understanding an African Kingdom: Bunyoro.* New York: Holt, Rinehart and Winston.

Beteille, Andre, and T. N. Madan, eds., 1975, *Encounter and Experience: Personal Accounts of Fieldwork.* Honolulu: University Press of Hawaii.

Brim, John A., and David H. Spain, 1974, *Research Design in Anthropology: Paradigms and Pargmatics in the Testing of Hypothesis.* New York: Holt, Rinehart and Winston.

Casagrande, Joseph B., ed., 1960, *In the Company of Man: Twenty Portraits of Anthropological Informants.* New York: Harper & Row.

Crane, Julia G. and Michael V. Angrosino, 1974, *Field Projects in Anthropology: A Study Handbook.* Morristown, New Jersey: General Learning.

Chagnon, Napoleon A., 1974, *Studying the Yanomamo.* New York: Holt, Rinehart and Winston.

Freilich, Morris, ed., 1977, *Marginal Natives at Work: Anthropologists in the Field.* Cambridge, Massachusetts: Schenkman.

Georges, Robert A., and Michael O. Jones, 1980, *People Studying People: The Human Element in Fieldwork.* Berkeley: University of California Press.

Golde, Peggy, ed., 1970, *Women in the Field: Antropological Experiences.* Chicago: Aldine.

Jongmans, D. G., and P. C. W. Gutkind, eds., 1967, *Anthropological in the Field.* Assen, Holland: Van Gorcum.

Kimball, Solon T., and Janes B. Watson, 1972, Introduction. In *Crossing Cultural Boundaries: The Anthropological Experience.* San Francisco: Chandler.

Kimball, Solon T., and James B. Watson, eds., 1972, *Crossing Cultural Boundaries: The Anthropological Experience.* San Francisco: Chandler.

Kimball, Solon T., and William L. Partridge, 1979, *The Craft of Community Study: Fieldwork Dialogues.* Gainesville: University Press of Florida.

Lawless, Robert, 1979, Differing Perspectives on Work Among the Pasil Kalingas of Northern Luzon. Asian Profile 7: 481-490.

Levi-Strauss, Claude, 1963, *Tristes Tropiques.* New York: Atheneum (first published in French in 1955).

Malinowski, Bronislaw, 1935, *Coral Gardens and Their Magic, Vol. I: Soil-Tilling and Agricultural Rites in the Trobriand Islands.* London: George Allen & Unwin.

1967, *A Diary in the Strict Sense of the Term.* New York: Harcourt, Brace & World.

Maybury-Lewis, David, 1965, *The Savage and the Innocent.* Boston: Beacon.

Mitchell, William E., 1978, *The Bamboo Fire: An Anthropologist in New Guinea.* New York: W. W. Norton.

Pelto, Pertti J., and Gretel H. Pelto, 1978, *Anthropological Research: The Structure of Inquiry.* Cambridge, England: Cambridge University Press.

Powdermaker, Hortense, 1966, *Stranger and Friend: The Way of an Anthropologist.* New York: W. W. Norton.

Read, Kenneth E., 1965, *The High Valley.* New York: Charles Scribner's Sons.

Shaffir, William B., Robert A. Stebbins, and Allan Turowetz, eds., 1980, *Fieldwork Experience: Qualitative Approaches to Social Research.* New York: St. Martin's Press.

Spindler, George D., ed., 1970, *Being an Anthropologist: Fieldwork in Eleven Cultures.* New York: Holt, Rinehart and Winston.

Spradley, James P. 1980, *Participant Observation.* New York: Holt, Rinehart and Winston.

Turnbull, Colin, 1961, *The Forest People: A Study of the Pygmies of the Congo.* New York: Simon and Schuster.

1965, *Wayward Servants: The Two Worlds of the African Pygmies.* Garden City, New York: Natural History Press.

Wax, Rosalie H., 1971, *Doing Field Work: Warnings and Advice.* Chicago: University of Chicago Press.

CHAPTER 1

Learning Fieldwork: Guatemala

CHARLES WAGLEY

Once when Alfred Kroeber was teaching at Columbia University after his first retirement from the University of California at Berkeley, I consulted him over lunch about a course on fieldwork methods which I had decided to teach. I had been hoping for some words of wisdom as to how to organize my course, but instead I was cut short. "Some can and some can't," he said (if I remember his words correctly), and he passed on to a more interesting subject.

I then began to reflect on how, when, and where I had learned fieldwork methods. In the late 1930's when I had been a graduate student at Columbia University, Margaret Mead had given some lectures on fieldwork methods which I had not attended but of which I had heard second hand. Ruth Benedict had asked us to analyze ethnographic monographs from the point of view of what one might ask in further fieldwork in view of theoretical interests of that time. We had at hand a lengthy set of questions called "Psychological Leads for Field Workers" in mimeographed form which I understood had been prepared by Ruth Bunzel, Irving Hallowell and others (it was unsigned). All of us studying at Columbia in those days had talked at length about fieldwork with our slightly older colleagues who had been "in the field." In fact, the line of prestige rank which set off the "lower" from the "upper class" graduate students was field experience. Gene Weltfish, Jules Henry, Edward Kennard and George Herzog tried to teach me phonetic transcription of native texts, but without much success. In fact, I had never had any formal training in field methods per se. It was, I suppose, something expected of any professional anthropologist, to be learned as part of anthropological culture transmitted informally from one generation to another. I did teach the course on field methods but I cannot remember how it was organized or what I said. I did not teach it again.

In 1937 in my second year of graduate study, I remember that I was frankly tired of study and of listening to lectures. In modern terms, I was a good candidate to drop out of graduate work for a year or more. Instead, I began to think about escaping into field research. I had taken a course on

Middle American ethnology with Ruth Bunzel in which she had allowed
me to read her then-unpublished study of Chichicastenango (Guatemala)
(Bunzel, 1953) and she had lectured on her rather recent field experience
in Chamula, Chiapas state of Mexico. Middle American sounded far more
interesting to me than the Blackfoot, the Paiute, the Ute or the North
American southwest where colleagues had recently done fieldwork. At
this point, I had no specific problem in mind, although out of Ruth
Bunzel's Chichicastenango monograph the pattern of land tenure and the
disruptive effects of land inheritance on the family (i.e. among brothers)
had interested me. So I set about preparing myself for field research in
Guatemala without any idea as to how I might finance it or when I might
be able to realize it.

To prepare myself for fieldwork, I began studying Spanish. I had had
two years of the language in high school and could read it with some
difficulty. I soon discovered an Uruguayan widow living in an apartment
near the university who agreed to give me private lessons in conversation
for the, even then, modest price of seventy-five cents per hour. For over
two months, I went to her apartment each morning from eight to nine
a.m. for conversation. After about three weeks, my Spanish lesson
included a free breakfast, for she soon discovered that I arrived in jejune.
Dona Maria — I wish I could remember her last name — was not a professional teacher, but by instinct she used the most modern methods.
After establishing the time and price of my lessons in our first interview,
she never again used a word of English. In Spanish we conversed during
our breakfast and discussed the headlines of the New York Times, and she
told me of her life in Montevideo and of her children who had migrated to
New York. She also taught me Spanish etiquette — not to place my hat on
the bed (bad luck) and, in time, how to kiss her lightly on one cheek as
I arrived and left. Little did I know that some of the vocabulary I was
acquiring was Porteno Spanish and would be puzzling or totally unknown
in Guatemala. With extra study in my room and five conversation lessons
each week, my Spanish became passable and understandable but hardly
fluent.

I also read anything I could find on Guatemala. Oliver La Farge and
Douglas Byers' *The Year Bearer's People* (1931) was particularly helpful.
Sol Tax's article describing each Indian municipio as a distinct endo-
gamous ethnic unit appeared that year and it clarified for me the problem
of the unit of research and the local community to be considered (Tax,
1937). This had been vague before. The German scholar, Schultze-Jene
(1933), had discussed the Quiche (a linguistic group) almost as if they
formed a "tribe." I also read history and called on Professor Frank

Tannenbaum whose books on Mexico I had read. Tannenbaum was always a maverick. He reeled off a list of books I should read but he urged me to go to Guatemala as soon as I could. "Spend some months or a year in Guatemala and then the books will have some meaning" he said – at least that is what he said that he said when years later we discussed my visit.

I soon learned that Oliver La Farge lived in New York and Ruth Bunzel knew him, so I made a date to visit with him in his small apartment at 79th and Madison Avenue. La Farge had received an MA degree in Anthropology from Harvard, and had worked for a time on the staff of the Middle American Institute at Tulane University from which his field trips to southern Mexico and Guatemala had been financed. He was also a successful author: his novel *Laughing Boy* won the Pulitzer Prize and was made into a movie; and he regularly published in the *New Yorker* and later in *Esquire*. At the time, he was a free lance writer and also served as Executive Secretary of the National Association on Indian Affairs (later changed to Association on American Indian Affairs), the office of which was his apartment. I liked him at once and he was tolerant enough to give his time to a curious graduate student. Also, I suspect he liked a one-man audience to listen to his stories of travel and ethnographic study in Chiapas (Mexico) and Huehuetenango (Guatemala). His income, I discovered after several visits, was precarious for the moment, for he had successfully run through the small fortune which *Laughing Boy* had brought in. He invited me to dinner and our meal was brown beans and bread ("a substitute for tortillas," he explained). I learned that he had an unpublished monograph on Santa Eulalia, a municipio in the Cuchumatanes mountains of north-western Guatemala (La Farge, 1947), and was pleased when he allowed me to take chapters of it home to read. I visited La Farge perhaps a dozen times. Some of these visits were almost formal ethnographic lessons, while others were "bull sessions" in which he transmitted to me problems, methods, and general advice on field work in northwestern Guatemala. By the end of 1936, I was hooked on Guatemala and more anxious than ever to go.

In January of 1937 I took my problem to Ruth Benedict. She listened carefully to what I had done to prepare for fieldwork and seemed to approve. At the moment, however, there were no funds: work outside the USA did not qualify for WPA which had granted some support for anthropologists through a writer's project, and I was not far enough along in my studies to qualify for an SSRC or NRC fellowship which were very few in number and highly competitive. I was not disappointed in these prospects, for I had little hope for a grant at that time. However, by the end of the month Benedict called me to her office and informed me that

she had found $600.00 for my field trip. Just where she "found" this sum
I will never know — from departmental funds, from private sources, or
from her own pocket book? I do know, however, that I was asked to take
a metal, dismountable doll which Dr. David Levy, a well known New York
psychiatrist, was using to work with disturbed children. I was instructed
how to observe children playing with the doll — Did they identify it with
little brother, big brother, sister, mother, or father? Did they tear off its
head, arms, legs, or just cuddle it? The same "doll play technique" was
being used among the Pillaga in the Chaco by Jules Henry. It was understood that this was to be only a side product of my research. (I did do a
few tests in Santiago Chimaltenango and wrote a short report for Ruth
Benedict.) It is more than probable that Dr. Levy underwrote part of the
costs of my Guatemala field trip.

It may seem improbable today that $600 could support a field trip to
Guatemala of almost six months duration, but it did. The fare on the
United Fruit Lines from Philadelphia to Puerto Barrios was $100.00. I
sailed late in February for Guatemala, and returned by railroad through
Mexico, arriving in New York late in September of 1937. The overland trip
proved more expensive with one week in Mexico City, so I had to borrow
money from Texas relatives to make it to New York. My short stay in
Guatemala City in a small hotel seemed expensive, but in my small village
my expenses were fifty dollars a month including a small house, the salary
of an interpreter-assistant, and informant fees. There was little margin for
equipment — I borrowed Ruth Benedict's old folding Kodak and had no
typewriter. All of my clothes, equipment, and other personal effects fitted
into a small army locker.

When I sailed for Guatemala, I was as well prepared bookwise as was
possible in 1937. However, I was ill prepared to be seasick off of Cape
Hatteras. I bought a second class railroad ticket from Puerto Barrios to
Guatemala City and suffered through the day with crowds and lack of
food. I bought a plantain from a vendor at one station and thinking it but
a very large banana began to eat it raw — until my fellow passengers stopped me. I bought a papaya already parted in half and ate the black seeds
thinking they must be a spice (they are a good laxative). Arriving in
Guatemala City about seven p.m. I quickly bathed and changed clothes. At
eight p.m., I rushed to the hotel dining room only to find it closed — I
thought, for the day. I tried to explain to the clerk that I needed dinner
badly and he explained that the dining room, in good Spanish-American
style, would open at nine p.m. I was rather disoriented and in low spirits
for a day or two but carried letters to the staff members of the Carnegie
Institute of Washington (A. L. Kidder was excavating at Kaminaljuyu at

the time) and they gave me good advice and urged me to visit Sol Tax who was then in residence in Panajachel on Lake Atitlan.

My most valuable letter of recommendation, however, was written by Ruth Bunzel to Antonio Goubaud Carrera. At that time Goubaud was almost 30 years old. He had graduated from high school and had had some collage education in California. Although he was a member of a well known and aristocratic Guatemalan family (his grandfather had been President of the Republic) Tono, as I came to call him, earned his living as a tourist interpreter-guide for Clark's Tours. Anthropology was his hobby and he dreamed of doing graduate studies and then devoting himself to research.[1] He was even then well-versed in Guatemalan ethnology and had traveled throughout the country. He spent hours with me pouring over maps, giving me the names of hotels or pensiones at different places where I might stop, and arranging official letters for me to the *Jefes Politicos* (appointed governors) of several "Departamentos" (similar to States), as well as letters to several of his personal friends in Huehuetenango, the Departamento where I hoped to do my research.

In the middle of March 1937 I traveled by bus from Guatemala City to Panajachel hoping to consult with Sol Tax. There I found the Hotel Monterrey, recommended to me by Tono Goubaud, and after lunch the next day was guided to the little house in Panajachel where don Sol (Tax) lived. I was still very much a neophite — I arrived unannounced just after lunch at siesta time and had to arouse Tax and his wife from their rest. They were both charming, and Sol Tax took me for a walking tour through Panajachel. In one shady retreat, I met what seemed to me an Indian in the process of interviewing another Indian. I was confused until Tax explained that one was his assistant, Juan de Dios Rosales,[2] and the other was a Panajacheco informant. Tax persuaded me to remain another day since the staff of the Carnegie Institute was to meet there and I could meet Robert Redfield. Tax invited me to give up the Cuchumatanes and to do my research in nearby San Marcos de la Laguna, and the next day Redfield agreed, since I could then have Sol Tax's guidance from time to time. It was tempting, but I had spent too many hours with Oliver La Farge talking of the Cuchumatanes to modify my plans suddenly. I was able to catch a ride in a Carnegie car to visit Chichicastenango, Santa Cruz Quiche, and Momostenango, and was dropped off in Totonicapan where I spent 24 hours.

It was in Totonicapan that culture shock caught up with me with a vengeance. Totonicapan is over 8,000 feet above sea level. It was raining and cold. People walked through the damp dark streets wrapped in ponchos and blankets with their faces covered with head-kerchiefs or mufflers. My cheap boarding house was humid and drab. I remembered that I had a letter to the Jefe Politico so without anything to do decided to pay him a visit. My spirits improved in the Palacio. The Jefe Politico spoke some English. He invited me to tea, and I met his wife and young daughters who were rather fluent in English. We sat in a parlor waiting for tea and cakes when two aides suddenly arrived and the family and their visitors were moved quickly to another room on the other side of the Palacio. I enjoyed my tea and conversation and after a time, took my leave. The Jefe Politico accompanied me downstairs to the portico. There he explained our hurried move — it was to spare the sensibilities of his wife and daughters. He had forgotten that an execution by firing squad of two Indians, "nothing but vagrants who had robbed in the market," was to take place at five p.m. just below the parlor. He knew that I would understand the feelings of ladies and his grave problem of trying to keep order among brutes. I returned to my ugly pension in shock and spent a night without sleep. I would have liked to have returned as fast as possible to New York.

Instead I traveled on by bus to Huehuetenango, which I found to be a pleasant small city. A visit with the departmental Jefe Politico resulted in a circular letter to municipal *Intendentes* (i.e., appointed executive and judicial officers of each *municipio*) requesting that they provide transportation (a saddle horse) and a *mozo* (Indian guide) from one pueblo to another. A visit to Recinos Hermanos, the largest general store in town, soon resulted in some extra supplies and their acting as my bankers. I deposited my total funds (which were by then around four hundred dollars) with them and arranged to charge purchases and to draw cash from time to time. Again, this was a favor I owed to Tono Goubaud, for he was a friend of Andrian Recinos, who had written a rather good descriptive account of the Department of Huehuetenango many years earlier.

I took off by horse back down the Selegua River Valley to San Sebastian, then up into the heights of the Cuchumatanes mountains, the highest and most rugged range of Central America with peaks rising to as high as 12,000 feet above sea level. My route led me through Santa Isabel, San Juan Atitlan, Todos Santos, Concepcion, San Miguel Acatan, Santa Eulalia, Jacaltenango, San Antonio Huista, Petatan and finally Santiago Chimaltenango. For each of those *municipios*, I had rough statistics — census data, products, and the like. Among them I selected to study Santiago Chimaltenango for several reasons, both ethnographic and personal. Ethnographically it seemed a good choice because the people spoke Mam-Maya about which little had been written, because the population was small in comparison to other *municipios* with only approximately 1,500 people, and finally, because 908 of these people lived in a compact village rather than scattered about the rural zone in homesteads and small hamlets as they did in other *municipios*. A "full village" rather than an "empty village" as Sol Tax had characterized Guatemalan Indian *municipios* seemed logically easier to observe than scattered households. Then, by the time I reached Chimaltenango I was exhausted, suffering from a cold, tired of sleeping on the floors of town halls, and my behind was raw from the unaccustomed horse back travel. In Santiago Chimaltenango, I found a decent meal in the house of Dona Amalia Rojas and a cot in an empty house normally used to store maize. There were only five *ladino* (non-Indian) families in the village. They urged me to stay and explained that Santiago Chimaltenango was "muy alegre" while the other *municipios* with predominantly rural populations were "sad" and "cold." Raymond Stadelman, an agronomist contracted by the Carnegie Institute who was stationed in Todos Santos to study maize cultivation, had recommended Santiago Chimaltenango (of. Stadelman, 1940). Chimaltecos, he said, were "open, friendly, and pleasant" as compared to those inhabitants of San Juan Atitan and Todos Santos.

Thus, I stayed, and in time Santiago Chimaltenango proved to be a happy choice, for the Chimaltecos were just as Stadelman had described them to me.

At first, however, the Indians did not seem friendly at all. They stopped talking when I approached. Children fled into their mothers' arms and women withdrew into their homes as I walked through the village. Only the ladinos were friendly. I contracted with Dona Amelia to have three meals a day in her simple house for $20.00 per month — which was quite a bargain for she fed me eggs, beans, chicken, tortillas, and the bread which she baked on Saturdays. She allowed me to stay in the storage house without rent, which soon became my residence and in time my research office. Her husband, don Amalio Rojas (the same first name as his wife) was a taciturn character, short and heavy, with a long Pancho Villa-type mustachio. He made a poor living recruiting labor for coastal coffee *fincas* and buying maize (when he had the cash) during the low prices at harvest to be sold later when maize prices climbed. In contrast, Dona Amalia was talkative, eager, and motherly. She arranged for an Indian woman to launder my clothes and to clean out the store house in which I had settled, as well as two Indian youths to walk to Huehuetenango to fetch some supplies for me at Recinos Bros., to bring me some cash, and to carry back my rather heavy foot locker. Dona Amalia had two sons by a previous husband (a common-law husband according to other ladinos) whom she described as a tall gringo from Spain. One of these sons, Carmelo, who was about 20 years old, lived with her and I soon came to know him. He was almost six feet tall and badly dressed. He seemed to do nothing and she complained that he was "lazy" but that he was "well instructed" (i.e., at least four years of primary school). Carmelo took to walking with me through the village. I found that he spoke Mam fluently (he was born in Santiago Chimaltenango) and that he had an easy, bantering friendly relationship with the Indians. In fact, it was Carmelo who explained that the Indians thought that I was a Protestant missionary, but they wondered how I could be Protestant yet still smoke and drink aguardiente. The Indians had been warned against missionaries by the Padre who occasionally came to the village. Carmelo corrected this misapprehension and in his company I came to know in the course of two weeks a few Indian men. I realized that only a few spoke Spanish and that with the few months at my disposal, I would not learn Mam. So I hired Carmelo as my "secretario" (his title for the position) to act as my interpreter assistant. His salary at 50 cents a day was considered liberal, for this was five times the local pay for Indian day labor and about the same as the ladino "secretario" of the *municipio* received. With Carmelo's assistance serious field work began and during the next four months I worked more intensively and longer hours than I have ever worked before or since then in my whole lifetime. I was insecure about my ability and training, so made up for it by devoting myself perhaps too intensely to my task.

My main early problem was training Carmelo. He was proud of his white-collar occupation and eager to help. He found that his friendship with Indians impressed me; he treated them as intimates since they had known him as a boy. Carmelo was a ladino, however, and had all of the stereotypical prejudices against Indians characteristic of ladinos in Guatemala — they were "brutes," uncivilized," and mentally "inferior." But Carmelo's attitudes toward Indians in Santiago Chimaltenango were ambivalent and tempered by the fact that he had grown up often with only Indians as his playmates and friends. He was somewhat irritated by his foreign employer who treated Indians with respect and sought consciously to ingratiate himself with them. Carmelo taught me a list of Mam words and phrases including terms of address and polite expressions. I pent considerable time explaining what I wanted to learn. I stressed that I wanted to hear cases and examples and not just merely generalized explanations. After a few days he arranged for Gregorio Martin, a Chimalteco Indian of about forty years of age, to come to my house to teach me about Santiago Chimaltenango. Gregorio spoke considerable Spanish but he was not at ease in that language. He preferred to speak in

Mam and then to let Carmelo translate into Spanish for my benefit, but Gregorio often intervened in the translation process correcting Carmelo when he left out a detail. For over two weeks, Gregorio came each morning from about nine a.m. until midday to my house and each day interviews improved as Gregorio learned that I was interested in details of stories (myths and folklore), family life, and village affairs and Carmelo lerned to translate literally and not to embellish, abbreviate, or inject his own opinions. I was aware of the dangers of working through an interpreter but as weeks went by Carmelo developed into an excellent one. He even learned to translate texts of prayers I recorded phonetically in Mam word by word. Yet I checked and rechecked information garnered from such interviews and have reason to believe from ethnography done later in the same region of Guatemala that my data was generally sound.

I also had to train native Chimalteco informants. After the first two weeks, Gregorio did not return for a time since he had work to do in his garden, but he did serve as a major informant at different times throughout my stay in Santiago Chimaltenango in 1937. I worked with many others: Diego Martin, Francisco Aguilar, Diego Jimenez, Miguel Dias, and others too numerous to mention. The only woman who worked with me as a regular informant was Andrea Martin, a widow of about 55 years of age. Beginning with Gregorio I worked out a system of work with regular informants. I found a table around which the informant, Carmelo, and I sat. I took notes as Carmelo translated the information, reworking these same notes in the afternoon or at night into more coherent form. An interview would last from two to three hours after which the informant, the interpreter, and the anthropologist were exhausted. I paid such regular informants in cash after each interview at the rate of 15 to 20 cents (10 cents was a day's wage) per interview. The interview was as casual and informal as possible. I provided local cigarettes (crude tobacco rolled in yellow paper) and coffee from my thermos bottle. I made it clear that I paid for the time lost in other occupations and not for information. Thus, I never paid for information garnered when I visited a family in their home or when I sat outside the *Juzgado* (town hall) covering in Spanish with the young men serving as *Mayores* (town clerks). People seemed to understand this system and eventually found it fair, for in 1944, when Juan de Dios Rosales visited Santiago Chimaltenango to carry out a nutritional survey, he recorded in his diary:

> The ten or more Indians in the village whom we count among our friends are very humble when they come to our house. They speak with us with care and answer our questions well. They are never arrogant or haughty toward us, as are the Indians of other villages which we have visited. We give them cigarettes, and they

smoke them with satisfaction, taking care to keep our house clean. Pop (Augustin Pop from San Pedro la Laguna who was Rosales' companion) learned that our informants counted on being paid for each time they served as informants for us, because this was the method used by Wagley. Now we have to decide how much to give them each day or for each visit. (Rosales, In Wagley, 1949: 130)

Later in comparing notes with Rosales, I found that he had worked with some of my regular informants.

But training informants, or more specifically, learning how to work with informants, included more than organization of interview settings. A crucial problem was the specificity of the data. For example, at least four informants gave me a description of courtship and marraige with all of its complexities and all agreed on the major steps and events: the use of a "go-between," four visits by the father of a prospective groom and the "go-between" to the father of the girl, his refusal, a divination by *chiman* (priest divinator) as to the future success of the union, the acceptance, a party offered by the groom's family, a bride price of five *quetzales* ($5.00), prayers for the couple by the *chiman*, and twenty days of matri-local residence before the young couple move to their own house built for them by the groom's father in a patrilocal compound. Yet, as I began to ask each informant: "Exactly how did you get married?." not one had courted his wife according to the articulated "ideal pattern." Some had been accepted by the bride's father on the first visit, another had never called a *chiman* for divination or prayers, another had paid a bride price of as little as two *quetzales*, and at least one had side-stepped the whole process by eloping with his wife. So I learned to distinguish between "ideal" and "real" culture or between "emic" and "etic."

There was the problem, too, of the sensitivity of subject matter and the range of knowledge of each informant of his own culture. I soon learned that land ownership and even household economic data were almost as sensitive a subject as one's personal sex life. There was then a Guatemalan law which declared any person a vagrant who did not have 64 *cuerdas* (about 9.2 cuerdas to one acre) in cultivation or a labor contract for 100 to 150 days generally at a plantation. Such "vagrants" were put to work on road gangs. In addition, there were taxes on sweatbaths and identification cards which few Chimaltecos paid. It was hard for people to believe in the first months that I did not work in some way for the government or perhaps for some powerful coffee plantation. In fact, a variety of rumors spread about the anthropologist — even that I was a supernatural Guardian of the Mountain looking for souls to man a plantation believed to be situated inside one of the tallest peaks. In time such suspicions and rumors

subsided but one had to be careful of the subjects introduced into interview.

There were some subjects, while not entirely taboo, that were beyond
the scope of my key informants such as Gregorio Martin, Diego Aguilar,
and others. Only Andrea could tell me in any detail about the women's
role in Santiago Chimaltenango. She was among the few women who
spoke Spanish and preferred that I come to her house for interviews when
her younger children were generally present. She also preferred to converse
with me in Spanish rather than have Carmelo present. Our interviews were
never very successful, although she seemed at ease and joked with me
about my need for a wife. After many interviews, I finally broached the
subject of menstruation. She did not avoid the subject but told me that
she knew little about it! According to Andrea, she had only menstruated
once when she was about 14 years old just after she had married. Then,
she was pregnant nine times (five children lived) and since the birth of her
last child her menses ceased. She promised to discuss menstruation with
other women but the subject never again was mentioned. So, except for
what I could observe and learn during frequent visits to Indian homes
when husbands were inevitably present, all of my information came from
males.

Religion was a specialized subject. Gregorio, Diego, and others knew
family prayers and ritual but they knew little or nothing of the esoteric
aspects of religion controlled by the *chimans*. Once I asked Carmelo about
the day names of the Mayan calendar. After hearing my description of
the twenty day names collected in Kanhabal-Maya in Santa Eulalia by
Oliver La Farge, Carmelo assured me that such a system did not exist in
Santiago Chimaltenango. Yet in one of our interviews with Gregorio some
weeks later, Gregorio made mention of the day *Ik* and that it was pro-
pitious to make *costumbre* (a generalized Spanish word for prayers and
ritual) for maize. I recognized the term and pounced on it. Did he know
the names of other days? "Only a few" he said; "only the *chiman* know
the good days for *costumbre*." Gregorio promised to speak with Pedro
Martin, his kinsman and *Chiman del Pueblo*. Perhaps he would agree to
teach me the day names and their significance. Negotiations with old
Pedro Martin were slow and tortuous, but finally he agreed. So, Pedro
Martin, Gregorio, Carmelo and I sat together while Pedro slowly gave me
the twenty day names and explained the *costumbres* most successfully on
each day. This led to work with other *chiman* into the realm of esoteric
religion and ritual which only they knew. Carmelo was amazed. He had
lived over 20 years in Santiago Chimaltenango and he had seen the overt
ritual performed again and again, but like all ladinos he had never been

aware of the covert meaning and organization of what was before his eyes. Much of this information was provided rather secretly and I requested that Carmelo not speak of it with his ladino friends and family.

Not all of my field research was accomplished by formal but open ended interviews with informants. As time went by, I enlarged my circle of acquaintenances and I made a point of paying visits as well as attending a party on the occasion of the roofing of a house. I joined a *chiman*, who was carrying out a costumbre to cure a fever of one of Gregorio's sons, following him from the church to various prayer stations in the nearby mountains. All of these attempts at participant observation had limited ethnographic value, for without fluency in Mam I could record only the overt behavior. Later, with the help of Gregorio, I was able to record some of the prayers and to understand why certain sites were selected for prayer and the offering of candles and incense. I was certain, however, that field-work should include participant observation for I had, of course, read with admiration Malinowski's introduction to *Argonauts of the Western Pacific*. But my enthusiasm for the "participant observer" technique was weaken-ed by working at weeding a garden for three days with my neighbor, Manuel Aguilar, and his two sons. We left the village at about six a.m. each morning walking about a half mile to the garden. We hoed between the rows of maize planted on an incredibly steep mountain slope. About 11 a.m. Juana, his wife, arrived bringing some *tortillas, posol*, and slightly warm coffee. We then returned to work until about four p.m. I could hardly even keep up the pace with Pascual, a boy about 13 years of age. There was considerable amusement about my awkwardness. Each after-noon I arrived so tired that I ate my early dinner and retired to my cot without recording notes of the day's experiences. I soon decided that this was not productive ethnography. It was much better to walk out with them at six a.m., return at 3 p.m., and sit under a bush to measure their progress during the day rather than trying to fully participate. Many years later a colleague at Columbia University dubbed this as the "passive participant observer" technique. Ever since then I have always been a "passive observer." It is obvious that the anthropologist is an outsider and often inept in local skills. He or she must achieve the role of the tolerated intruder. Most of those who attempt to "go native" may fool themselves but not the natives. Chimaltecos were pleased when I danced local style to a *marimba* at a house warming and on the occasion of the fiesta for Santiago (Saint James) but they did not expect me to dance till dawn as so many of them did.

In July I took a break from fieldwork. Tono Gouband had written that he would like to spend three weeks with me in Santiago Chimaltenango and I had suggested the weeks of the patron saint (July 25). A week before, I traveled to Huehuetenango (a long day on horse back) to wait for Gouband and to consult a doctor, for I had been suffering with diarrhea for more than two weeks. I enjoyed the small city and the comparative comfort of the local hotel. A local MD prescribed a mixture of paragoric and lemonade which controlled the diarrhea. Gouband arrived and we returned to Santiago Chimaltenango where we enjoyed the Fiesta and talked long into the night about local ethnography. We then traveled San Pedro Necta which had a large ladino population and a small pharmacy. I needed a refill on my prescription, for my diarrhea had started again — undoubtedly as a result of drinking aguardiente and eating tamales during the Fiesta of Santiago.

In San Pedro Necta, we encountered Werner Yaggi, a Swiss who owned and operated a small coffee finca nearby. Hearing of my ills, don Werner insisted that I return to his finca to rest and to allow his wife, a trained nurse, to care for me for a few days. It was time for Gouband to return to Guatemala City, so he returned alone to Huehuetenango and I went with don Werner to his finca. A note was sent to Dona Amalia to send an Indian with some of my clothes and the next day an Indian youth returned with everything I had asked for. I stayed a week with the Yaggis, sitting in the warm sun at an altitude of only 5,000 feet above sea level, eating Swiss cooking, and speaking English with don Werner and his wife.

When I returned early in August, I was rather amazed at my reception. Many people came to visit me in my house asking about my health. (The rumor had spread that I was very ill.) When I walked through the village, people (even children) greeted me — Buenas Tardes, don Carlos! I learned from Carmelo that people had said that I had left, never to return, disappointed and sad with Santiago Chimaltenango. Thus, I learned an axiom which I have always passed along to my students. There comes a time after three months, four months, or more, when the anthropologist needs to break away from his village, tribe, band — or urban neighborhood. Anthropologists are uncomfortable intruders no matter how close their rapport. The anthropologist loses objectivity and becomes entangled in the lives of the people. A short respite is mutually beneficial. One returns with objectivity and human warmth restored. The anthropologist returns as an old friend; it is proven that he wants to live with them.

With added confidence and greater rapport I began to inquire about land ownership, size of gardens, family budgets, and other economic questions that had been sensitive in the past months. Obviously, I could not measure milpas nor do even a large sample survey on family budgets. I did record family budgets of those families I knew best in some detail, however. I came to know the *Alcalde* (mayor) rather well, for one of the reasons he held that office was the fact that he spoke Spanish. I probed the subject of landholdings with him. He was very knowledgeable, but vague about the size of landholdings. One day he made the suggestion that the *Regidores* (the municipal councilmen) might find out for us. We reached an agreement that I would pay the *Regidores* to do a survey, which they did during one full week going from house to house asking only two questions: How much land do you own; How large is your *milpa* (garden) this year? I sat with the *Alcalde* in the town hall writing down the results. In my first monograph on Santiago Chimaltenango (Wagley, 1941: 253) I record the results of this survey. I recorded the landholdings of 253 men. But I did not personally measure these plots nor did I find out whether the areas were actually owned by the men reporting or only available to them, but ultimately owned by their father.

I have always felt uneasy about this data on the size of landholdings in Santiago Chimaltenango, and even more so because I did not state in my monograph (Wagley, 1941) exactly how the data was collected. On the other hand, the data is both internally consistent with the calculations of the size of maize fields planted, the consumption needs of a nuclear family, and my direct observations of Chimalteco family farming. Chimaltecos are people who measure the world about them – the time, distances, weights, areas, and relative values, not with a clock, a tape measure, a scale, or monetary units, but with a keen sense of accuracy. I believe even today that the *Regidores* did provide me with a relatively accurate picture of the range of landholdings among their fellow villagers whose situation they knew well. At least, my data on landholding, size of gardens, size of yields in maize, consumption of maize per family, and system of cultivation is in agreement with similar data collected by Raymond Stadelman in the neighboring *municipio* of Todos Santos in the same year. Stadelman spent over one year in Todos Santos studying maize cultivation and actually carried out measurements of gardens and their yeilds (Stadelman, 1940). Still, if a student presented me today with this sort of data, I would demand better evidence than I was able to gather in 1937.

In the month of August and part of September a new element entered my field research. By then I had acquired a series of Indian informants who spoke adequate Spanish for interviews. Working with them, I did not need Carmelo to interpret. It was Carmelo who suggested that we work separately. Each evening I discussed with him a subject or subjects (e.g., quarrels between brothers over land, stories of Owners of Volcanos, etc.) to collect the next day and with whom he would work. Each afternoon I read over his interview notes asking him often to return to clarify details the next day. In these weeks, Carmelo became a valuable co-worker. Since I was interviewing simultaneously, my files of notes grew rapidly and I was able especially to enlarge the number of case histories involving specific key situations and people. I understood how Sol Tax, and other anthropologists, were able to train native assistants who fully participated in data collection.

During those last weeks in Santiago Chimaltenango, I achieved an intimacy with several Indian families but none as great as with the family of Manuel and his wife, Juana, and three sons — Pascual, 14 years of age, Manuel, 10 years old, and Francisco, three years old. I made a habit of going to their house each afternoon to have coffee when Manuel and his two older sons returned from the garden. (I, of course, made periodic presents of unground coffee.) In fact, each day they would send little Chico (Francisco) to call me for coffee. On the days when Juana heated up their sweatbath, I would join Manual and the boys for a bath, a habit which I thoroughly enjoyed. Several times when Juana needed to run an errand she would leave Chico in my care. He loved to swing in a fiber hammock which I had hung in my veranda. Juana did not speak Spanish, so communication was poor. She directed conversation with me through one of the older boys who had spent two years in school. In the evenings after dinner, both Pascual, Manuel (son), and their cousin Francisco Aguilar (aged 11 years) would come to my house. They would say little but they spent hours looking at copies of magazines I had received from friends in the United States. Then, questions would flow in my direction. Did I come to Chimaltenango on such a big boat (an advertisement of the French Lines)? Did I live in such a tall house (a picture of the Empire State Building)? I fielded these and hundreds of other questions the best I could. I was often glad when their father came to call them home and I was able to return to work on my notes.

What the three boys liked best was to wrestle with me on a patch of grass near my house. It was typical play, but I took on two at once and they could soon pin me down. They were especially delighted when I walked six kilometers with them on Saturday to the large market in San Pedro Necta. I bought candy, fruit, and each a hat (smuggled across the border from Mexico) and we ate tamales made by a ladino woman in a market stall. I took careful notes on my experiences with the Aguilar family but in some way, I could not consider it as fieldwork. Time spent with them seemed more like recreation with a family I enjoyed. I never paid Manuel (father) my regular informants fees, although he did spend many hours talking with me. But I did give them presents from time to time and when I left they inherited many odds and ends such as a kerosene lamp, a flashlight, and a few kitchen utensils which I had never used.

When I left Santiago Chimaltenango in 1937 the Aguila family accompanied me to Huehuetenango. I rode a rented horse as did Carmelo who accompanied me to Guatemala City. Two *Mayores* carried my bags but Manuel (father), Pascual, Manuel (son) and their cousin walked alongside. We fired off some rockets from the *cumbre* (mountain pass) as a farewell to the villagers. In Huehuetenango, the Aguilar family took their leave for they would return afoot (about 40 kilometers) the next morning. Carmelo and I left the next day for Guatemala City where he was able to enlist in the police service. (He became sub-delegado of the Guatemala City police force.) In two days I began my trip by train via Mexico for New York.

I believed in 1937 that I had learned how to do field research during my experience in Santiago Chimaltenango. But in the years that followed after further fieldwork among two Tupi speaking tribes in Brazil and with Brazilian peasant communities, I realized that no two field situations are alike. Among the Tapirape Indians, for example, I had to learn the language at least sufficiently well so as to collect my data. There were no bilingual individuals who might serve as interpreters or informants, nor would I have wanted to use them since I had time (15 months) to learn Tupi. Nor could I count on regular interviews, for the Tapirape did not order their lives as did the people of Santiago Chimaltenango (ch. Wagley, 1977). What I had learned in Santiago Chimaltenango were certain basic facts and techniques of fieldwork, some adaptable to other situations and others purely local in application. I would not go so far as to say that fieldwork is an "art"; but like an art there are basic rules of the form wihin which the artist-anthropologist is working. The research anthropologist in the field must know, respect, and play with these rules. Beyond that, fieldwork is a creative endeavor, with some anthropologists more creative than others, and this is true in any discipline. One makes use of the most useful techniques available for the question at hand — ethnoscience, quantitative measuring and sampling, open ended and free flowing interviews with key informants, and other techniques now in the armory of field research. Creative science does not follow a handbook of rules, for it often results from developing insight which is then subjected to empirical verification. This is even more true when dealing as anthropologists do with human collectivity. In this sense, Kroeber was right when he told me that: "Some can and some can't" do fieldwork.

NOTES

1. Some years later he did take an M.A. in Anthropology at the University of Chicago. He returned to Guatemala to found the Instituto Indigenista Guatemaleca and later became the Guatemalan Ambassador to Washington before his untimely death.
2. He also later studied at Chicago University and returned to become a director of the Instituto Indigenista Guatemalteca.

REFERENCES CITED

Bunzel, Ruth, 1953, Chichicastenango: A Guatemalan Village. American Ethnological Society Publications, **Vol. 22.**

La Farge, Oliver, 1947, *Santa Eulalia: The Religion of a Cuchumatan Indian Town.* Chicago: The University of Chicago Press.

La Farge, Oliver, and Douglas Byers, 1931, The Year Bearer's People. New Orleans: Tulane University, Middle American Research Series, **Pub. 3.**

Recinos, Adrian, 1913, *Monographia del Departamento de Huehuetenango, Tipografia Sanchez y de Guise, Guatemala.*

Schultze Jeana, Leonhard, 1933, *Leben, Glaube, und Sprache der Quiche von Guatemala.* Indiana I. Jena, Gustav Fischer.

Stadelman, Raymond, 1940, *Maize Cultivation in Northwestern Guatemala.* Washington D.C.: Carnegie Institution of Washington.

Tax, Sol, 1937, The Municipios of the Midwestern Highlands of Guatemala. American Anthropologist **39**: 423-444.

Wagley, Charles, 1941, Economics of a Guatemalan Village. Memoirs of the American Anthropological Association, **No. 58.**

1949, The Social and Religious Life of a Guatemalan Village. Memoirs of the American Anthropological Association, **No. 71.**

1977, *Welcome of Tears: The Tapirapé Indians of Central Brazil.* New York: Oxford University Press.

CHAPTER 2

On First Being an Anthropologist

ROBERT LAWLESS

The title of this chapter is taken from an article by a sociologist writing about his first few days in a new cultural situation — that of a brothel (Stewart, 1972). In like manner I concentrate here on the first-event aspects of the first few months of my fieldwork in 1973-1974 among the Kalingas in the mountains of Northern Luzon, Philippines. Although I had done fieldwork before 1973, all such earlier fieldwork — carried out in 1965-1968 — was conducted as a graduate student among Philippine lowland neighbors in Manila and nearby peasant villages while I lived at home with my wife and daughter. Now for 12 months I would leave my family, abandon familiar urban and lowland peasant surroundings, and settle as a professional stranger among a people noted primarily for their headhunting.

My first concern when I arrived in Manila in July was to renew acquaintances with Rufino Tima, a college-educated Kalinga who had been my classmate in the mid-1960s at the University of the Philippines. It was quickly agreed that one of the Rufino's male relatives would be my guide and interpreter in Kalingaland. A member of a prominent family in the village of Dangtalan near the ancient Kalinga cultural center of Guinaang on the Pasil River in Kalinga-Apayao Province, he would be returning to school in November, after which I would be on my own.

A six-hour bus ride from Manila brought us to the mountain resort of Baguio City, which was no longer the sleepy town I had remembered from the early 1960s when I taught English there but a bustling city of some 83,000 permanent residents and about 47,000 students. My wife and daughter settled into a house on a beautiful hilltop overlooking the hospital where my daughter had been born, and I interviewed my guide about conditions in Kalingaland. My first question concerned the roads and trails in the area.

The following morning he and I left Baguio on the 8 a.m. provincial bus, headed for our first overnight stop on the way to Kalingaland. About nine hours and 146 kilometers later we arrived in Bontoc Town, the old administrative capital of the former Mountain Province and a site well known in the anthropological literature.

We stayed at a lodging house popular with traveling Kalingas, and at dinner I met Max Duguiang and Geronimo Alunday, two wealthy and influencial Kalinga figures on their way to Manila on government business. Duguiang had been a friend of Walter Franklin Hale, the first lieutenant governor of Kalinga Subprovince under the American occupation of the Philippines, and he was one of the informants of Roy Franklin Barton, an early ethnographer of the Kalingas, whose book (1949) I had brought with me. Since I didn't have any questions of my own, I only asked them about Barton.

The next morning we left Bontoc at 8:40 a.m. on the provincial bus, and we crossed into Kalingaland not far from the village of Bugnay at 10:10 a.m. I religiously noted all the times on the new Timex watch that I had purchased in New York City just for this trip. My only other supplies included a pair of flip-flops, an army surplus poncho, one change of clothes, two blankets, a Kodak Pocket Instamatic 10 camera, a small battery radio and battery shaver, a bottle of One-a-Day vitamins, and another bottle of kaopectate. About a dozen notebooks and ball-point pens took up most of the space in my backpack; I had horrible visions of running out of paper and ink.

At about 2 p.m. the bus arrived in Lubuagan Poblacion, the former capital of old Kalinga Subprovince and the only settlement in Kalingaland with vestiges of urbanism. We immediately set out hiking for Dangtalan, a village of 311 people several kilometers from Lubuagan. I thought hiking would be an improvement over bouncing up and down and back and forth on the hard seat of a crude provincial bus racing over rough, bumpy, twisting mountain roads, but I quickly learned that hiking could be even more uncomfortable. Since my feet were not as tough as the Kalingas', I had to wear shoes, and on wet trails I kept slipping. Since I had done little mountain hiking in my life, keeping up with my guide during that first short hike proved quite fatiguing.

The difficulties on the trail were compensated for by the sheer beauty of the landscape. My first sight of Dangtalan was from a high ridge called Lonong. I stood there out of breath from the hike and breathless from the splendour of the panorama before me. A kilometer or so off to one side is a terrific waterfall of a long, unmeasured drop. The village itself lies below on a lower ridge, a compact collection of 60 or so huts, behind which is a sheer cliff of about 300 meters with the roaring Pasil River crashing through the canyon. Terraced rice fields of all shades of green cover the mountain sides up from the village.

Later I realized that this scene is exactly the one featured in a photograph in Barton's book (1949: Plate III), which he captioned, "A View of the Region of Guinaang. Other Kalingas believe that the people of this region frequently change into were-swine."

I followed my guide stumblingly down the steep trail, across the fields — balancing on what seemed to me extraordinarily narrow dikes around the edges of the fields — and into the village. Few people noticed our arrival because most were out working in the fields. A group of about 25 kids gathered at the house where I was resting outside, and I did a few hand tricks. They giggled a lot, and then it started to rain and I went inside to drink a cup of water — a traditional sign that I was under the protection of the household. I was in my new home.

Darkness fell quickly that first day, and when I went outside to defecate, I learned first-hand what effective scavengers of human wastes were the numerous insolent pigs that roamed the village. I don't remember falling asleep that night, but when I woke up the next morning, among the first sounds I heard was the squealing of these pigs, blending with the hacking coughs of bronchitic children, the savage growling and barking of the half-starved dogs, the roar of the nearby Pasil River, and the never-ending thump-thump-thump of pestile and mortar as the women pounded the day's supply of rice. The first smells that assaulted my nose that morning were from the ever-present pig manure, from the wood burning in the hearth, and then from the always welcome mountain coffee.

Within a week I had settled into a routine and was rather surprised that what would have seemed exotic to me a short time previously so easily and so quickly became so commonplace. I bathed in rivers and dried myself with a flat rock. My shampoo was the ashes of burnt corn straw. I slept on a split and plaited bamboo floor. I ate with my fingers. The meals consisted of rice, of course, and all sorts of unfamiliar grass-like vegetables, as well as familiar ones like mung beans and bamboo sprouts.

In the coming months meat would be very rare. When I hiked to villages in sparsely settled, heavily forested areas, there was a fair amount of meat from bats, deer, wild pig, and lizards, but in Dangtalan meat came only from the slaughtering of domestic pigs and carabaos (water buffalos) for curing or funeral ceremonies, though twice I had some delicious dog meat at surreptitious gatherings of a few of the younger men.

My first experience at serious hiking with Kalingas in their territory at their speed came a few days after my arrival. One of the members of the household became very sick with a recurrance of malaria. She was treated by the local shaman, and the blood from a sacrificed pig was rubbed on her body — the same pig also served in the ceremony marking my welcome into the village.

Her condition nevertheless rapidly deteriorated, and the members of the household decided to take her to Kalinga Hospital in Lubuagan Poblacion. She was carried up the trail by two men holding on their shoulders one long bamboo pole with a blanket slung underneath and tied at the ends with rattan strands. One blanket under and tied over the pole supported the middle. Despite the fact that I had no load I could not keep up with the stretcher bearers ascending that fairly short trail to Lonong, and about an hour later I dragged myself into the outskirts of Lubuagan, exhausted and embarrassed and about 20 minutes behind the others.

Fortunately the one doctor was in, and she was well cared for. The stretcher bearers and the few other Dangtalan men that had accompanied us insisted on showing me around Lubuagan. I suspected that they were actually showing me off to the townspeople; Lubuagans have a bad reputation as arrogant cityfolks, but Dangtalan at that moment gained the upper hand by possessing a resident anthropologist.

Our group drank San Miguel gin at several establishments (a drink generally not readily available in the outlying villages) and then started back. Then came my first experience with what always happens in Kingaland when you "start back" during rainy season. It began to rain heavily, and it was already dark by the time we reached Junction Store, a small variety store that marks the outskirts of Lubuagan Poblacion. I refused to descend in the dark and in the downpour what I then regarded as a dangerous trail, and the men refused to leave "their anthropologist" in the clutches of Lubuagan people. One member of the group finally persuaded them to go ahead with the promise that he would keep watch over me at Junction Store throughout the might and that we wouldn't go back into the town proper. The next day I returned to Dangtalan and resumed regular interviewing and participation in the events of the village, centering mostly on agricultural activities.

My next trip was to a funeral in Malucsad, a village on the other side of the Pasil River from Dangtalan about one hour away. Funerals were to become a part of my everyday life in Kingaland. I was expected to sit with the village leaders and join in the conversation, a conversation that would more accurately be described as oratory. I never approached being an orator, and I never quite became accustomed to sitting on the hard logs for hours on end waiting for the carabaos to be brought and slaughtered and the meat distributed.

One of the good things to come out of the Malucsad funeral was that arrangements were made for me to travel to the village of Bagtayan in the forest northwest of Dangtalan, where a large amount of hunting is done. The trip took all day, and when I arrived I learned that a Kalinga hikes it

Lukas Gayodan, on the right, a Kalinga from Dangtalan, shows me, on the left, how to divine the hunting prowess of a dog through an examination of the nipples. A follow-up investigation in the hunting village of Bagtayan resulted in an article on Kalinga divination (see Lawless 1975).

in a little over an hour, as I was to do myself much later.

Another thing I learned on the short hike to Malucsad was the importance of omens. Our trip to Malucsad was delayed because someone had sneezed — a bad travel omen. On the way there several Kalingas instructed me in the reading of *idaw* omens. The *idaw* is a small bird about 12 centimeters long with a black bill, yellow breast, and dark red feathers; it is thought to be a variety of maya. Kabunian, chief god of the Kalingas, speaks through the *idaw* and foretells good luck or misfortune. A traveler wants good signs, e.g. a happy *idaw* dancing and jumping around, an *idaw* singing on the right side of the trail, an *idaw* flying across the path from right to left, and so many Kalingas purposely call the *idaw* when traveling, hoping to get a good sign. The call is an a-i-o-o-o-o-o-o-o sound uttered very loudly. I apparently never got the sound right, for I never was able to call an *idaw* out of the trees. The entire omen system is quite complex, and I'm sure I didn't learn it all; I did, however, find myself looking for omens during my later trips through Kalingaland — especially when I was by myself.

On the way to Bagtayan it started raining as usual — and the rain in Kalingaland comes down like someone was pouring it out of a bucket — and although I wore the army surplus poncho, I was generally as wet inside it from sweating as I would have been without it from the rain. So I arrived in Bagtayan wet, exhausted, and with aching knees from that inevitable end-of-the-trail steep climb up to the top of the ridge where perched the village.

My guide left me at the house of the outstanding village citizen and set out to strut around the village for the benefit of the young women, which was his routine activity whenever we stayed in a different village. For this and other reasons, when I felt I knew the territory, I gave up guides and interpreters altogether. Without an interpreter that first night in Bagtayan, however, I was unable to converse successfully with the members of the household, and we mostly just watched each other uncomfortably. I slept very little because at about 1,100 meters Bagtayan becomes cold at night — all the more so when one is sleeping in wet clothes. Nevertheless, during the next days I was able to participate in some hunts and to gather a considerable amount of data about Kalinga hunting.

After a few days we returned to Dangtalan where I had to make an important decision. My small supply of batteries could not keep both my radio and my shaver going for much longer. Obtaining batteries in this part of Kalingaland was quite difficult — and expensive. I decided in favor of the radio and began my beard; this was the period of the Nixon scandals, and I could not bring myself to miss the downfall of a man whom I had long regarded as a scoundrel. Unfortunately the radio didn't last too much longer, and the last bit of news that I heard was about Spiro Agnew being charged in connection with kickbacks in Maryland.

A few weeks later I made a hike to the village of Pugong where I stayed for a couple of weeks to talk with a wise old man named Andrew Coom. The images of Pugong are particularly vivid for me. I stayed in the house of a rich and prestigious Kalinga. The rich often build onto the small, indigenous bamboo hut a big room of hand-hewed lumber, i.e. a non-indigenous sala little used except as a symbol of prestige; Kalinga home life revolves around the hearth in the center of the hut. As a guest of some prestige I had the misfortune of being requested to sleep in the large empty sala, while everyone else slept around the hearth. These nights were the first times that I felt so acutely the ache of loneliness living as a stranger among the Kalingas.

The loneliness was deepened by a strange mixture of impinging images and events. One afternoon after starting a recitation of epidemics in the area with a story his grandfather had told him of a smallpox epidemic in the late 1800s that had killed over 50 people in this very village, Coom, an old man with asthma, went to relieve himself — which I knew from working with him for a few days would take a while. So I picked up a piece of a novel to pass the time. (I say that I picked up a *piece* of a novel because the few paperback books I came across generally had most of the pages torn out; they were commonly traded into Kalingaland for use as cigarette wrappers.)

This particular novel happened to be C. Y. Lee's *Lover's Point*, a story about an instructor at the Army Language School in Monterey, California. The Presidio of Monterey holds for me only the most awful memories of loneliness and despair; I stayed there for nine months separated for the first time from my fiancee and studying under enormous pressure a language in which I had no interest. My unhappy reading of the bits and pieces of this novel was interrupted by women's wailing from the main part of the village just down the hill — the eerie, shrill wailing that signalled another child's death from measles complications; a measles epidemic was spreading through the Pasil area, and just a few months before I arrived eleven children had died in Dangtalan.

The epidemic had reached Pugong almost simultaneously with my arrival there. In fact, a few days after I first slept in that big room the eldest of the three sisters in the household — a cute little girl of eight or so who had always giggled when I poked her in the stomach — was taken to the hospital in Lubuagan Poblacion to join the youngest sister, who had gone there a few days earlier. A crude affair with only one doctor, the hospital is patronized only by the wealthier Kalingas; it is widely regarded as a place where people go to die.

Coom returned, and after hearing the recitation of a diarrhea epidemic, a terrible cholera epidemic, and several measles epidemics, I lay down in my big empty room to rest. I was soon interrupted by a rare occurrence — a letter was handed to me. Mail usually reaches only the outskirts of Kalingaland and then may be carried haphazardly throughout the villages by whoever happens to be on the trails. The letter was from a friend of mine in Peru, who told me that her daughter was down with the measles.

I had just finished reading the letter when the wailing began again, and the news came that the youngest of the three sisters had died — for the last few days the household had been pounding rice in anticipation of a funeral gathering — but it turned out to be a fake report. Instead the death was of the daughter, an only child, of Rufino's brother.

A few days later at the funeral of the daughter I sat as usual on the front row of logs with the village leaders, who orated in English for my benefit, and I participated as best I could, e.g. on the difference between intelligence, knowledge, and wisdom; on would you save first your mother or your wife; then on why don't the rich Americans give to the Kalingas. And for the first time among the Kalingas I felt impatience. I was becoming weary of it all – and especially of one village leader from Dalupa, who was getting on my nerves by continually arguing that all Americans are rich. I began to get heated, but a Dangtalan friend of mine, seeing my difficulty, moved up to the front row and managed to change the subject – and I lapsed into silence.

The end of the funeral saw considerable shouting and shoving for the last parcels of meat since the one butchered carabao didn't provide enough meat for distribution to the entire crowd. When I asked my usual rhetorical question, "Why do the rich get the larger shares of meat" and had received the usual answer, "It is a sign of respect," I said, "Then the small pieces for the poor must be a sign of disrespect." My retort brought a laugh from some standing nearby and was quickly translated for the Kalinga masses standing on the fringes. They seemed to react with some restless movements. I noted the Dalupa leader staring straight ahead, silent for once, and felt a tinge of satisfaction.

We headed back to Dangtalan that night and were met by a lot of excited people on the trail; they were carrying word to the Dalupa leader that his son was dying of measles complications – the epidemic had spread to another village. We loaned our flashlight to one of the couriers and hiked on back to Dangtalan by moonlight. This was the first time I had hiked by moonlight in Kalingaland, and it was somehow a satisfying experience. Having been essentially a city boy all my life, all parts of the forest looked the same to me initially. (Perhaps I should mention that the first time I went outside the village of Dangtalan on my own – to take a bath at a spring not more than 500 meters away – I got lost and couldn't find my way back for the lack of any landmarks that made any sense to me.) During this first hike by moonlight I began paradoxically enough to see parts of the forest that I had never seen before and to feel and smell the forest and the trails and the rocks and the streams as though they meant something to me, and somehow I felt like dancing instead of walking down the trail. Then I suddenly remembered the passage in Colin Turnbull's *The Forest People* where he finds "in the tiny clearing, splashed with silver, . . . the sophisticated Kenge, clad in bark cloth, adorned with leaves, with a flower stuck in his hair . . . all alone, dancing around and singing softly to himself as he gazed up at the treetops. . . . 'I am dancing with the forest, dancing with the moon' " (1961: 272). Then we reached the rice terraces marking the boundaries of Dangtalan, and I awkwardly crawled up the walls using all fours, while the Kalingas with me marched vertically straight up the walls, their bare feet silently finding the tiny steps, their backs straight with dignity.

Things seemed unusually quiet in Dangtalan for the next few weeks, and I made a number of short trips to nearby villages slowly expanding my hiking capabilities in the hopes of being able to keep up with the Kalingas and rapidly expanding my ability to pick out good omens – which seemed to increase my confidence. By the end of September I thought I could make just such a hike to Colayo, the last village upstream on the Pasil River. My guide, a young cousin of his, and I left Dangtalan at 6 a.m. one quiet morning and set out for Balatoc and then Colayo. Stopping once to consume the rice we had carried with us, we arrived in Balatoc at about 2 p.m. A prosperous looking village of 846 people, the largest Pasil village, Balatoc sits in the middle of three active volcanoes, the nearest one to the village named Bommag. The trail passes over smoking rock and the air is full of the powerful smell of sulphur. Although the trail to Balatoc was not difficult, the last part, the entrance into the village, exhausted me; after crossing the Pasil River on a high, long, rickety old swinging bamboo bridge, we climbed straight up a mountain to the top of a high ridge – a typical village location for the defense-conscious Kalingas. I counted about 1,000 steps up the ridge to the village. I slept very little that night because I couldn't find a position to rest my aching knees.

We left Balatoc at 8 a.m. the next day and arrived in Colayo at around 1 p.m. The hike was continuously uphill; Colayo is about 1,500 meters in elevation, and there is nothing to the immediate west of Colayo but the misty mountain peaks that mark the east-west watershed of the North Luzon Highlands. It was the first time my two companions had been to Colayo – an indication both of its isolation and its reputation as a haven for headhunters.

At the entrance to Colayo are strewn huge, smooth, rounded boulders over which a visitor must awkwardly climb – a defense parameter as effective as the steep ridge on which Balatoc sits. As we ungracefully clambered over the boulders, a huge, powerfully-built man, the biggest Kalinga I ever saw, leaped from boulder to boulder and met us with a huge grin on his face. He took us to his hut and all that afternoon and evening he regaled us with stories, legends, and rodomontades. I noticed that my guide stuck close to me and translated everything very carefully – which was unusual.

We left late that night to go to someone else's hut to sleep, and my companions whispered to me that the man we had been with was a killer, widely noted throughout Kalingaland for having taken seven heads in the Colayo-Butbut feud in 1971.

The night the blanket that I wrapped myself in was full of bugs, but being half-asleep I didn't realize it until I was thoroughly bitten all over and the pain had awakened me. Everyone else was asleep and there were no more blankets. I put on my jacket – my old army jacket that I always carried with me – but it was too cold to sleep. I wanted to walk around outside, but it was pitch black, and having been brought to the hut after dark, I had no idea whether or not a precipice might lurk just beyond. So I squatted on a rock in the dark just outside the hut – and surprised myself when I later realized I was sitting Kalinga-style. My knees had begun to ache during the night from the strenuous hiking, and the squatting seemed to relax them.

I sat there for what seemed to be endless hours in reverie. Through my drowsy head surged the rude crowds of New York City, pounded the cacophonic cadences of the subway, and whispered the eternal phrases of love from a soft face on East 13th Street – all ghosts of my abandoned past and omens of my expected future.

Gradually at first the blackness turned to heavy purple and then to light purple. Bright orange-yellow ribbons began to hesitantly waft up from behind the distant mountains, and rather suddenly a big orange ball popped up just to the right of a peak, squatted on the slope, and stared silently, appraisingly at me. It was morning, and I was alive and in Kalinga-land. I heard some voices in the hut asking about the "alan," the ghost, meaning me; ghosts are white in Kalinga. Breakfast was prepared but I had no hunger; I had eaten the sunrise and was fully nourished.

Returning to Balatoc from Colayo, we took an old hunting trail. We had been warned that it was considered one of the most dangerous in Kalingaland, but at 6:30 a.m. we set out on it. There were no bad omens. There *were* three swinging bridges, one so rickety that my legs began shaking, and except for the laughter that would have assailed me I would have crossed it on all fours. During one stretch the ground was washed out underneath, leaving only a precarious web of rocks wedged against each other – all this with sheer drop-offs on each side down to 150 or so meters. One part of the trail simply went straight up the side of a cliff with most of the steps being worn machete notches. I counted 521 steps. Another section consisted of a rotted bamboo ladder for about 20 meters up the side of a cliff. It rained some on the trail and then started to pour as we reached Balatoc a little after 8 p.m.

For the next several days in Balatoc I began for the first time to acquire good data. Due to my experiences in Dangtalan I could ask intelligent questions of the Kalingas in the field, and I knew what topics to probe deeper into. I had a good idea of the gaps in my knowledge, and I felt I was rapidly filling them in. In the evenings seated around the hearth with its smoldering fire, I had informative discussions with the old men of the village, and I felt warm outside from the heat of the hearth and warm inside from the bottle of San Miguel gin being passed around.

Finally we had to return to Dangtalan. Once there I began for the first time to appreciate some of the inroads of the national government in Kalingaland. It was decided that I should see the "mayor"; the villages and hamlets of the Pasil area actually form an official municipality, according to an act passed a few years earlier by the national government. Also named Pasil, the municipality is one of seven in Kalinga-Apayao Province. And there is a mayor, who was elected in 1971 in the last election before martial law was declared throughout the Philippines in September 1972.

The mayor lived across the Pasil River from Dangtalan in an area known as Amdalao, which had been renamed Pasil Poblacion. There were only a few houses there, and some broken-down shacks passed as the municipal government buildings; a two-way radio and one typewriter made their home there.

Once past the awkwardness of introductions, the mayor and I quickly established good rapport, though he seemed a little disappointed that I had no official government papers with me about my mission (the first and last time I was ever asked). We had lunch there, and some old men from Balatoc told the now familiar story of having hidden and fed six Americans for four years in the mountains during World War II and of having never received any compensation from America. I replied to them that I would check into the matter, and they wanted to know what kin I was to Nixon. I assured them that I was as close to Nixon as they were to President Marcos, which brought a look of puzzlement and then laughter.

The mayor invited me to go along with him to a barrio council meeting in nearby Pugong, so I went to check out this instance of political acculturation. A barrio council meeting in Kalingaland turned out to be a group of men sitting around on logs. As honored guests, however, the mayor and I were given chairs; in fact, two boys were delegated to follow us around all afternoon with two rattan chairs, and I wondered where they had been during those interminable funerals when I sat forever on hard logs. The council finally passed an ordinance requiring pigpens, which is already required under national law but apparently nobody knew that. I was assured later that ordinances don't mean anything and that nothing is complied with unless the village leaders and the elders decide on it.

Actually the star attraction at the barrio council meeting was a drunk army sargeant from Pugong on home leave — and drunk not only on gin and sugar cane wine but on the new power of the army since martial law.

He was the first and last Kalinga I ever met who was in the Philippine army. Although not a member of the council, he took the handwritten ordinances and tried to read them, but they were in English and his English was not up to such a task. He kept trying to draw attention to himself by making the mayor and me his guests. In fact, we did finally have dinner in his house; he had already butchered a pig and a chicken for us. Most of the councilmen left before eating – a rank Kalinga insult.

When we were ready to go back to the mayor's around 9 p.m., it started to pour rain, so we sat around while the sargeant, quite drunk by this time, babbled on and on, and kept drawing attention to himself by pointing out his guest "Mr. Bob." The mayor pretended to be asleep in his chair, my interpreter excused himself to urinate and never reappeared, two others spent about an hour examining with rapt attention the four photographs stuck on the wall, and I smiled dumbly and nodded a lot.

Finally the rain stopped and we all got up to leave. The sargeant became upset because he had thought the mayor and I were going to stay overnight. I noticed the mayor fingering his machete and made my exit. The mayor came along and we walked the fairly short distance back to his house in the dark, ate venison, and went to bed. My interpreter showed up the next morning, and on the way back to Dangtalan it rained while the sun was still shining. When I was a young child, I used to think that that was magical.

The people in Dangtalan had heard about my difficulties in the sargeant's house and hastened to inform me that he had not been in his right mind since he had eaten tabooed meat at his wife's funeral. This indigenous explanation seemed somehow reassuring to me.

I spent the next few weeks visiting the six remaining villages in the Pasil area, often hiking in flip-flops and occasionally barefoot since my shoes had become worn and impossibly slippery. I even hiked into Lubuagan Poblacion for the first time since we had taken the sick woman these; the route had been closed for several weeks due to a dispute between Dangtalan and Lubuagan. The town of a little over 3,000 seemed like a big city to me now, and I caught myself wondering whether my country manners showed. I even gawked at seeing a newspaper there. Although many weeks old, the September 22nd Manila *Daily Express* gave me two items of good news: Agnew was expected to resign and Billy Jean King had beaten Bobby Riggs 6-4, 6-3, 6-3.

Soon came the moment for my trip to the village of Balbalasang. Located on the Saltan River, Balbalasang is about eleven hours from Dangtalan and is in a slightly different cultural area; the Balbalasangs are closer to the so-called Tinguians of Fay-Cooper Cole's ethnographies (1915,

1922) than to Barton's Kalingas (1949).

Balbalasang is the site of an active Episcopal Church mission dating back to 1925. I had known several Kalingas from there who had worked at the Episcopal schools in Baguio City — Easter School and Brent School — when I taught at Brent from 1963 to 1965.

My guide, another relative of his, and I left Dangtalan at the first crowing of the rooster, about 5:30 a.m. None of us had ever been to Balbalasang before.

The hike to Balbalasang was the most satisfying of my stay in Kalinga-land and the first time I had really enjoyed hiking there. I later read a description of a hike made in 1882 on the very same trail by Hans Meyer (Scott, ed., 1975: 85-89), and the trail has not changed much at all. The hike took us upstream along the Tabia River through a leech-infested, wet mossy rain forest. After about two hours of gently loping along I glanced over my shoulder and was surprised to see a village in the distance behind us unexpectedly far off to the northeast. "What village is that?" I asked. "Bagtayan," they replied, irritated that after all this time I still couldn't recognize the country I was in. So *that* was Bagtayan — the small village left far behind in our push up the Tabia River toward Balbalasang. Bagta-yan of the aching knees, of the day-long hike, of the wet, steep, final prostrating climb. Goodbye, little Bagtayan, I'm on my way to farther places. I felt good.

Around 11 a.m. we stopped in a clearing by the roaring Tabia River where we met some hunters from Bagtayan who shared their snack of rice with us. One spoke quite good English and gave me some information on trees. The forest was still wet, and I scrapped two silent, bloated leeches about five centimeters long from my ankle.

After the snack the trail began winding abruptly upward away from the river, and it went consistently up and up until we reached the end of the Pasil area and the beginning of the old Banaw area, which is now the municipal boundary between Pasil and Balbalan. A little past noon there at the top of the pass I tied a knot in the end of a runo stem and stuck it in the ground among some others wilted now and drooping — the traditional entreaty for a good welcome in Balbalasang.

From the pass down to Balbalasang was beautiful hiking. We traveled just around the pine-tree line. Part of the time we would be in the wet, mossy, soggy rain forest with its tangle of vines and branches, its smell of decay, its dark closeness, slippery grounds, and clinging leeches. Next we would suddenly emerge up into the clean, dry pine forest with its brown needles on the floor of the broad open spaces between trees, and my nose filled with the acid, tingly pine smells. We stopped once at a gorgeous pine tree clearing, and I felt intoxicated. I pulled a fat leech from my calf instead of scrapping them off as the others were doing, and blood flowed from the wound — as it would continue to flow for the next couple of days. We crossed the Saltan River, where I washed the leech bite, and entered Balbalasang.

What struck me at once was the foreignness of Balbalasang. Its appearance was overwhelmingly different — and seemingly prosperous. The pigs were fenced, the dogs appeared well fed, and the children didn't cough. All the houses were made of hand-hewed plank boards, and many of them had two stories with separate, connected kitchens. The houses were built far apart with surrounding fences. There were outhouses and even refuse holes. Since none of the Brent-connected families that I mentioned seemed to be in the village at that time, we were directed to the barrio captain. His house contained furniture! Chairs, beds, tables! As the barrio captain spoke to my guide in Kalinga I felt a sudden surprise that he could speak Kalinga, though with what seemed to me to be a distinct accent. I realized with a shock that I saw the people of Balbalasang as foreigners, and I was frankly startled for the first time at the degree to which I had assimilated the Guinaang-Dangtalan folk model of Kalinganess.

Due to some machinations of my guide, which are not quite clear to me, and to the fear of his relative that if he stayed any longer in this Christian village he would somehow become Christian, we left Balbalasang the next morning at 8:30 a.m. From Balbalasang all the way back to Ableg (a Pasil village only 50 minutes from Dangtalan) we took the one single-lane dirt and gravel road that wanders through Kalingaland — a distance that comes out to an even 50 kilometers, according to the road surveyors' maps.

Hiking on the road seemed quite strange to me. There was a laziness about it that came, I suppose, from the complete uneventfulness of the hike and the levelness of the walk. We met no vehicles until we caught the weekly bus for the last 12 kilometers, and we met very few people; Kalingas use the trails, which are shorter though vertical, while the roads follow the elevation contours and wind around mountains for endless kilometers. Neither of my companions, however, knew this territory so we had to stay on the road to avoid getting lost in the forest or walking into someplace where we wouldn't be welcomed.

Somewhere between Balbalasang and Salegseg, a 26-road-kilometer stretch, my guide began to complain of aching knees and leg cramps, and I gloated to myself over the fact that I had out-hiked my first Kalinga. We decided to stay the night in Salegseg, especially when we ran across a group of people from Guinaang who were attending a "postponed funeral" and who greeted us as clansmen. A piglet was butchered for us, and I relaxed in a spirit of camaraderie, relieved to be away from the foreignness of Balbalasang.

The next morning we slowly hiked 12 kilometers to the village of Balbalan, where my guide proclaimed that he could hike not a step farther and that we must wait for the bus no matter how long, and nobody seemed to know when — and I mean what day — the bus would come through. (I was anxious because I understood the bus ran only between Salegseg and Lubuagan once a week — or whenever it was in running condition — and we hadn't seem a bus in Salegseg.)

While waiting by the roadside for the bus, I had the unexpected pleasure of striking up a conversation with a woman who was exceptionally well informed about Kalinga politics. It was the most information-packed few hours that I spent in Kalingaland. The bus did come and we took it into Ableg. There was a funeral there, and for some stubborn reason that seemed valid at the time I refused to go to it. It was the first funeral I didn't attend in Kalingaland. Since it would have been a breach of etiquette for me not to attend, I hid out for several hours in the house of a friend I had met on my first visit to Ableg.

When we did start back for Dangtalan my guide was limping, and it took us over an hour to reach the cliff overlooking our home village, and he wanted to rest. His relative left us there over some disagreement; I think he was embarrassed that my guide could not hike "like a Kalinga warrior."

It began to pour and the trail down the side of the cliff became a rushing stream as we descended. We were literally washed down to the bottom. As a final token of my victory, I ascended the stone walls of the rice terraces outside Dangtalan standing erect without holding onto anything, and as darkness fell I strolled into Dangtalan far ahead of my Kalinga hiking partner.

A few days later we got up at 3:45 a.m., packed, and left Dangtalan silently about an hour later. I now hiked rapidly up the familiar trail to Lonong without a light. We sat there on the ridge, where Barton had taken his photograph of the village of were-swine, and waited in the darkness for the first crowing of the rooster and the flickering of lights as the women got up to fetch the firewood and stoke up the hearths. A few hours later we caught the bus in Lubuagan, and my erstwhile guide was on his way back to school in Baguio City, and I was on my way back to see my family, straighten up my notes, find the gaps in my information, and prepare for the next trip into Kalingaland on my own.

34   ROBERT LAWLESS

REFERENCES CITED

Barton, R. F., 1949, *The Kalingas: Their Institutions and Custom Law.* Chicago:
    University of Chicago Press.
Cole, Fay-Cooper, 1915, *Traditions of the Tinguian: A Study in Philippine Folk-
    lore.* Chicago: Field Museum of Natural History.
1922, *The Tinguian: Social, Religious, and Economic Life of a Philippine Tribe.*
    Chicago: Field Museum of Natural History.
Lawless, Robert, 1975, Effects of Population Growth and Environment Changes on
    Divination Practices in Northern Luzon. Journal of Anthropological Research **31**:
    18-33.
Scott, William Henry, ed., 1975, *German Travelers on the Cordillera (1860-1890).*
    Manila: Filipiniana Book Build.
Stewart, George Lee, 1972, On First Being a John. Urban Life and Culture **1**: 255-
    274.
Turnbull, Colin, 1961, *The Forest People: A Study of the Pygmies of the Congo.*
    New York: Simon and Schuster.

CHAPTER 3

From Structure to History in Malaya

DAVID J. BANKS

When I arrived at the site of my fieldwork in Kedah, West Malaysia, in September, 1967, I intended to write a definitive study of Malay kinship. The study was going to concentrate upon the symbols of kinship among Malays and upon their ideas about social relationships. When I concluded my stay, some fourteen months later, I had begun to question the value of a symbolic study divorced from historical scholarship. I believe that my field experiences brought about this change from the study of symbol and structure to a study of the role of symbols in history. In this essay I will trace the developments that changed my thinking about the study of kinship.

The intellectual results of fieldwork would be difficult to describe without some mention of the crisis atmosphere of the time. The 1960's was a decade of American internationalism and social anthropology was, for many of us apprentices, an extension of it. We were unhappy with the Vietnam involvement with which we were forced, by historical circumstance, to identify. To be a successful anthropologist meant to successfully complete a field study. This would involve establishment of adequate working relationships in the field, finding a suitable place to live and usable methodology, carried through to a series of workable field methods. Later on, of course, the position of anthropology changed in the American academic world. Many anthropologists now receive certification without fieldwork experience.

I decided to settle in Kedah rather than the more familiar southern regions or in the idiomatic Kelantan region of the northeast for several reasons. The large Chinese and Indian populations around Kuala Lumpur and north of Singapore suggested that it would be difficult to perceive Malay culture without reference to the cultures of the immigrant groups. I thought that I could best study Malay culture in a predominantly Malay area. The decision in favor of Kedah rather than an area on the east coast was more subjective. I traveled to the east coast states of Pahang, Trengannu and Kelantan and was especially intrigued by the reports of a cultural revival in Kelantan, but I was also aware that several anthro-

pologists were working in Kelantan and Pahang and that Firth's study of
the Bachok district of Kelantan (Firth, 1966) addressed many problems
that would be found in the coastal state of Trengannu. Kedah had not yet
been the subject of social anthropology as far as I was then aware and this
was appealing in the atmosphere of individualism of the day. My trip to
Kedah via Penang in early September firmed my resolve to stay in that
area. I met some American Peace Corps workers there who discussed the
various regions of Kedah and the lore associated with each. This was a
great help although their observations were not always completely
accurate.

Kedah was rainy when I arrived. Cloud alternated with rain for most of
September and part of October. The east coast had been sunny when I had
visited them but somehow Kedah had a strong appeal. Kedah had never
been directly ruled by Britain and had maintained its independence from
its powerful Thai neighbor through several turbulent centuries during
which it lost much of its sovereignty. The Sultan of Kedah sold Penang
Island to the British East India Company, beginning the colonial drama in
Malaya. Britain ruled Kedah indirectly through an advisor. Kedah was not
part of the original Federated Malay States.

I entered Kedah via the northern trunk road along the Wan Mat Saman
flood control canal. From this road one can see the surplus producing
Kedah Plain and the hills in the center of the peninsula to the east. Then I
went up into the Kedah hill districts. If the Kedah Plain had been, by dint
of its political status, isolated from the rest of Malaya, then its hill
districts, with their recent roads, must have been more isolated. I did not
think that there would be a pure Malay kinship system in the hills of
Kedah but I felt that the study of the kinship system of an isolated Malay
area would be useful, if only for its comparative value. There might also
be more continuity with pre-colonial patterns.

MY HEADMAN

Once I had chosen the District of Sik, southeast of Alor Setar, administrative capital of Kedah, located in its hills and received permission from the
State Secretariat to reside there, I turned my attention to finding housing.
I had been staying in the district town's rest house. One day while driving
up the main district road I spotted some teenage boys by the roadside and
asked them the name of their village and its headman. I arranged to meet
with the village headman in the evening. Later I found that my visit had

caused considerable stir and that the headman, Tok Im, was as curious as were the teenagers to know the purpose of the black foreigner's visit. I returned at dusk using the road marker stones and my memory of the house indicated to me to guide me there. Tok Im greeted me from his veranda, a well constructed wood structure with concrete stairs, trimmed with carved wood panelling. He was a small man (about 5'2") about 50 years old with a rather long face and a pasty light brown complexion. He beckoned me up with a sheepish grin. We sat down together across a wooden table on the veranda and I attempted to explain to him, using the Malay that I commanded, what the purpose of my visit was, from the desire to reside in the district to the academic purpose of my stay. He listened carefully and tried to repeat back some of my ideas to me using his version of Malay that I would understand and I found that he had understood much of what I had said, but he could not, at that time, distinguish the objectives of my stay from those of the United States Peace Corps. This should not be surprising since he did not assume that Americans in the Peace Corps were an undifferentiated category. If some did rural development, perhaps others did research.

He said that he would be glad to have me live in his village, but I would need a house and someone to cook for me. There were no old or unused houses in the village that were usable for my purposes. (Actually, there were several houses rented to rubber tappers for $5.00 per month. These structures would have been too small in retrospect.) Building a house would involve an outlay of money for lumber and to pay the builders. He also talked about a payment to his wife as my cook since she would need a larger kitchen to cook for her new boarder. The initial expenses would come to several hundred American dollars, and I was told that I could sell my house or its lumber upon my departure. The house constructed for me was simple and divided into four sections. It was a sixteen foot square area with a slanting zinc roof. The veranda was 8' by 4' and one of the four 8' by 8' quarter sections inside of the main section (the NW quarter) became my bedroom with a door attached, while the rest of the house, an L-shaped space, was used for an audience chamber and a combined study and kitchen. The zinc roof was very hot, producing afternoon heat over 30 degrees Celsius, and I somehow never got around to having leaves woven over it. My house was to be located on the headman's land next to an old, abandoned graveyard. It was constructed by a crew of workmen led by the elder brother of the headman's wife.

Soon after my house was completed a large kitchen addition was added to the house of the headman, as inducement for his wife's expanded culinary efforts. The cooking was actually, I later found, assigned to the headman's adopted daughter, who was also has wife's niece, daughter of the chief carpenter who made both house and kitchen. I had paid for the labor on my house but the carpenter had provided the labor on the kitchen, free. After all, his sister and daughter were to be recipients of its benefits. So while I was preparing to begin a study of the symbolism of kinship I became gradually aware of operation of an elaborate and complex kinship surrounding the family that had agreed to take me in and accept the major responsibility for my welfare while in Malaya.

Living under the protection of the headman of the village of some 250 persons caused me some concern. Was I not a ward of a member of the ruling group? I tried to include interviews with members of factions opposed to my protector as much as possible, but I never was completely relieved of the feeling that I was getting one side of the story. For example, the headman's fiercest rivalry was with a man whose grand-father had been headman and who coveted government recognition of his right to inherit the post. They had had fisticuffs in the past over access to the local stream, which the headman's rival had cut off. The situation was settled for the time by the Assistant District Officer. There were several other enemies that the headman had to deal with periodically. The leader of the religious committee who was responsible for the building of a local *madrasah* (prayer hall) was accused of being lax in his efforts. They eventually cooperated in the completion of the structure which was to be subsidized by the District Office. The village was to provide the labor for construction. Government policy was for a committee of local prominent men to lead the village but the headman simply regarded this as a deroga-tion of his skills in organizing labor. Tok Im had also made an enemy of a man who wanted to start a group of villagers who would dig graves for a fee. He said that such a group would be a violation of tradition. He did not oppose gifts for grave digging, however. Of these individuals, I met and chatted with two and had a lengthy genealogical interview with the third in which he aired his views frankly.

Every night at between 6:30 and 7:00 I went to the headman's house for rice and fish, or, once or twice a week, for a bit of meat. We would sit and eat across the table, or, on the floor inside with an open flame lamp between us. Our relationship became more than warm. His wife fixed me special meals when I looked ill in one way or another, or simply to help me sleep. (Americans snore more than Malays think is healthy.) Her specialty was fruit or vegetables boiled in sugar and coconut milk. She sat in on many of my conversations with her husband and discussed the woman's side of things unashamedly. Toward the end of my stay her husband went on a hunting and fishing trip for three days. During this time she fed me in the normal way and used the opportunity to tell me a lot of things that she thought that I had missed as a result of speaking to her through her husband, about her own life's disappointments and about the economic distress that she perceived as general in the region. She had not had any natural children and her husband had only one (who had a checkered reputation). This commensality certainly helped us develop relationships patterned upon Malay paternal and maternal ones. As time passed, the paternal orientation of the headman's role and the personal comfort that my host felt in that role became apparent.

My headman was a remarkable man by local standards and by my own. His life had brought him into contact with a large number of people from many walks of life and he had participated in the growth of the district from an area of primary and secondary forest to an inhabited one. He had been a trader, a transporter of goods by elephant and a lumberman both independently and working for a contractor from the state capital. He spoke Malay in a variety of dialects, a little Thai (he said, though I suspected he spoke it fluently) and a little Chinese (Hokkien). He was not literate in Roman letters but he could read figures and could calculate rapidly. Tok Im had been naughty in his youth, for a good boy would have stayed behind on the land and not pursued his fortune in distant regions.

Tok Im was an expert woodsman and since much of the distinctive lore of the district and environs concerned the wild animals there and their spirit familiars, I was fortunate in meeting someone who was an authority on the local definitions of their properties. I later found out that he was the cousin of the most renowned shaman in the area. Some of my warmest memories of Malaya concern gatherings when the older men recalled the days when tigers and wild elephants terrorized villagers and special parties of men had to try to bring them under control. These stories made the skins of the assembled males tingle as did mine. Every night we would discuss one topic or another related usually to my social anthropology. I tried to explain to Tok Im the practical implications of existing theories of human behavior and the Malaysian context. He seemed to be keenly interested, and did not take them lightly. Probably the most helpful advice that he gave me was on regionalisms in kinship nomenclature and the variation in the names for categories in other parts of the Malay Peninsula and in the structure of kinship terminologies and rules of inheritance.

GENEALOGIES IN SIK

My interest in the history of Sik began when I started to collect genealogies. Much as Rivers tells us in his several discussions of the genealogical method (ch. Rivers, 1968: 97-100) the collection of information about family lines and ongoing social relationships led to inquiries concerning the second and third ascending generations and the geographical origins of the members of those generations. I soon found out that it was almost unknown for a middle-aged person to know about a grandparent who had been born in Sik. I could not find one. The most important shaman said that Sik had been inhabited about three hundred years. I was skeptical about this but duly recorded it. Later I found out that the shaman was referring to a mythical time in which the spirit familiars of the ancestors arrived. For my assessment of the actual length of habitation I asked several people and they generally did not know. Tok Im gave me a fairly precise guess. He suggested that I got to the areas with dead coconut trees and count their rings and then add this to the number of rings on neighboring living trees. Malays plant new trees near old ones and when one dies they plant another. The trees record the succession of rainy and dry seasons in horizontal rings on their trunks. Using this measure, he said that Sik had been inhabited under one hundred and twenty years. I checked this myself and even allowing a few years overlap it appeared that Sik had been inhabited by Malays since the middle of the last century. Before that there had probably only been ancestors of the modern *orang asli* (aborigines). After that I began to look around for old stands of coconut trees, but my estimate, using his method, remained close to his. The historical record, nonetheless, does not go back nearly far enough to confirm or disconfirm Tok Im's hypothesis but it was an intriguing suggestion.

The Malay population of Sik has several origins. One element speaks Thai, with Malay as its second language. Its members probably came to Kedah as Thai troops and converted to Islam. Another element came from Yala in Thailand and a final group came to Sik from the west coast of Malaya. I had originally thought of this district as pristine and separate from the explosive changes that had taken place on the coasts of northern Malaya and southern Thailand, yet it turned out to have been populated as a result of them. I needed to know about the origins of Sik's people simply to isolate and classify the dialects spoken there. Two major Malay dialects are spoken in Sik. One is similar to Penang Malay which has been described in at least one article (Hamilton, 1922). This dialect, among other things, involves a series of regular sound shifts from standard pronunciations. The most glaring of these shifts occurs in words with final syllable *us or as* these syllables being transformed into *ui*, or *ai*, respectively. Similarly, final *ul*, *ol* or *al* become *ui*, *oi* and *ai*. In the Sik dialect, which was said to

correspond with Yala Malay, a parallel shift was made but the high vowel
i in the final dipthong is replaced by a lightly articulated final aspiration
(*h*). Sik's dialects included many nuances in vocabulary distinguishing
them from Standard Malay, Penang Malay and from the Malay of Yala.

MY VILLAGE FRIENDS

I had a paid assistant during most of the period that I was in Sik. He was
an immense help with my field data collection and we might have even
developed a warm personal relationship had it not been for the jealousy
of his wife. This poor man could not leave home for even a few hours
without an extended interview from his wife, who accused him of being a
flirt. This was embarrassing to me even though our work did not involve
such as could, by standards of Malay custom, destroy a marriage. Later in
my stay his wife escalated her complaints against him and began to throw
blunt objects at him: pots, pans, etc., and the headman had to intervene.
I found out that the escalation had been occasioned by events about which
I initially had no knowledge and over which I had no control.

Several months after I arrived I was befriended by two young men who
were about fourteen years old and who had both gone to the government
Malay-medium middle school. They came to my house at least once a
week to play chess, tell jokes or just chat about much of nothing. They
were my eyes and ears in the village and I hope that they learned even a
small amount as much from our association as I did. They helped to
translate local idiom into concepts that could be compared with similar
Malay concepts elsewhere. I came to respect their opinions on many
matters especially when they would contest what their elders presented as
definitive local usage, often suggesting that everyday usage was much
different from the normative statements of local wise men.

Through my young friends I learned how much my work depended
upon an improved understanding of Malay. When I arrived in Malaya I felt
that one could learn to command a local dialect and complete one's
research by means of it. Gradually, I came to see that language is an open-
ended historical process that can be viewed, imperfectly, as a system. The
Yala derived upland dialect differed from the coastal one, while Radio
Malaysia and the national school system had made a major impact on
everyone's speech. People were becoming more proud of their national
language and were proud to speak it correctly to me. The language that
I used had been a problem from the time that I arrived. I had studied

Bahasa Indonesia (Indonesian) at the University of Hawaii. The excellent aural — oral training that I had there prepared me for early comprehension and speech, but I spoke with a very bad accent from the Malay point of view. The syntax was all wrong. The Indonesian preference for subject — verb — object sequences, particularly when discussing complicated subjects just did not hold in Sik among any Malay speakers, and the local syntactical forms were the most difficult aspect of Kedah speech that I had to try to learn to use. I found that proper speech for teachers and educated Malays was closer to Indonesian syntax than to rural peasant speech. Kedah speech had rules of its own which I had to learn but I was expected to speak more like a teacher than like a farmer. This was difficult because there were no teachers in my village with whom I could interact in Malay. Therefore, in the matter of language, my young friends played a crucial role. They tried (I think subconsciously) to use an appropriate idiom of speech for me through our interactions. Our conversations were a great help. When I play tapes of my initial use of Malay and compare them with later interviews I can see their influence which supplemented the process by which confusion and discomfort changed into easy familiarity in most situations.

I began to read Malay novels late at night by the open flame light that everyone there used (brighter lights attracted many more insects). First I chose some from authors whose styles were close to Indonesian and gradually shifted to more Malaysian ones. Kedah has produced several important Malay writers and one of Malaysia's most prominent novelists, Shahnon Ahmad, was born in and had a residence in Sik. My friends, particularly Man, who was still in school, took an active interest in my reading. While at first I could read only ten pages in an evening, and it seemed that I had to spend more time with the dictionary than with the text, gradually my reading speed went up and I began to use the dictionary more for connotation than denotation. My breakthrough in vocabulary probably came when I was about to conclude my stay but it was real. Every day I went to Sik Town on my bicycle and picked up the Malay newspaper that was waiting for me at my local newsdealers. Some days I thought that Malay studies were an endless task. I learned to have patience. If literary Malay was hard for me, I could assure myself that it was not so easy for the Malays themselves.

Discussing Malay novels also gave me a chance to compare my insights into the personalities of the characters with those of my friends. I was surprised to find how similar our points of view were. There was one important difference that we had: the interpretation of a novel about a Malay politician who is experiencing mental problems because of the moral dilemmas inherent in his job. Man said that these mental troubles were inevitable because the politician's role necessitated excessive study of the minutiae of office. The "head full of cares" conduced to aggravation and moroseness. I had discovered here a source of perduring conservatism in Malay folk theories of mental illness (cf. Resner and Hartog, 1970: 372).

MY ETHNIC IDENTITY

I never fully understood how my ethnic identification as a black American affected peoples' relationships with me. That I am black was known and commented upon. Black skin is not positively valued in Malay society, and is considered a liability in physical appearance. Many Malays in my village had similar skin coloring to my own, but I was of African descent and my physical appearance concomitantly different. Much as I tried to learn local stereotypes of Africans I was only able to collect a few and they appeared to be similar to stereotypes of Africans found elsewhere: poor, ignorant people, probably not Muslim. There was a strong positive identification with Muhammad Ali, the then heavyweight champion and there were inquiries about the strength of Islam among black Americans. People asked questions about the treatment of black Muslims in America. Was there freedom of worship or did the Christians oppress Muslims? These were tricky, difficult questions.

If I could not identify a clear African stereotype, or a cultural conception of what a black American was, I felt that white Americans were assimilated more to the cultural pattern reserved for British than I was. Kedah was never directly ruled by Britain and there had not been British district officers, nor had there been many British employees of Kedah. The British that came were consultants and specialists in areas in which the local Malay population could not immediately supply manpower. There were surveyors, engineers and doctors who had served the state government. Officials from the central government of the colony visited from time to time and were accorded deference. There was a feeling among the less educated that white people were more powerful than Malays, although this feeling was changing rapidly. Farmers told stories of complaints made to the British about the evil deeds of Malay civil servants and that their complaints were heeded, wrongs were righted and officials transferred. The Peace Corps volunteers in Sik found the deference paid to whites too much of the colonial sort for their liking and some complained that people were secretive and not forthcoming. Perhaps it is well to note that the volunteers in the northern portion of Malaya were married couples who did not board, who cooked for themselves and lived, from the Malay point of view, in self-contained households. This appears to have supplemented the deference normally shown to whites and made the going difficult for some. There were also stories of black Peace Corps volunteers in Malaya and a common feature of the stories was their affinity for Malay speech and the many cultural events that they attended.

As people got to know me, they were naturally more familiar with the purpose of my visit. They knew that I was not a Peace Corps volunteer and that I had come to learn about Malay customs and values. A white anthropologist could have had a similar identification, but I feel that it probably would have taken him longer. Having been exposed to a wider range of social situations in Malaya my assessment of the advantages and disadvantages of being a non-white in a traditionally white role became more provisional. I do know that villagers in Sik were forming a consciousness of racial problems in the West. They wanted to know how it felt to be black in America. Does Muhammad Ali suffer discrimination? Why was Martin Luther King killed? What is discrimination like? These questions came at unexpected times and in unexpected places and made for categorical solidarity: We were non-white in a world in which whites have the most power.

THE VILLAGE BOMOH

My relationship with Tok Din, the village *bomoh* (shaman) had an important influence on my comprehension of the Malay language and upon my eventual interpretation of Malay ideas about social relationships. I had expected the guardians of village folk religion to provide helpful insights into social relationships and I was not disappointed. Tok Din was able to explicate a complex system of genealogical categories that were transmitted bilaterally through a series of kinds of substance that realized themselves in kinds of abilities and aptitudes, by providing physical propensities toward expressive movements. These propensities are explicated in terms of *angin* (winds, similar to the Western concept of humors) that are part of the body. These *angin* also made people liable to illness by attack from evil spirits since it was thought that the past members of genealogical lines used them to establish relationships with spirits, particularly in order to perform theatrical forms or mediate with the supernatural. The way to cure illness caused by wayward spirits and troublesome *angin* was to perform a trance exorcism which revived the *angin*, attracted the evil spirits and eventually drove them away.

I had read about such exorcisms in Skeat's *Malay Magic* (1967) and in works by Winstedt (1961) and Firth (1967 and 1974) but I had not read of an attempt to see them as systematic ideological elements for segments of Malay communities. All previous works tended to regard them as simply supernatural ideas as opposed to ideas about nature. I was able (Banks, 1976) to show that these so-called beliefs were parts of a comprehensive Malay theory of the natural order and not part of a theory of a supernatural, transcendant order outside of nature.

I first met Tok Din about six months into my stay. We met after a trance exorcism being given in our village. I went to his house to discuss it with him after I had collected some material on the ideas that non-specialists had of its rationale. He provided me with several long interviews which I was able to transcribe and use to get more detailed future interviews. Tok Din was a warm and jovial personality. He was about 55 years old when I met him and he had been an entertainer in his youth and had later became a *bomoh*. What I liked most about Tok Din, although it would be hard to pick one attribute, was his ability to tell a long story well, without excessive elements, digressions or compromises with his vocabulary. His pronunciation of rural Malay was superb. His voice had a musical ring. His total style was of a public official, careful of his words and conscious of the serious problems that his expertise was called upon to solve: sorrow, death, disappointment. The relationship between us was modelled on that between a *guru* and his protogee. I was advised by the headman to bring him a couple of pounds of sugar when I went to visit: to sweeten his coffee for the evening.

In addition to his explications, Tok Din loved to give examples, especially when they involved recitation of an invocation (*jampi*). He told me that these did not sound right to the spirits when simply spoken and that was why he did not hesitate to recite them in isolation. I found out what he meant by this later in my stay during an elaborate exorcism performed at the far northern end of the district. Performed in context these invocations or spells were like musical cadenza passages recited to the accompaniment of the *gendang* (two faced drum) which punctuated Tok Din's phrases. The first (*ibu*) *gendang* player (there were two) turned out to be Tok Im, who could not agree on a fee for playing in the ceremony but who came anyway on the first night to play for fun. The total band consisted of two *gendang*, and a set of two gongs along with sticks of bamboo clacked together (*cerek*) by children. The band played several set rhythms, but the *jampi* were always performed as a duet between *gendang* and *bomoh*. The tempo became faster and faster as the *jampi* unfolded in a subtle crescendo. The total effect of the performance was awe inspiring. What had been spells to attract spirits evoked joy in the assembled audience through their pure aesthetic value. Gradually, as each spell reached its climax and denouement, the drums and gong re-entered in regular rhythm and the clacking of the *cerek* began again. This went on for hours and hours as one spell built upon another, one spirit came to join another. The spirits spoke to the *bomoh* through the members of the kinship group for whom the exorcism was being given. The spirits' requests and complaints would be answered by more *jampi* and conferences with those not in trance.

After the conclusion of the three days of ceremonies necessary for a successful exorcism, I visited Tok Din and we discussed them from a variety of perspectives. I have continued to discuss similar matters with him in subsequent visits. He enjoyed hearing my tapes of his performance and adding spells that it had not been necessary on this occasion to include. A new skeptical outlook about the village world and its supposedly hostile spirit environment was growing, augmented by the deaths from an epidemic of dengue fever subsequent to my first field trip. The attacks resembled syndromes attributed to spirits. One suspects that use of traditional medicine without aspirin and vitamins increased the death toll.

PEER GROUP RELATIONS

I did not really have a group of same age friends while in Malaya, save some salaried government employees in Sik Town. The village's youth about my age (22 years) were too busy during a major portion of the day for us to spend leisure hours together. Our activity patterns were different. The young men of my village went to tap rubber before sunrise and returned and were finished their activities preparing the latex that they had collected by ten or eleven, that is, by the heat of the day. They would then either go to town or tend to fields, if they had paddy land. Many of the youth about my age did not have land and simply dawdled during their hours after work. It must have been a boring existence all in all since many of them had been to middle school but really couldn't put their educations to use in the simple work of tapping rubber (cutting open the tree, collecting the cups of dripped latex, coagulating it with acetic acid and rolling it into strips of latex). They dressed in urban clothing with tight pants of synthetic fiber (called *seluar yengki* or *seluar ketat* which were disapproved by older village males), wash and wear shirts and shoes without socks or Japanese thong sandals. A group of men would rent a shack for five dollars a month and share the cooking.

My villager peer group must have envied my affluence. I had the use of a car for part of my stay. I did not tap rubber and had a steady source of income. Many of them were either landless or were headed for small landed inheritances. Virtually all were looking for employment and would travel far for a chance to work in a factory. Such employment appeared to them to be more exciting and the cash more certain than rubber tapping. This group contained some strong scoffers at Malay magic as espoused by Tok Din. Every few weeks one or another of these young men would visit me and provide me with the benefit of his opinions concerning what I was interested in or concerning his own predicament. Often I heard long analyses of the political changes sweeping the Malay community throughout Malaysia, particularly of the advances of the Islamic Party (P.A.S.). I was given descriptions of the economic arrangements made between the rubber tappers union on the estates and the workers and the superiority of working on an estate as opposed to tapping for a small-holder and dividing the proceeds in two. My sympathy with the plight of these Asian youths made me more interested in the extent and implications of landlessness in Sik and I began to study man — land relationships and rice yields through government publications and interviews.

SOME AFTERTHOUGHTS

When I came to Malaya I intended to write a study of the symbols of Malay kinship, using genealogical interviewing and participant observation. I studied my genealogical interviews and re-played recordings that I had made of them. Each informant's theories about the social system received my attention and I tried to fathom common elements and distinguish them from variants. As I did this I saw that the variants were related to situational, historical factors. The old residents of Yala ancestry had different ideas about sibling order terms than did those from the west coast. The former had greater optimism since they had come heir to an abundance of land over the last several generations while the latter had inherited landlessness from their parents. Although the village was divided about equally between old residents and those from the west coast it appeared that the migrant population would soon have a controlling voice since they were the most active members of the community in matters of religion and community activities. There was a floating population of rubber tappers in their late teens or early twenties.

48   DAVID J. BANKS

I could also see the influence of Radio Malaysia upon the consciousness of the peasants with respect to health and disease. The folk religion espoused by Tok Din and Tok Im was coming under attack from the Ministry of Health's clinics and from a new Islamic orthodoxy which sees itself in conflict with the old animistic beliefs. The conflicts that I saw between rival ideologies of kinship and of disease curing, for example, were not simply inherent in a static social structure but were parts of dynamic social changes sweeping Malay communities across Malaya. I decided that the old ideas needed to be recorded in order to understand the processes of change. One could hardly predict the direction of all of the changes beginning to take place. Would the Malaysian government significantly lessen the Malay dependence on rice and rubber as sources of income? Would steps be taken to lessen the explosive growth of population (Banks, 1972)? What kind of Islamic theology would involve the increasingly literate peasantry? What kinds of compromises would be made between the Malays and other racial and ethnic groups? I come to see the anthropologist's role as that of an historian of pre-modern ideology, of those aspects of life not generally recorded by other scholars: ideologies of social relations and of the relationship of man to nature. Anthropologists would record aspects of quality of the life of peasant populations as human possibilities without romanticizing them, of symbols in change and not of structural systems.

REFERENCES CITED

Banks, David J. 1972, Changing Kinship in North Malaya. American Anthropologist 4: 1254-1275.
1976, Trance and Dance in Malaya: The Hindu-Buddhist Complex in Northwest Malay Folk Religion. Special Studies. Council on International Studies. State University of New York, No. 74.
Firth, Raymond, 1967, Ritual and Drama in Malay Spirit Mediumship. Comparative Studies in Society and History 9: 190-207.
1974, Faith and Skepticism in Kelantan Village Magic. In Kelantan: Religion, Society and Politics in a Malay State. William Roff, ed., pp. 192-224. Kuala Lumpur: Oxford University Press.
Hamilton, A. W., 1922, Penang Malay. Journal of the Straits Branch of the Royal Asiatic Society 85: 67-86.
Resner, Gerald and Joseph Hartog, 1970, Concepts and Terminology of Mental Disorder among Malays. Journal of Cross-Cultural Psychology 1: 369-382.
Rivers, W. H. R., 1968, The Genealogical Method of Anthropological Inquiry. In Kinship and Social Organization. New York: Humanities Press.
Skeat, W. W., 1967, Malay magic. New York: Dover (originally published 1900).
Winstedt, R. O., 1961, The Malay Magician, being Shaman, Saiva and Sufi. London: Routledge and Kegan Paul.

CHAPTER 4

Field Experience in Three Societies

ENYA P. FLORES-MEISER

My field experience includes the study of child-rearing practices among Moslem Samals of the Sulu archipelago, Philippines (1963-1964); compadrazgo and socioeconomic patterns among a southern Tagalog group, Philippines (summers 1969 and 1971); and ethnicity and religious attitudes among Japanese-Brazilians in the state of Parana, Brazil (for a total of six months, 1975). I suggest that these studies are probably no more dramatic or boring on occasions than some others. Certainly, none delivered exotic data. While each is a unique experiences it is the nature of the "self in the field" and its continuity and discontinuity to which I shall address myself.

In the first case, I worked among a people with whom I shared common citizenship at the time of the study (although I have since acquired U.S. citizenship) but who belong to a non-Christian minority group in the predominantly Christian Philippine society. Thus, at the start of fieldwork I was to locate myself in the insider-outsider continuum veering slightly to the left when compared to a western anthropologist. The second study was conducted in the community that nurtured me from childhood to early adulthood. In this instance, I was definitely an insider when compared to the first, However, my American acculturation sometimes got in the way and was not dismissed lightly. Lastly, in the third study, I felt very much an outsider altogether who periodically gained insight into being an insider.

BEING A CHRISTIAN WOMAN IN A MOSLEM ISLAND

My field trip to Sulu (specifically Sibutu island and the last one within Philippine territory) was the result of a number of considerations. During the first part of the 1960's the Philippine government in cooperation with foreign agencies and missionary groups launched vigorous measures directed to the need to integrate non-Christian groups into the national society, including the ever resistant Moslems to the south. In part, because of this institutional support, and in part, due to my childhood fascination of the area (as depicted in grade school books), I chose Sulu to be the site for my anthropological rite of passage. There was also the equally important consideration on which my faculty adviser and I agreed: that doing my first field experience in Sulu may not prove to be as traumatic as perhaps doing it in Indonesian New Guinea for which funds would have been made available to me had I decided in favor of the latter alternative.

Through the Bishop of Sulu and the Coordinated Investigation of Sulu Areas project, I obtained both funds and other facilities for the research on Sibutu island. The people of Sibutu island in common with the Moslems in Sulu and Mindanao regions and other non-Christian groups constitute minority status in the Christian Philippines. Unlike the typical Suluan who would tend to be a fisherman, the Sibutuan made their living by building boats they called *kumpit* which were sold to merchants in North Borneo, Zamboanga or Cebu when finished.[1]

For the first week in the island, I occupied temporary quarters in the compound where the mission high school is located a distance of less than a mile away from the coastal barrios. Determined to be inconspicuous throughout my stay, I underplayed my status, i.e., that of an educated woman; avoided unnecessary contact with other Christians in the island (high school teachers and their families who lived in isolation in the compound); and made no effort to contact other fieldworkers in the archipelago. In four months, I learned to undertake an intelligible conversation in the native language, siamal.

Working through students primarily, and bypassing the leadership of the barrios altogether, I found a family in the smallest of three contiguous barrios which reluctantly took me in as a lodger. Under the circumstances, it was the best accommodation available then, with the exception perhaps of a *datu* (nobleman)'s house located in the central barrio.

At this time my paramount consideration was personal convenience. The datu's house was much too crowded. I would realize later, however, that this decision would have its toll.

There were only three members in my host's family: father, mother, and a young son. The fourth member was a daughter whom I never met because she was away to school at a university. She was visited by her father twice a year but was not permitted to return home before her college degree was obtained. In the course of fieldwork, I became the daughter surrogate, a fact which later brought difficulty to my subsequent attempts to transfer residence, as originally called for in the research design. The idea was finally abandoned, and thereafter, forced my participation in and observation of village life to concentrate in the section where I lived making it necessary in the end to employ more structured interviews to cover greater ground in other barrios.

My presence in the barrio was welcomed but not fully understood. "Why after all would anyone leave the United States to study a bunch of poor people like us," asked an *imam* (Moslem priest) once, "unless of course she is crazy." The comment was made in jest, but certainly well meant. I was after all, not a teacher in the mission school, or a Chinese merchant, or a medical or paramedical personnel, or a government agent. I was nobody with respect to the structure of roles and statuses associated with prestige. I was nothing and of no consequence to the barrios. Therefore, as the novelty of my presence wore on and I became a permanent part of the barrios, I was generally ignored. This became more apparent during the big social and ceremonial events sponsored by the noble families in the central barrio and to which I did not often get invited. My attendance, in these affairs however, was always welcomed but it made me no less self-conscious. I did not cherish being taken for granted especially when other Christians received a fair share of the people's attention. Even when I could rationalize on the merits of being ignored and left alone, my personal inclination to desire the same esteem accorded to the other Christians sometimes became a source of personal anxiety. In the confines of the barrio and the island, my need for esteem becomes very real and probably exacerbated by my identification with the Christian group. As the community progressively took me for granted, I spent more time at home transcribing field notes. Even note-taking became laborious and boring in the end, which I finally abandoned weeks before leaving the island. Having done so, retrospective moments sometimes make me wonder how much information had been missed during that period.

In my attempt to maintain the outsider-insider balance, I would periodically leave the island for another, hoping to recapture upon returning the qualitative impressions about the island culture as it was experienced at first entry. Sometimes I was successful, sometimes, not.

The daily transformation from being insider to outsider and back, cannot be measured in the field situation, so that ultimately what counts in a reasonably successful research is the mutual accommodation of each other's differences which both the observer (anthropologist) and the observed have learned progressively to accept. As a Christian woman anthropologist, I noted elsewhere[2] that I was allowed to sit with the men, as no unmarried woman to my knowledge was permitted to do in public feasts and prayer chants. On these occasions I was routinely offered cigarettes to smoke among them. Also, I was admitted to the front part of the mosque during the Friday service while the few women, who attended those services sat in the back. How many times I had unknowingly desecrated their world, I'll never know except at least once. While waiting for the Friday Prayers to begin, Mr. Ali, a public school teacher, came to sit next to me and engaged me in a conversation. It was rather lively, and a few other men came near to join us. But as soon as the prayers began, Mr. Ali quietly slipped away, and did not come back until 10 minutes later. When the prayers were concluded, we walked out of the mosque together and continued our conversation. When I asked why he left as the prayers began, he gave me a very vague answer. It would be months later when I would be told that he left to ritually cleanse himself all over again since I "supposedly touched his hand and inadvertantly polluted him." I, of course, apologized. My interest that my informants live as good moslems is met with similar interest in my landlord that I also live a good Christian life.

On Sundays, my landlord woke me up earlier than other days so as not to miss Mass. Despite my repeated assurances that the mission priest would not start without me, I found myself awakened at the first hour of dawn and incessantly warned not to be late. His concern over my religious obligations only equalled mine and no doubt was enhanced by the fact that I was a guest at his house. Many times he took me to the mission on his motorcycle and fetched me after Mass. Once he came too soon and waited outside the chapel for one half hour. We never really discussed religion except to compare fasting practices during which time we decided that the Moslem way was more strenuous. He seemed glad about it. Implicitly, we saw each other as model persons relative to our respective cultures. Although I attended the Friday prayers at the mosque quite often, neither he nor his family ever came to Mass. His tolerance was exemplary when he told his wife who later told me in English the following:

"Enya is a good Christian. I am sorry she is not a Moslem. I think
she will make a good Moslem, too."

In consideration of the preceding, it was obvious that my person was judged not in the context of their own cultural values, but in terms of mine as they perceived and presumed them for which I was more than grateful. For my part, I never once entertained the idea of eating pork even when opportunity presented itself and the temptation was nagging. I was on a few occasions privy to the young men's surreptitious hunting trips for wild boars. Yet I never considered their offers of meat after a successful hunt. Such an acceptance to my mind would not only have destroyed rapport but more seriously, it would have defiled their world. During the fasting season I tried also to observe their rules (i.e., no food or drink allowed from dawn to sunset) to the level of toleration beyond which my inability in numerous instances to continue further was always forgiven. It is on this common ground as noted above no matter how narrow that humanity is bridged, at the same time that the insider-outsider distinction is periodically assessed.

There is perhaps one detail of this fieldwork which I wish had been different. I feel that in retrospect, had I located myself in the central barrio (which is also the oldest of the three), I might have sensed much earlier than I did, the fundamental split attendent upon the barrio organization, and perhaps avoided any seeming identification that might have been hinted by my association with one group or faction rather than another. Jealousies between the nobility and commoner I found later usually translated into open rivalry and political struggle, and created two main factions, the nobility vs. the commoners (See Flores-Meiser, 1969).

Although the Sibutu community is not as status-stratified in the sense that the Indian villages were described to be (Berreman, 1962; Mencher, 1974; and Morris, 1973), the overall upshot of my strategy of entry bore some resemblances to the problems recorded for the Indian villages.[3] When finally, I was ready to move into the sphere of the noble families, the members of this group had turned cautious, reluctant, and for most of the time indifferent to my questions. For example, when I asked Datu Bandung to confirm the facts about the controversial nature of his daughter's marriage, he grew diffident and sarcastically responded that should not I "ask Mr. X, my landlord, since he seems to know everything. He will tell you." Since my landlord belongs to the commoner group the sarcasm was unmistakable.

Thus my information about the nobility was obtained in general from the commoners and for the most part unconfirmed. It is difficult to assess whether a reverse strategy of entry would have made some difference. Admittedly, I should have been more persistent in pursuing the noble families. Perchance this would have been made easier had I sought residence in the datu's household, despite its relatively larger membership. How much more information would have been made available to me had it been the case, is academic. Would going through the barrio leadership have altered the nature of my data?

STUDYING RELATIVES AND FRIENDS[4]

My second fieldwork was undertaken in a city of over 100,000 inhabitants, in a southern Tagalog province where I was born and raised as a child. Until a martial law government was imposed on the Philippines, I managed to return often to visit family and friends and renew ties with the less immediate kinsmen. But for the summers of 1969 and 1971, I returned for the purpose of studying the community. This feat was indeed most difficult to say the least, and fraught with role conflict and clashes as one might imagine. To draw the lines between the scientific, professional role and that of a friend and kinsman was a task next to being impossible. Wittingly, I chose an area of inquiry with little emotional involvement and controversy, that of compadrazgo and socioeconomic stratification.

From all appearances, the homecoming part of the trip seemed to dominate over the research end of it. Rarely aware of the professional objectives I had set to do, informants often construed my interviewing activities as no more than friendly visits and mere curiosity. Being a native of the community, I was able to visit households with practically no assistance and little introduction. I kept no notebook and jotted down notes only after each interview. In a foreign setting, one naturally proceeds to record all that is observed and learned often with little discrimination in anticipation of much later sorting process. But in this particular situation I was always sifting information to determine what was appropriate and relevant datum. It was easy to dismiss note-taking. Yet fieldwork in this situation is no less trying. From my vantage point, the dichotomy between relatives and non-relatives is easily invoked. For example, damaging facts about the former hardly found themselves in the journal; whereas, similar data on adulterous liaisons, bribes and political corruption were entered for non-relatives. Indepth and enduring interviews from relatives and friends were decidedly pointless as they tended to become counterinterviews, at best, and reminiscences about a distant past. There were constant interruptions created not only by informants but also other people as well, leaving me with unfinished interviews most of the time. Relatives known to have difficult personalities were deliberately left out. Curiously, it is in this fieldwork, among relatives of different gradations and casual acquaintances that I also became engaged in extensive patterns of gift-giving which I found it altogether unnecessary in Sulu or Brazil.

In the role of relative or friend and member of the community, I bore the option to define the preferred social sector toward which the expression of loyalty, affection and unqualified support was encouraged and with which social participation and interaction were maximized. But in the role of the anthropologist and social scientist, the need to break out of this confinement, so to speak, into the other sectors of the community was not only mandatory but sound research. The consequence of course was my greater exposure to the community, its judgements and its sentiments which I did not have to deal with in previous homecomings. In this context, my acculturation to another society (and therefore, transformation in my personality) was subject to greater scrutiny and evaluation. My effort to uphold the traditional behavior and etiquette received both approbation and skepticism.[5] Approbation seemed to me to say in effect "good show for not forgetting or giving up the old customs, and permitting yourself to be transformed only superficially;" while the skeptical reactions suggested the same behavior to be pure affectations, a "put-on" and therefore, unreal. The presence of these two points of view in a sense indicated the limits by which the insider-outsider determination hinged. How much deviation indeed is a native daughter allowed to remain a genuine member of the community, despite long absence from it, was not clear. The genuine member should after all be morally responsible to the community and its cultural integrity. Thus from this vantage point, one cannot exhibit too much or too little acculturation without constant reassessment of her membership in the community. On the psychological level, I found my own marginality sometimes counterproductive and hindered me from coping with daily social demands or trying harder to do so. This was after all the community I left in the first place, presumably, because it seemed wanting then. Thus the tension between restoring maximum membership in the community and maintaining a sense of detachment not as an anthropologist but as a former member who has outgrown her community demanded constant management. To this might be added the experience of a deep sense of betrayal and vulnerability incumbent upon this type of research. After all, does not one who lays bare his community lays himself bare as well?

One cannot afford to relax in fieldwork — even in one's own community. Here the gossip and rumor seemed considerably more engaging, if not interesting. On two occasions while seeking information on a number of matters, I was named the source of a rumor which embarrassed two relatives who vowed never to speak to me again. Reflecting now on this matter, it is clear o me that whatever miscalculations I might have caused in this field situation might have been altogether inconsequential in another. In a different setting I would perhaps have exercised more caution, if not greater sensitivity. There is also, I think, an inherent advantage to being an outsider: he is allowed to make mistakes! On the contrary, similar accommodations for the insider are superfluous. I should have known better for I definitely know better than a stranger does. My inadvertant involvement is lesson enough but the fact remains that gossip and rumor provide significant insight into the alignment, segmentation and cohesion within groups and a perspective otherwise not viewed from ordinary interviews.

The segment of the community with which I found relative unease was the local upperclass. To begin with, I knew only a few of them although my parents have friends among them. As a child from the middle class, I established little contact with them and avoided forming friendships among classmates from this group, even when opportunities to have done so presented themselves. Conceivably, my protracted absence from the community prevented me from cultivating friendships among members of this group. Consequently, in attempting to reach this population, I needed assistance to be introduced to intended subjects. At the interview sessions that normally took place in their homes, I found discomfort in their hospitality, which I welcomed and took for granted, however, from the lower and middle classes. In this community where the individaul's esteem and prestige continue to be judged, regardless of his achievements, in the context of the kindred (*angkan*) and its socioeconomic position, I found interviewing among the local upperclass personally excruciating. The behaviors that attend interclass relationships, I came to realize and admit, were another reason for my leaving this community. And so, my data about upperclass informants were minimal requiring supplementary information obtained from the other classes.

By being at once an anthropologist, kinsman, and friend, I found it much easier to acquire information from mere acquaintances than from relatives and close friends. In my effort to achieve greater objectivity as a social scientist, it became necessary in the end to apply more standardized and formal interview procedures used by sociologists in studying their own societies. Even when questionnaires were returned anonymously, I often speculated whether the respondent may have been a certain cousin or another.

AN ASIAN-AMERICAN AMONG JAPANESE-BRAZILIANS

A sabbatical leave brought me to Brazil to conduct an ethnographic study, albeit a short one, in the State of Parana. My increasing interest in Asian immigrants, dilettantish fascination for the Japanese, and attraction to Brazil made the decision unequivocal. Without any knowledge of the Japanese or Portuguese languages, I opted to learn some Portuguese before fieldwork. It proved to be more a sensible decision, despite my great reliance on interpreters.

The Japanese-Brazilians, unlike the two groups described earlier in this paper, do not constitute an exclusive community in the physical sense, but rather, they are widely dispersed in many towns and cities in the States of

Parana and Sao Paulo and the Amazons. They constitute a minority status in these communities except in a few cases.[6] I was particularly interested in the adaptation of the Japanese in the Brazilian culture and thus formulated my design accordingly. My choice of Parana was dictated by the fact that although the Japanese culture in Brazil was well documented for Sao Paulo, little had been written about the Parana counterpart.

One learns very quickly the rigor that attends the bureaucracies of Brazil and subsequently, the wisdom to turn to informal channels.[7] In this connection a former graduate student in my university assisted me in locating us (my children and myself) in her hometown. Through her I also obtained an office in the local college (*faculdade*) which I occupied throughout the duration of my research. She was also responsible for finding a family who provided us temporary quarters.

Falcão (a pseudonym) was a town of 65,000 inhabitants, about 18% of them were Japanese (immigrants) and Japanese-Brazilians (descendants). Many of them have kinship connections in Sao Paulo and the western states; consequently, they travel with frequency and in great distance. Despite the agrarian nature of this community, the people, as in most of Parana, were less entrenched in their communities. This point is immediately evident when comparison is made with the Philippine communities discussed earlier. Quite clearly this is understandable since Falcão is only a few decades old. The people of Falcão, like other Brazilians in this region of the country were constantly busy, hardworking, and optimistic – even proud of the development and potential of their country.

Against this background, I entered this community equipped with a cultural baggage of "odds and ends" with anticipation that these contents will prove helpful in transcending the insider-outsider barrier which any stranger is bound to experience. Bearing Hispanic (maiden) and German (married) names; being a professed Catholic; speaking English almost exclusively (despite the accent and little Portuguese, but not Spanish); and being an American national of Filipino origins, *my identity was as confusing to my informants as it was revealing to me.* Members of the community who bore interest in the "Yankee" culture and American English and who desired to study in American Universities naturally sought me for information and sometimes patronage. Curiously, none of them were Japanese-Brazilians at all. The latter seemed more interested in maximizing participation in their society and showed no inclination to visit the United States or Japan.

It was undoubtedly my ethnic origin and phenotype which contributed in some measure to my acceptance among the Japanese-Brazilians. As they defined their ethnicity primarily in racial terms, so did they view my identity in similar light. In this context attempts by informants to span the chasm between insider and outsider were made on at least three occasions, by speculating about my ancestry. In the opinion of an old man, *an Issei* (immigrant), although my parents are Filipinos, "it is quite possible that in the very distant past, there could have been a Japanese ancestor in your family. Isn't it a shame to lose track of one's history." When I assured him that to my knowledge this was not the case, but that instead the probability of a Chinese ancestor was much greater indeed, he was quite disappointed. Such a gesture surely reminds us of my Sulu landlord who wished I had been a Moslem. The temptation thereafter to pass as an American-Japanese came my way on several occasions. For one, there loomed the possibility for greater interpersonal relationships with informants; for another, there was the chance to simplify my identity as a person and the affinity I bore with them. Racial affinity requires geneaological accounting, and in this case, a Japanese ancestor somewhere along my geneaological tree might have made the difference in their contextual definition of the insider vs. the outsider. To the Japanese-Brazilians, race and ancestry bind their ethnic group.

Most social relationships in Falcão other than those encompassed by kinship or friendship have rationalistic foundations. It is probably fair to say that their most pressing motivations are related to the acquisition of material possession and gaining upward mobility. The people of this community and most of Parana have faith in their industry and sel-reliance. In short, they are committed to the ideals of the middle class culture, regardless of ethnic affiliations. Majority of the Japanese-Brazilians whom I came to know were decidedly middle class and middle class aspirants. Save for three families, the Japanese-Brazilians of Falcão, live in the center and margin of the town. The outlying areas beyond it are in contrast modest homes of wood and galvanized iron roofing in unpaved streets. Here the poorer families live. However, similarly modest homes are found within the town, and are generally occupied by Japanese-Brazilians.

The obvious difference between Japanese-Brazilians and non-Japanese-Brazilian middle class lies mainly in the relative size of their respective families. Japanese-Brazilians tend to have larger families — a fact easily explained by their relatively recent rural experience. Although their life style conforms to the middle class standards of the community, priorities seem to point to encouraging their children to enter professions (i.e., send their children to the universities.) This is done sometimes at the price of deferring gratification of other needs. For example, they wait to paint their wood and frame houses or anchor them in concrete materials until the children are sent to college. The movement from the colonia (farming colony) to town and subsequently, maintaining residences in both places, are all linked together to bring the children closer to schools.

In consideration of the above, it became obvious to me the necessity to restrict research to the sphere of the middle class culture of the community — a prospect I thought unchallenging and unpromising. Consequently, my contact with lower class Brazilians was limited to the servants of the middle class families, just as my experience with the upperclass was pertinent only to the few Japanese-Brazilian families. At the initial stage of the study, I did not then think it necessary to pursue the upperclass of the community per se. When later the matter was reconsidered, time had virtually run out, and gave me an excuse for not knowing them. The Japanese-Brazilians are quite proud of the overall economic gain they have experienced in Brazil.

From my vantage point, participant observation or observation-in-participation meant largely a twice-a-week trip to the supermarket or *quitanda* (stalls of vegetables and fruits in the traditional market place); a weekly attendance in church, laundering clothes with the aid of the old lady (an Issei) next door; getting invited to private homes for dinner (few and far between); occasional social club functions and charity drives or parent-teacher meetings. Added to the above activities were scheduled personal interviews undertaken at informants' homes. On a well spent day, I would have accomplished two of them. An interview schedule proved to be valuable. In addition a questionnaire in Portuguese was administered to Japanese and non-Japanese-Brazilians alike.

I felt toward the close of my study that my comprehension of the Japanese-Brazilians did not pose any great contrasts to my knowledge of other Brazilians. Admittedly, my knowledge of the latter group was not systematically obtained, and very cursory. Still my general observations led me to wonder where all those Japanese exotic customs known in the traditional Japanese culture might all have gone and why the Japanese-Brazilians seemed less exotic than the ones I have read about in mainland Japan. This seemingly efficient group of people and their growing contractual society continually remind me of how like they, Japanese and non-Japanese middle class, are to the "Yankees" of the north. Because Brazilian wages are not at par with those in the United States, most middle class Brazilians need to work at two or three jobs to maintain a socioeconomic level which in some way approximates that of their North American counterpart. Consequently, they have very little time except for themselves and their families and I left the community with only very few friends. After having subscribed to the objectives laid out in the research design, I felt in the end very much still an outsider. I rarely visited

60   ENYA P. FLORES-MEISER

informant's homes more than once, and enjoyed the intimate friendship
of only two key informants. On the other hand, the middle class orientation of this group, made me feel "at home."

CONCLUSION

The three field studies briefly summarized in the preceding pages, although
quite distinct in their research objectives, represent varying points on the
insider-outsider continuum of participant observation. In her natal community, the anthropologist was considerably more insider than outsider
because she left the community to live abroad. In the Sulu community she
was an outsider primarily for being Christian in a Moslem island. And in
Brazil where the sojourn was brief, she was a foreigner who spoke little
Portuguese and phenotypically resembled a Japanese. At the base of the
insider-outsider dilemma, is a social-psychological experience in which the
anthropologist is brought to terms with her identity vis a vis informants
and others. Attendent to this is an occasional unfolding of the self: in Sulu-
the need for personal esteem, and conscious projection of the personal
culture in its ideal patterns; in the home community, conflicting sense of
loyalty and betrayal toward the subjects; and in Brazil, the unsettling
feeling of being a stranger. Despite the uniqueness of each case as
established by the surrounding circumstances, there seems to be a common
thread that runs through all three studies. This commonality points to the
anthropologist's general failure, inability, or, at best, self-consciousness to
strike more than sporadic rapport with the high status/socioeconomic
segment of societies described. One wonders, in fact, how many of us,
anthropologists, have been adept at studying the upperclasses of human
communities. I cannot offer a sound personal analysis of the matter in my
case yet, but knowing full well this limitation, is it fair to ask if such a
deficiency ought to be systematically corrected, or should it be treated as
a constant variable in the past and future field work of this anthropologist?

NOTES

1. Presumably, the present conflict between Moslem insurgents in Sulu and the
   Philippine military forces has temporarily altered this pattern.
2. See Flores-Meiser (1980).
3. I do not wish to imply in the least that the nobility — commoner relationship

is one of separation in the sense of the Indian caste or the traditional Polynesian structure. Rather, the individuals' loyalties to their respective groups are markedly obvious and predictable.

4. This section was the focal point on which Flores-Meiser (1980: 24-28) was based and presented in the Symposium, "Anthropologists and Origin Cultures." 77th Annual Meeting of the American Anthropological Association, in Los Angeles, November 14-18, 1978.

5. For example, gestures of respect toward the elders like kissing their hands or carefully using in speech, the Tagalog word pô which indicates humility, low status, lack of presumption, etc., and thus enhance the status of the person to which the speech is directed.

6. Asahi (var. Assai) in Parana is a town that is almost exclusively Japanese-Brazilians and Japanese is the dominant language. Similar communities, are found as farming colonies in the Amazons, Parana, and Sao Paulo. In some Japanese colonies Afro-Brazilians live nearby and are employed as field laborers by the Japanese-Brazilians.

7. In both Brazilian and Sulu studies, my reliance on the informal network to facilitate entry into the respective communities is parallel.

REFERENCES CITED

Berreman, Gerald, 1962, Behind Many Masks: Ethnology and Impression Management in a Himalayan Village. Society for Applied Anthropology, **Monograph 4.**

Flores-Meiser, Enya P. 1969, Division and Integration in a Sulu Barrio (Sulu, Philippines). In *Anthropology Range and Relevance.* Mario D. Zamora and Zeus A. Salazar, eds. Pp. 511-526. Quezon City, Philippines: Kayumanggi Publishers.

1980, Doing Fieldwork in One's Own Community, In Research Bulletin (Association of Third World Anthropologists) 2 (1): 24-29.

Mencher, Joan, 1975, Viewing Hierarchy from the Bottom Up. In *Encounter and Experience.* Andre Betteille and T. N. Madan, eds. Pp. 114-130. Honolulu: The University Press of Hawaii.

Morris, Patrick G., 1973, Problems of Research in a Stratified Little Community. Anthropology Quarterly 46: 38-46.

CHAPTER 5

The Conversion of A Missionary

VINSON H. SUTLIVE, JR.

The heat shimmered in waves off the sun-baked streets of Sarikei as the *S. S. Pangkor* eased alongside the dock. Although we had sailed through the Suez Canal and the Indian Ocean without the aid of air-conditioning, nothing we had experienced had the impact of this white hot Sarawak port. As we disembarked and walked the mile or so to the missionary bungalow, our eyes teared, forcing us to wipe them continuously. Sounds of strange languages — Malay, Iban, Foochow, and Hakka — and smells from open drains and the town market assaulted our senses. After exchanging pleasantries with the resident missionary, we were treated to a catered meal of fried noodles, garnished with pork, greens, and black mushrooms, all thoroughly saturated with garlic browned in peanut oil, from one of the local coffee shops.

The *Pangkor* was to continue on to Sibu, the port town where we were to live and work, but our hosts insisted we should travel by outboard-powered longboat that afternoon, for we could make the trip in three hours and thus save ourselves the inconvenience of another two days travel by ship. Making our way back through the market to the docks, we descended to a jetty where a longboat, equipped specially for our comfort by one of our colleagues — our senior by some six months — roled easily in the waves and echos. In addition to my wife, Joanne, our three-year old son, Vins, our four-month old daughter, Susan, and me, our party consist-ed of our driver and five English missionaries. Six tiny cane chairs lined both sides of the 24-foot boat, and we seated ourselves with chins on knees. The gunwales had only three inches clearance and, once underway, glistening columns of water, at times as high as the boat's roof, flew past, thrown up as we proceeded upriver. Utterly unschooled in boat travel, we could not know that the three-hour trip was the most uncomfortable — made so by the cane chairs on which we were forced to sit — and fully as perilous as any we would make in our 11 years in Sarawak.

After unloading our baggage and taking everyone to the missionary residence on Island Road, our colleague and I returned to the boat and continued down the Igan River — which divides from the Rejang at Sibu —

to the Malay village where he moored his boat. As we slipped alongside the mangrove post to which the boat was secured, directly behind the house of a Malay driver employed by the missionaries of the Women's Division of The Methodist Church, the driver descended the wooden stairs leading off his kitchen to help tie the boat. My colleagues attempted to tell him that he would be using the Women's Division speed boat and wanted the driver to buy four tins of fuel for the trip. I later discovered that the driver was fluent in Iban — a cognate of Malay — but he feigned confusion and pretended not to understand. An impasse was reached and my colleagues asked if I could explain to the driver in Malay. I had just completed a full year's study of Malay at the Kennedy School of Missions in Hartford, Connecticut, in a course designed by the U.S. Army and began with such critical questions as *Di mane stesen kereta api?* ("Where's the train station?"), and, *Di mane tempat buang ayer?* ("Where's the latrine?"), facilities all but missing in Borneo. Despite the course I quickly discovered that there was a great gulf between my untried Malay and the Sibu dialect, and got nowhere in trying to get the message across to the driver.

On my first day in Sarawak, I learned my first lesson; viz., that the linguistic prescription of listening before speaking is indeed a sound one. Chagrined by my inability to communicate, I determined to keep my ears open and my mouth closed until I knew what to say and how to say it. (It must be noted, however, that some discomfort in language learning, particularly in a fieldwork situation, is unavoidable. Any effort to speak in the vernacular is self-exposing and may evoke responses ranging from approval to ridicule, but it is a risk one must take.)

Our arrival in Sarawak was the climax of three-years' preparation for work as missionaries. Joanne and I had applied to the Board of Missions of the Methodist Church during my middler year in the Vanderbilt School of Religion. I had wanted to be a missionary in my early teens, had abandoned the idea in college when I was fascinated by clinical psychology and seriously considered graduate work in that field, before deciding to enter seminary. A visit by a personnel secretary of the Board rekindled my interests and, after discussing the decision with Joanne, I made application for missionary service.

As part of the screening process we were required to undergo rigorous physical and psychological examinations, and to write a statement of our beliefs. Joanne wrote a profoundly simply one but I, giddy with theological concepts and jargon, produced a very involved statement. As a result, when we were interviewed by the Regional Committee she was asked only two questions, but I was soon challenged to debate by the personnel secretary and a college president. To my enormous relief, another member of the committee, a professor of philosophy at Vanderbilt, rallied to my defense. We thus survived the interview and were informed shortly afterwards that we had been accepted as candidates.

During my senior year at Vanderbilt we began the study of Japanese, having been told that our appointment would be in Japan. After one semester's study, however, we received word that the Methodist quota for Japan was filled and that we should choose a new appointment from Hong Kong, of which we had heard, Malaya, of which we had heard, and Sarawak, of which we had not heard. Consulting an encyclopedia we read about the British colony, land of headhunters and White Rajahs, and other exotica, all of which intrigued us. When we learned of the rapid conversion of indigenes to Christianity — a "people's movement" in missiology — and that we would be working in a pioneering situation, we knew that was the place we should work.

Upon completion of my seminary training, we moved to Hartford for a year's training in linguistics, anthropology, Malay, Southeast Asian societies and cultures, missiology and, perhaps most important, "how to keep healthy in hot climates," the last course taught by a physician who had gone to Egypt in the first decade of this century! (A book the physician had written proved a God-send when our third child, Thom, developed digestive problems. After months of unsuccessful treatment and almost at the point of despair, my wife and I — at 4 a.m. after an all nighter with Thom — read that some Caucasians had difficulty synthesizing food in tropical climates because of a vitamin B deficiency. As soon as the local apothecary opened we bought a bottle of liquid B, started Thom on it, and our problem was solved! Several years later we solved a similar problem with a gibbon who also had problems digesting his food.)

After our commissioning service by the church and final visits to our families and supporting church, we sailed from New York in September, 1957, on H.M.S. Mauretania for Southhampton and, after a week in London, from Southhampton to Singapore on the Willem Ruys. Asian flu struck while we were in the eastern end of the Mediterranean and we were all confined to our quarters with high fevers. To compound our discomfort, the air-conditioning system malfunctioned as we were in the Sea of Reeds, awaiting formation of the convoy of ships to proceed through the Suez Canal which had just been reopened. We stopped overnight at Port Said, and then entered the Indian Ocean. The second evening out of Port Said, Celeste Amstutz, wife of the bishop of the church in which we were to work, told us that we were to establish an Iban department in the Methodist Theological School in Sibu. (Perhaps the regional committee had seen more in the debate than we had realized, for we had been so anxious to be accepted we both were convinced that we probably would not be approved for service.)

Joanne and I held high — and we now realize, unrealistic — images of "the mission field" and of the people who comprise the church in relatively new situations. She had been a member of a small church, now Christian and Missionary Alliance, before our marriage, after which she became a Methodist. Our expectations of the missionary experience had been fed by the highly selective presentations of missionaries on furlough, during which they visited congregations to share information and solicit support. Understandably, such presentations describe the best and the worst of overseas situations, but not the normal frictions of social life which exist in varying forms and to different degrees wherever people must adjust to one another.

We were almost totally unprepared for what proved to be the greatest shock of all — one far greater than heat, humidity, sounds and smells. And it hit us immediately. After dinner on our first evening in Sarawak, we sat down with the missionaries, husband and wife, with whom we were to live for the next month until they were posted upriver. We had known them in Hartford, and they had preceded us by six months. For reasons which later became clear, they began our socialization with a description of the feud they were having with the local head of the Women's Division. Out poured the resentments and hurt feelings that had accumulated over several months, climaxing in a refusal on their part to even speak to the other person. They felt compelled to characterize in turn each of the missionaries and local people with whom we were to work. They described conflicts and confrontations which left us aghast at the intensity of their feelings, and which created biases which in many instances took years to overcome. We discovered that our society was virtually polarized by differences in personalities and policies. We realized that persons who choose overseas service are characterized by strength of personality and decisiveness, but our naivete was shattered and we felt devastated by the pettiness which our colleagues described as permeating the institution we held in such high esteem. It is scarcely any exaggeration to state that, had we had the funds to purchase return passage, we should have left Sarawak on the first available ship.

In the short period of another five hours we had learned our second lesson, viz., that human beings are human beings and in overseas situations in which people are removed from the familiar cultural milieux, the worst *and* the best in personality traits tend to be exaggerated. We subsequently realized as well that we had received in one evening — and at the end of a journey half-way round the world — an "overwhelming dose" of what a good and wise colleague called "the normal friction of social life."

We set in almost immediately studying Iban, the language in which we were to teach. Arrangements had been made with an Iban student in the Methodist Secondary School to tutor us. He came to the house twice each week and we worked on pronunciation, vocabulary, and memorization of short phrases. A month or so into our study one of our colleagues who had worked in China and was fluent in the Foochow dialect — but who spoke no Iban — commented how fortunate it was that we were studying Iban which, as everyone knew, had only 500 words, unlike the much richer Chinese dialects. We soon discovered the unfounded nature of the remark, as we built our vocabulary to several thousand roots. N. C. Scott's *Dictionary of Sea Dayak* (Iban) had just been published and we worked through it soon to discover that, as valuable as it was, it was quite incomplete. After "mastering" the Scott lexicon, I began compiling my own list of roots and the morphophonemic changes each underwent. As I began to travel extensively, I recorded each word that was new to me, or new usages of words I knew. Iban were genuinely appreciative of a person who was interested in learning about them and their language, and they patiently provided new words, phrases, and an introduction to the many subtleties of the language. My fascination was amply rewarded in each community as I was plied with common and uncommon terms. From the notebooks in which words and phrases were recorded, I transferred each root or headwork to a separate 3" X 5" card to be kept in my files. The lexicon which began as part of language study has grown over the past 24 years and now exceeds 51,000 roots. I now estimate that the dictionary of Iban and English when reasonably complete will include between 80,000 and 100,000 words, comprising everyday terms and archaisms used by the bards and shamen in dramaturgical events.

A month after our arrival in Sarawak, I traveled upriver to the mission center at Seputin where I met Professor Derek Freeman. I had read Freeman's *Iban Agriculture* and asked him about the language and its forms. Freeman commented that Iban is an exceedingly rich language and that the folklore "probably exceeds in sheer volume the literature of the Greeks." At the time I thought his estimate excessively generous, but now, almost a quarter of a century later, I do not.

Three months into the study of Iban I reached a plateau. I felt I had learned all I could and was making no further progress. Providentially, Dr. William Smalley of the American Bible Society, a gifted linguist and a capable chess opponent, visited us in preparation for a literary project and a program for translation of the Old Testament into Iban. Smalley suggested that I begin transcribing and memorizing folktales. With the tutor I began with the stories of *Apai Salui* ("The Father of Stupidity"), an anti-hero and notorious character whose example Iban are exhorted to avoid, then went on to numerous stories of the mousedeer, the tortoise, and other animals. From a small beginning I put together an admittedly incomplete collection of 109 narratives, 18 published collections, transcriptions of 27 rituals, and more than 1,000 pages of aphorisms, proverbs, and riddles. (Much more complete collections exist in the Sarawak Museum, the *Biro Kesusastraan Borneo* (formerly, the Borneo Literature Bureau), and Radio Malaysia-Sarawak.) I memorized large blocs of the folklore, particularly proverbs and aphorisms, which I found extremely useful in lecturing and preaching, and even in informal conversations. And, as so often happens, knowledge begat knowledge, i.e., upon hearing a reference to a particular proverb or folktale Iban would suggest variants or other forms which came to mind.

The study of Iban led to recognition of a third lesson, viz., that "simple" societies may produce unbelievably elaborate and complex cultures. Though less developed in other arts forms than Bornean societies at approximately the same techno-economic level, the Iban have excelled in creating, editing, transmitting, and retaining enormous amounts of oral literature. (Happily, much of this material has been taped by Radio Malaysia-Sarawak which regularly transcribes a variety of the forms, thus helping to perpetuate the rich tradition of the Iban.)

The trip to Seputin mentioned above was pedagogically significant for several reasons. Seputin itself was fascinating. About half-a-mile upriver from the Rejang port of Kapit, Seputin had been purchased by the Methodist Church from the Borneo Company, Ltd. which had cleared the site for the housing of elephants used in the collection and transshipment of hardwood logs. On the way to Seputin I experienced my first — but by no means last — incident of outboard failure. About 50 minutes out of Sibu the motor died and refused to start again. We drifted for almost two hours before the late Pengulu Buah, an Iban chief, and his party towed us to the port town of Kanowit. To my astonishment, the Iban refused any payment for their service and tendered an invitation for us to visit them in their longhouse at any time, an invitation we later followed up on. To the best of my knowledge, Pengulu Buah never became a Christian despite the efforts of several missionaries and local ministers, but a gentler and kinder person I have not known. It was he and his party who impressed upon me the quality of hospitality which is universally characteristic of the Iban.

At Seputin our host was Burr Baughman, senior missionary to the Iban. Burr and his late wife, Tek Lyn, provided accommodations for my colleague and me, and introduced me to the variety of culinary delights which even now evoke involuntary salivary and gastronomic responses. One item, however, required both courage and getting used to: the durian fruit (*Durio zabethinus* Linn.). After a delicious curry dinner, Tek Lyn brought to the table a platter piled with what I thought were pieces of spoiled fish. Anticipating my discomfort and amused by my indecision about whether to eat the durian, Baughman told me that the pieces were sections of a fruit which in the words of another guest, "smells like a monsoon drain and tastes like cream custard." (For a humorous description see the *Encyclopedia Brittanica*.) Encouraged by my host, I took a section of the mooshy fruit and found that, indeed, it was not at all bad, in fact, it was quite delicious. In time, all members of our family became addicted to durian – as well as the other delicious fruits such as the mangosteen, the mango, pomelos, and naturally ripened bananas – to the consternation of overseas visitors who, when offered some, more often than not refused.

The experiences with Pengulu Buah and with the Baughmans provided a fourth lesson which was amplified and reinforced throughout our years in Borneo, viz., be aware of the biases you bring to new situations, and be willing to accept what is offered and available by your hosts. As a product and practitioner of my own American sub-culture, I scarcely expected the consideration and kindness of so many Iban, Malays, Chinese, and others. Having been convinced that, in the words of the writer of the First Letter of John, "all who love are children of God," I had to revise my narrowly particularistic view of revelation. This became even more necessary when I met and was befriended and extended courtesies by persons of a wide range of ethnic and religious backgrounds. The confrontation with and fondness I quickly developed for durian convinced me not to reject any gift which – most commonly – was food. Consequently, I ate everything I was served, at least once. One was enough for *jukut* or *pekasam*, "pickled meat," a great delicacy for most Iban. *Jukut* is made of pork, venison, or fish, the meat being mixed with rock salt, packed into earthenware crocks and covered, then left to ripen for about three months. When opened, the crocks are a seething mass of meat and tiny organisms. I ate *jukut* once, but thereafter politely declined with the familiar excuse, quite understandable to Iban hosts, that *jukut* had been taboo to my ancestors and hence to me.

Although it seems hardly necessary to comment on, I feel compelled nevertheless to emphasize that refusal to accept the gifts of one's hosts and especially to eat food they have prepared, is almost certainly to obviate the close relationships essential to successful fieldwork. One of the most piteous situations we observed involved a young Englishman who had a number of hang-ups about local foods which he refused to eat, to the annoyance and shame of Iban. Sadly, his fastidiousness about cleanliness and his sensibilities about food-borne illnesses climaxed in a bothersome, but fortunately not serious, case of colitis.

My opportunities for travel and language study were made possible because of Joanne's willingness to assume primary responsibility for the home and our children. After our colleagues' assignment upriver and their departure, she also served as hostess for government officials, Iban who might stay a night or a month, and overseas dignitaries. Maintaining our home, caring for our children, and managing the guest house made it impossible for her to spend as much time as I did in language study, and altogether impossible for her to travel extensively. We had agreed prior to going to Sarawak that we would not neglect our children for the sake of "the mission." And, although subtle − and less subtle − pressures were brought to beat on us for Joanne to turn the children over to an *amah* or governess and later, when they were school age, to send them to boarding school in Singapore, we flatly rejected any such suggestions. Joanne's encouragement for my study of the language and travels to longhouses, and later for studies of the society and culture, made my fieldwork possible. While these remarks may seem gratuitous, they are important to me for I suspect that all-too-often the emotional support and encouragement provided by the field-researcher's wife, together with her assumption of a major part of responsibilities which in other situations would be shared, are ignored and unappreciated.

In September, 1958, having acquiring an adequate ability to understand and speak Iban, I began teaching in the Methodist Theological School. Actually, my first teaching was tutoring a brilliant and altogether remarkable student, Henry Ajat Buah. Ajat, better educated and in many respects intellectually superior to his classmates, had been sent from the first Iban seminary in Seputin − facilities having been built in the old elephant barn − to Sibu where his former classmates were to move the following year. As is so often the case, the teacher learned far more than the student. Ajat and I devoted mornings to theological studies − scriptures, theology, church history, ethics − and each afternoon he came to our house where he taught me Iban folklore. It was in this context that I first really appreciated the enormous volume of oral material the Iban had produced, filled with details about humanity, nature, and the universe. (Twenty years later, while attending a *Gawai Antu*, literally, "Festival of the Spirits" (and "Skulls"), I was still staggered by their literary creativity as I heard six teams of six bards each sing the praises of *Oryza sativa* − rice − from 11 p.m. until 4 a.m., identifying hundreds of sub-species and the varieties of use to which rice is put.)

Ajat was my constant companion and as good a friend as I had. As well as being exceptionally intelligent and articulate, he was unbelievably strong. Two demonstrations of his strength had amazed me. The first occurred when our colleagues moved upriver and Ajat hoisted a gas-powered Maytag washing machine, still in its crate, on his shoulder and carried it some 30 yards up a hill. The second incident involved a kerosene refrigerator, also still in the crate, which we had to get up a narrow flight of stairs to a house we had built. After several minutes' deliberation about how to proceed, how many men it would take, and whether men and case would fit in the staircase, Ajat ordered us to put it on his back and with no hesitation walked it up and into the house.

As I began to travel extensively in the middle and lower Rejang, Ajat and I spent days together talking about "the Iban world." It was he who told me creation myths, who explained the role of the shaman, who introduced me to the omen birds, and who demonstrated again and again the sensitivity of the Iban to every part of their environment. One hot Saturday afternoon as we were moving slowly up the Sarikei river, we passed a floating island of nipa palms. "Just like some people," commented Ajat. "How's that?" I asked. And he explained that nipa palm islands are rootless, they drift with the tide, with no bearing or direction.

The Methodist Theological School had been founded in 1955 in response to an obvious need for leadership in the rapidly growing church. The Methodist Church had been established formally among the Iban with the baptism of 32 Iban in Kapit in 1949. The next two decades were to seen an astounding growth in the church, a "people's movement," surpassing in numbers older denominations which had worked among the Iban for more than a century. Three reasons account for this growth. First, the Iban have been a physically and culturally mobile people. Their mobility has predisposed them to accept, appropriate, and adapt external ideas, values, and patterns of behavior, much more rapidly than most other Bornean societies. Second, contacts with members of Euro-American societies and exposure to new and foreign phenomena were greatly accelerated after mid-century. And third, the Methodist Church, unlike other major denominations, established its congregations in longhouses and developed its liturgy in response to the felt needs of Iban. (Other churches had been predominantly urban-based, requiring members to come into towns for worship and other services which followed European traditions.) These, and other factors, resulted in some years in as many as 2,000 Iban joining the church.

Recognizing the need for leadership for new Christians, missionaries developed a strategy for training ministers who would serve up to a dozen (and sometimes more) congregations, and lay leaders who would lead worship services and work as volunteers in their own communities. Thus, two seminaries were begun, the one in Sibu in 1955, the other in Seputin in 1957. The Sibu school began with 10 Chinese students and one Iban, the former instructed in Mandarin, the Iban in English, and the school in Seputin began with 12 Iban students who were taught by Burr Baughman and Lucius D. Mamora, a Batak, in Iban.

It soon became apparent that maintaining two seminaries was expensive, duplicative, and unjustifiable, so a merger was sought. The location of the Iban-Chinese seminary was a matter of considerable debate, leaders of the Chinese church insisting that it be in the town of Sibu to take advantage of local instructors, Baughman and others arguing that it should be in a rural setting similar to the situations in which most pastors would work. When a decision was made to unite the two schools in Sibu, Baughman was adamant that Iban be instructed in their own language by someone familiar with their culture. For this purpose, when the students from Seputin moved to Sibu to join Ajat and the first class of Iban admitted to the Methodist Theological School, Mamora, who had worked among the Iban from 1938 and whose family had been hidden by them from the Japanese during World War II, became my colleague.

I had worked in Iban with Ajat but I was intimidated by the larger number of students, many of whom were unfamiliar to me. Thus, I began the year lecturing in English. Two weeks into the quarter Mamora came to my office and told me that the students were unable to understand the theological terms and concepts in English, and that it was imperative that I begin to teach them in Iban. With understandable anxiety and hesitation, I began a daily discipline of writing out in Iban each of the five lectures I was to give the following day. Thus, it seemed, I finished one day's lectures and just had time to get the next day's lessons written out.

Predictably, the discipline of writing in Iban had two results: First, my familiarity with vocabulary, grasp of subtleties, and catalog of important expressions grew exponentially. And second, I discovered again and again one of the first rules in approaching a new language, viz., realize that it will be arbitrary and does not follow rules with which you are familiar. The arbitrariness of Iban produced many humorous incidents with the students as I delivered my lectures constructed of Iban words which often — and decreasingly — were arranged according to English rules of morphology and syntax. One afternoon, I was discussing an assignment and told the students that they were to submit the work in a manila folder. The word for folder or cover is *kulit*, and to form a verb I followed the procedure of replacing the initial /k/ with the prefix /ng-/, the ordinary morphophonemic change. The students erupted with laughter and, after I was able to calm them and ask the source of their amusement, they told me that the verb form I had produced, *ngulit*, meant "to mourn the dead," and there was no "indicative form" to be derived from *kulit*.

This, and similar episodes brought home yet another lesson, viz., you may be instructed about the arbitrariness of language – and the unpredictable experiences one will encounter in fieldwork – but there is no substitute for the personal experience itself. As my fluency in Iban increased, so did expectations of Iban, who delighted in adding to my vocabulary and, not infrequently to my confusion, by engaging me in word-play. Concurrent with awareness that there is no substitute for the experience itself was recognition that fieldwork must be balanced between a minimum of self-seriousness and a maximum of good humor. Having seen a film taken by another anthropologist who worked in Southeast Asia about his fieldwork experiences, I am convinced that the researcher often must appear a Dostoyevskian "idiot" to his hosts.

Insistence that lectures be given in Iban had another result; I was forced to seek terms and similarities for Iban beliefs and rituals and Christian theology. Not surprisingly many existed. "Wrong-doing" was readily comprehended, and in their customary law Iban recognized scores of misdemeanors, felonies, and even "sins" for which sanctions and penalties existed. "Forgiveness" and even "redemption" were easily grasped, Iban recognizing the importance of seeking forgiveness for a discourtesy, an unintended slight, or *faux pas*, and the institution of slavery had as a component a ritual by which captured slaves could be "redeemed" and made full members of society.

The notion of monotheism, predictably, was problematic. Iban mythology acknowledges three creator gods – Seremugah, who made the land; Segundit, who made the sky; and Segundi, who made the water – as well as spirits of land, water, and life, the omen birds who serve as messengers of the gods, and numerous culture-heroes who are but slightly below the gods. Most Iban have ascribed the capacity for sentient thought and action to *anything*, so that, for example, the incubus may actually be the transformed human shape of a rhesus macaque, a crocodile, a carrying-basket, or a rice motar. I still recall my astonishment at the description by one of our students of an heirloom jar that "moaned" for lack of attention, and stopped moaning only after her mother had placed a new piece of cloth with an offering of rice over it. As difficult as monotheism was to comprehend, the doctrine of the trinity was even more perplexing: three in one, one in three? The result was an Iban invention (independently) of modalistic monarchianism, the ancient heresy which described God as One

Being with three "modes" (appearances). Not surprisingly, the resolution of these and other theological concepts has been in syncretism so that, as one Iban put it, "the cross adorns the door but amulets still hang over our sleeping mats."

Syncretism was apparent one morning as we were dedicating rice-fields at the beginning of a new agricultural year. A Christian service of worship for blessing land, seed, tools, and people had been developed along the lines of a traditional Iban ritual, and we were moving from field to field — altogether 21 farms — standing in water up to our knees, singing hymns, reading Psalms, and having prayers of dedication. We had moved on from Umpi's field and were proceeding to the next, when I saw him out of the corner of my eye somewhat surreptitiously slip back to his farm carrying a small knife and a gunny sack. When he thought no one was watching, he removed a pullet from the sack and deftly slit its throat, letting the blood run into the water. Umpi was taking no chances and was playing both sides against the middle. He had become a Christian, had wanted his field dedicated to God for His blessings, but just in case, he also was going to ask *Sempulang Gana*, Lord of the Earth and Fertility, for a good harvest.

From the traditional Iban-Christian syncretism, a source of much alarm to some of our theological purists and more conservative colleagues, came another lesson, viz., that in a situation of contact between practitioners of different religious traditions, borrowing may occur by all parties. Some values in Iban culture were clearly more consistent with Christian theology than the distorted interpretations which had developed in middle-class American society. "Pure religion and undefiled," wrote the author of the Letter of James, "is to care for the widow and orphan, to befriend those in need, to express one's faith in considerate action," and by these criteria, the Iban are a "religious" people. As valuable as theological studies at Vanderbilt were, there were many lessons about living responsibly and ethics which were much more effectively taught by Iban. A major concern of some of our colleagues was that Iban abandon their beliefs and rituals and embrace completely Christian faith and worship (i.e., the tradition from which the missionary came). Although the lesson was a long time aborning, it finally occurred to me that if Yahweh could work patiently with the people of Israel from the Exodus in 1250 B.C. until 621 B.C. (or later), tolerating their practices of polytheism and monolatry, He probably would be as patient with Iban who only a decade or so earlier had decided to become disciples of Christ.

In the first class to enter the seminary in Sibu was another outstanding student, fully the equal in intellectual abilities of Ajat. Jawan Empaling —

currently, the Honorable Jawan Empaling, Member of Parliament and Parliamentary Minister of Health for Malaysia – was in the first group of Iban I had baptized after arriving in Sarawak. He came from a relatively poor community near the mouth of the Assan River, and was himself at odds with members of his longhouse. Aware of his somewhat troubled past we were surprised when he applied for admission to the seminary. During his first two years he seemed to move from crisis to crisis, in one scrape and out of another, until the final semester of his sophomore year. Taking a course on the history of Methodism, Jawan identified with John Wesley in the personal ordeal the Englishman suffered and, remarkably, underwent a resolution of his own conflicts. He emerged a person of discipline with a focus of his considerable abilities and energy. He established himself as the most capable leader in the Iban Methodist Church and, in 1969, after several years work as a pastor, entered Concordia College where he received a bachelor's degree and earned a master's degree in political science from New York University. Currently, he is a member of the Malaysian delegation to the United Nations.

The establishment of the Iban Department in the Methodist Theological School and the training of Iban ministers was in keeping with the position already established by church leaders, viz., that the church should be Iban, affirming traditional values of Iban culture which were humanizing and consistent with the Judaeo-Christian principles of justice, mercy, and acceptance, and that the leadership should be Iban. Thus, in attempting to develop an Iban church, it was essential to understand "traditional values of Iban culture" and to re-affirm them to Iban who were becoming exposed with increasing rapidity and intensity to Euro-American values. (In some respects, long before anthropologists appropriated Kenneth Pike's concept of emic perspective, we were seeking precisely that perspective in church development.)

Understanding Iban culture required "standing-under" the tutelage of Iban – students, bards, shaman and, the newly-established worship leaders. The rapid growth of the Iban Methodist Church – from 32 members in 1949 to almost 20,000 in 1981, from 18 congregations in the district to which we were appointed in 1957 to almost 150 at present – required each student to serve as pastor to several longhouse. Without question, the most valuable experiences for the staff and students of the seminary were (1) the Monday afternoon meetings in which field-trips were discussed, problems analyzed and programs planned, and (2) the extensive programs of lay-training which were organized for each group of longhouse churches.

The shortage of leaders in the rapidly growing church required staff and students to travel each week-end. We left Sibu on Friday afternoon or Saturday morning, conducted four to six services in as many longhouses, counseled local church members, and engaged in the institutionalized "verandah discussions" (*randau ruai*) until two, three, or even four o'clock in the morning. In the first decade of Iban Methodist there were only two church buildings, and all other congregations met on the longhouse verandah. The "church-in-the-home" was a God-send, in which ministers and members were forced to seek the relevance of a new faith to their lives. The practice of augury had provided a basis for agriculture, travel, and house-building. What is its place in the life of the Christian Iban? Do Christians observe rituals after they have had a bad dream? Heard a barking deer? Seen an omen bird such as the red-crested woodpecker or white-rumped shama? Is it necessary to sacrifice a chicken to the lord of the earth to begin the farming year? If someone dies outside the long-house, what payment is appropriate to other families if the body is return-ed to the house? Should the period of mourning be observed? Should there be a longer period of mourning for a politically important person? Is it necessary to employ a shaman to ritually sever ties between the dead and the living? Should Christians consult shamen? Should traditional patterns of courtship be changed? The closest term for "religion" in Iban is *jalai aki-ini*, "the way(s) of the ancestors." (I do not consider the loan word *ugama/agama*, from Arabic via Malay as meaningful to Iban.) By logical extension, Iban were keen to explore all implications of *jalai Keristin*, "the way(s) of the Christian," for which reason they discussed and debated endlessly the above and many, many other topics of moment.

The lay-training programs were intensive, interdisciplinary events, involving government and church personnel, held from Friday until Monday in centrally located longhouses. All worship leaders were invited, along with their friends, family members, and anyone else who might be interested. The programs included instruction in agriculture, home and family life, health and hygiene, the scriptures, and always, Iban religion and Christian faith. Lessons in agriculture were designed to introduce what has come to be termed "appropriate technology." Recognizing the impact of modern agriculture, extension agents attempted to learn problems Iban were having in adapting new technology, and, in consultation with farmers, work out practical and inexpensive solutions. Home and family life staff, nurses, and midwives identified problems of unbalanced diets, infant care — some practices of which contributed to a mortality rate of 50 percent — and the benefits of hygiene. Discussions of scriptures and faith were occasions for social dialectics in which *apo logia* for two different value systems were developed. In 1959, we held 44 lay-training programs, each in a different region, and for the next seven years we averaged 35 courses each year.

Out of the week-end services, lay-training programs, and Monday afternoon discussions, came an increasing awareness of and appreciation for the complexities of Iban culture. As Director of the Iban Department, I felt it important that each member of our staff make a continuing study of the culture, that such studies always involve students, and, for the sake of community and understanding in our bicameral seminary, that Chinese students should be exposed to representative and significant aspects of Iban culture. The first goal was accomplished through the assignment of a series of topics of which each staff member prepared a research paper and presented it for discussion with the students. We inaugurated courses in field research and folklore, in which Iban students made ethnographic studies of each community in their pastoral charges quite literally "from the group up," and collected previously unrecorded folktales. Although the field studies were varied in quality and thoroughness, several were rich in detail beyond our expectation and included information about soils, vegetation, water supplies, land and its ownership, census data on each longhouse, leadership roles, political processes, and evidence of acculturation.

The course in folklore was established as part of the curriculum because we discovered that most Iban students had been exposed to western-style education but had had limited contact with knowledgeable adult Iban. Using publications from the Borneo Literature Bureau and materials collected by staff and students, we developed a course which for some revived their appreciation for the richness of the folklore, for others made them aware for the first time of the value of their own traditions.

Our education of Chinese staff and students about Iban society and culture required overcoming decades of disdain in which Chinese held Iban. To paraphrase Nathaniel's question about Jesus, a Chinese might easily have asked, "Can anything good come from a longhouse?" Chinese-Iban relations had been marked by both competition and cooperation. Seeking refuge from nationalistic Boxers, the first Chinese Methodists immigrated to Sarawak in the early 1900s to be followed by thousands more. Most lived in cloistered communities with but little interest in Iban or other indigenes. Iban were looked down on and as recently as the early 1960s were called by a particularly offensive and irritating epithet. (When I wrote a chapter for a book about Chinese-Iban relations and subsequently discussed the work with a group of Chinese, the sensitivity of the subject – and the abreaction it produced – elicited enormous resentment and resistance among the Chinese. Eventually, the unwillingness of the Chinese to accord Iban equal representation on church committees

resulted in the division of the church into a Chinese conference and an
Iban conference.)

The first effort at educating Chinese staff and students was a program
on Iban augury. Derek Freeman had sent me a pre-publication copy of his
paper which appeared in Smythies' *Birds of Borneo*, and this excellent
analysis formed the basis for our presentation. Both groups of the Chinese
department were astounded that Iban divination contained such attention
to detail, such discernment of differences in calls and flight patterns, and
such elaboration into the mythological system of the brahminy kite and
his seven sons-in-law. From this program we proceeded to present others,
portraying Iban beliefs and practices.

A lesson we derived from these experiences was that human cultures
may form bridges — or barriers — to understanding. Previously, no efforts
had been made to interpret and enhance Iban culture to the Chinese. Nor,
for that matter, had the Chinese considered Iban culture worth studying or
spending the time to understand. Once interpreted positively, however,
Chinese staff and students developed appreciation and respect for the Iban
and their abilities.

In 1960, out of our shared concern for promoting understanding and
mutual respect between students of the two dominant groups in Sarawak,
Dr. Ivy Chou, Principal of the seminary, and I started classes in Iban, for
Chinese students, and Mandarin, for Iban students. The success of the
language courses was limited, and only a few students developed com-
petency in the second language. However, two significant events did occur.
One of our professors was a retired Chinese pastor, Lau Nai Buoi. Feeling
it inappropriate for him to sit in a class with his students, he sat just
outside the classroom where he heard, wrote down, and later practiced
Iban words and phrases. So convinced was he of the merit of the language
courses and the potential for greater understanding and better relations
that for the next eight years he worked with Iban students on an Iban-
Chinese phrase book which he published in 1968. The second development
out of the language courses was the decision of a Chinese student, Hsu
Chung Hou, to seriously pursue the study of Iban and to request appointment as a pastor to the Iban. Following his graduation, Hsu became the
first Chinese ordinand to work among the Iban.

The growth of the Iban Department and its involvement in the life of
a rapidly growing church impressed upon many the necessity for further
training in order to understand Iban society and its members. There were
— and still are — numerous differences between Iban, Chinese, and
expatriates, which created confusion and tensions. In my own case, I had
taken courses in anthropology but recognized the importance of a more

comprehensive program. I was aware that, while I had a certain perspective on life and the ultimate issues of human existence, developed through theological education and work as a missionary-educator, my view was necessarily limited and skewed by professional training and experiences. I knew that I had been "doing" anthropology, in the fieldwork and student projects, but that graduate training would enhance the work I wanted to continue.

In contrast to a majority of anthropologists, I had undertaken field research prior to professional graduate education. There were advantages and disadvantages in my reversal of the common order of events. The advantages lay in the experiences I brought to my course work and in the fact that I had a more clearly defined goal for my graduate program than did most of my peers. The disadvantages lay in the all-too-clear realization that there was much I had overlooked in the early years of fieldwork and things I would have done differently, had I had formal training.

In 1961-62, I completed the course work for a master's degree and investigated a doctoral program which I began in 1966, after another four years in Sarawak, and completed in 1972, after another three years in the field. Upon completion of my course work for the Ph.D. in 1979, I returned to Sibu. During the next three years, I was Principal of the seminary, and conducted research on urbanization among the Sibu Iban for my dissertation.

"Is it possible for one person to be both anthropologist and missionary?" I have been asked frequently. My response is that, obviously, I believe it is possible. I do not believe there is an inherent antithesis between the discipline of the anthropologist and the work of the missionary. My understanding of "the work of the missionary" undoubtedly is different from that of some of my former colleagues and that of many non-missionaries. I did not see my wife's and my roles as "proselytizers" but as "witnesses" to Jesus Christ and the meaning we have found in our lives. The decision to invite and respond to the missionary is the prerogative of the host community. I do not believe one must be more than slightly schizoid to play both roles concurrently.

Regrettably, both anthropologists and missionaries have been caricatured unfairly, the former as the student of the primitive and (by extension) the irrelevant, the latter as a heaven-bent agent of change among the irreverent. On the contrary, both groups have had as the focus of concern the situations of human beings and, unfortunately, there have been the "uglies" among each.

It is instructive to recognize that the entire missionary movement has undergone enormous and radical changes in the past quarter century, one being the incorporation of the anthropological principles of holism, pluralism, and relativism in their programs. It is equally encouraging to note that there has been a virtual spate of courses in applied anthropology and applied Christianity (both titles striking me as patently redundant!), each approach bringing its best insights into problematic and programmatic studies of humanity, nature, and universe.

I went to Sarawak with a relatively narrow view of the work of God and human response, and of the vocation I was assuming. My fieldwork among the Iban and reflection on experiences shared with practitioners of other cultures led me to recognize that agapaic theology must acknowledge the worth in all people and the interdependence of all life. My conversion has been from "biblical particularism" to the conviction of St. Paul who quite correctly wrote, "God has at no time and in no place left Himself without witness."

CHAPTER 6

Contrasting Experiences in Fieldwork

DANIEL T. HUGHES

In 1966 I spent eleven months on the island of Ponape in Micronesia studying the interrelation between the traditional and the introduced political systems and in 1973 I lived for five and a half months in Malolos, Bulacan in the Philippines studying local-level politics. During my fieldwork on Ponape I was a priest and a member of the Jesuit order with mission stations on Ponape and throughout most of Micronesia. Having left the priesthood in 1969, I was accompanied on my Malolos fieldwork by my wife and son. This chapter will discuss some contrasting experiences that I had in doing fieldwork as a priest and as a non-priest and also as a single person and as a man accompanied by a family.

Even before my fieldwork on Ponape I had had three years of experience in Micronesia. In 1955-1958 as a seminarian I had taught at a mission high school on the island of Truk. It was a boarding school with students from various districts of Micronesia. During those three years I visited most of the other districts in Micronesia and many of the Jesuit mission stations in the islands. Thus when I went to Ponape in 1965 for fieldwork I had already met the ten Jesuit missionaries stationed there. In fact, four of them had been contemporaries of mine in several seminaries in the U.S. and three had taught with me in the mission high school on Truk.

When I arrived on Ponape I explained to my fellow Jesuits that I wanted to take precautions to minimize any adverse effect my being a priest might have on my fieldwork. I wanted to avoid any parish ministry responsibilities that would take time from the research. Since I was being supported by an N.I.H. fellowship and research grant, there was no problem about my devoting full time to fieldwork. But I was also concerned that simply being a priest and being associated with the mission might make it difficult to obtain reliable information on some subjects. My fellow Jesuits were most understanding and helped me arrange to stay in a vacant house in Lohd Pah, a remote section in the southern part of the island fairly distant from any mission station. Because the residents of Lohd Pah spoke very little English, it was a good place to study Ponapean.

The house that I lived in belonged to Mr. and Mrs. Bob Hawley, a Ponapean-American couple who lived in Kolonia in the northern part of the island. Bob had built the house because they owned a large track of land in Lohd Pah and the family sometimes vacationed there. The house was quite comfortable and, most important, it was only about 100 yards away from the house of a Ponapean family, Luen and Maria Pelep and their four year old daughter, Juanita. Luen and Maria worked for Bob Hawley and took care of his land. They are both very intelligent, very kind, and seem to have an almost inexhaustable supply of energy. All during my stay in Lohd Pah most of their time and energy seemed to be devoted to helping me. They were a tremendous help and one of the most rewarding experiences of my whole Ponapean research was the deep friendships that developed from my daily contact with this extraordinary family.

I stayed in Lohd Pah for three months concentrating my energies on increasing the knowledge of Ponapean I had acquired from four months of study with a linguist and a Ponapean student at the University of Hawaii. By keeping my religious ministry activities to a minimum, I tried to establish the identity of a priest-athropologist rather than a priest-missionary. This was not too difficult to accomplish since a number of anthropologists (Riesenberg, Bascom, Fischer, and Mahony) had done studies on the island and many Ponapeans were familiar with the way that they had worked.

At Lohd Pah I divided my time between formal sessions with some local residents who acted as language informants, informal conversations, and participant observation at some Ponapean feasts and other social activities. Almost every evening I joined a kava-drinking group just outside my house and this became a source of vital information and welcome relaxation. Before leaving Lohd Pah I drew up a schedule of open-ended questions for the pilot study which followed and which marked the beginning of the strictly data-gathering stage of the research. During the course of the two and a half month pilot study the Ponapean District Legislature convened for one of its semi-annual sessions in Kolonia, providing an opportunity to observe the Legislature meetings and to interview the Legislators. In addition to the Legislators I interviewed forty-four other Ponapeans from all six municipalities of the island.

Interviews were conducted privately with only myself and the person being interviewed present. I was able to conduct the interviews almost entirely in Ponapean except in cases such as some of the outer-islanders who preferred to use English rather than Ponapean. Open-ended questions were asked about traditional and elected leadership roles and interviews ranged from one to six hours. The place of the interviews both in the pilot study and the later final study varied widely but was always left to the informant's convenience; his or her residence or a feast house nearby often serving as a suitable place.

Using information gathered in the pilot study I drew up a pre-coded schedule of questions to test certain hypotheses and to find out the extent to which Ponapeans shared common views on essential issues raised in the course of the pilot study. In this final phase of the study I interviewed 415 people, 300 randomly selected from the Ponapean population over twenty-one years of age and 115 purposefully selected from the various traditional and elected leadership roles under study.

As mentioned earlier, originally I was concerned that being identified as a priest might make it difficult to obtain reliable information in the research. As I went around the island and talked to more and more people, it soon became apparent that the reverse was closer to the truth. The population of the island is about half Catholic and half Protestant. Among both groups many of the Catholic priests had an extraordinary reputation. Fr. Costigan, who had been working on Ponape since 1947, was given a special commendation by the District Legislature in 1966 for his service to the people by his work with the Matolenihmw Housing Cooperative. He has also been the leading figure in building and staffing the Ponape Agriculture and Trade School, the most successful trade school in Micronesia. Fr. McGarry had been stationed on Ponape for about six years and was already acknowledged by many Ponapeans as an authority on Ponapean custom and tradition. Several other priests who had arrived more recently were noted for their speed in learning Ponapean and their work with Community Development programs. To be identified with these men was a definite advantage in my research because the people had so much respect for them and so much confidence in them.

Because I was a member of the mission group I was also able to receive a great deal of logistical support from them. The N.I.H. grant enabled me to pay for food and transportation, but the use of mission facilities proved advantageous in a number of ways. In 1966 the population of Ponape was approximately 13,000. About 2,000 people lived in the port town of Kolonia and the rest lived in small sections (*kousapw*) mostly scattered along the coast of the island. Sections were not villages because people did not live in any concentrated groupings. They lived in farmsteads consisting of two or three houses clustered together. The farmsteads of a section might be separated by several hundred yards or by a mile.

Once I left Lohd Pah the nature of my research design required that I interview people in many sections in each municipality of the island. Ordinarily therefore I would not be working in one section for more than a day or two before I would have to move on to another. At first I accepted invitations to stay overnight in the feast house of a section I was working in. But that was obviously too much of an inconvenience to the people of the section because they prepared special food for their visitor. So I quickly worked out a routine of using different mission stations as bases of operation. Ordinarily I left the mission station early in the morning by foot or by canoe and returned the same evening. Thus the use of the mission facilities proved a great help in the research.

Besides my being a priest and a member of a missionary group active on the island, another factor was significant in my research on Ponape. This was being without a family. Because I did not have a family to care for, I was able to move about the island quickly and easily. I changed residence from one mission station to another and went from the mission stations to whatever sections were necessary to follow a rather complex sampling design for my interviews and to observe significant socio-political events such as the District Legislature session and feasts of tribute for the traditional high chiefs. It would have been quite impossible to do that much traveling if I had been accompanied by a family.

The circumstances for my five and a half month fieldwork in Malolos, Bulacan in the Philippines in 1973 were quite different from those of my Ponape study. By 1973 I was no longer a priest or a member of the Jesuit order. My Malolos research was funded by the National Endowment of the Humanities, and I had arranged for an appointment as a Research Associate at the Institute of Philippine Culture, a research institute based at the Jesuit university, the Ateneo de Manila. But my official relation with the institute was no different than that of any other anthropologist.

Malolos is the capital of Bulacan Province and has a population of about 50,000 people. We rented a house in Santiago, a barrio within walking distance of the town plaza. Like other barrios near the center of town, Santiago was densely populated and most houses were clustered close together along the side of the road. From the windows of our house we could reach out and almost touch three other houses. So we came to know our neighbors very quickly.

In Malolos I was not known as an ex-priest, but simply as an American anthropologist with a Filipina wife and a son. Because martial law had been declared only the year before, a study of the political system in the Philippines, even on a local level, was a touchy business. By a most fortunate coincidence the Mayor of Malolos, Mrs. Purificacio Reyes, and my mother-in-law had been schoolmates in college in Manila. My mother-in-law sent a letter of introduction for me to the Mayor, and she was most helpful. She and her staff made town records available to me. She allowed me to sit in on the meetings she held with the town Council, and she asked the Kapitan of our barrio to help me in any way he could.

Without doubt Mayor Reyes' informal sponsorship of my work in Malolos was an important factor in my research there, but there were also other factors involved. One was my being an American. When I had taught at the Ateneo de Manila in 1967 –1969 there had been a growing nationalistic movement in the academic community with definite anti-American overtones. So I was pleasantly surprised to find that in Malolos I encountered almost no anti-Americianism. In fact, the reverse was much more often the case. Being an American was a definite advantage there because of the positive image the people had of Americans and the close ties they felt with their relatives living in America. I very quickly lost count of the number of times that I was stopped in the streets, often by complete strangers, and asked what part of the States I was from. Invariably the people then told me of one or more relatives living in the States or serving with the U.S. Armed Forces. This positive attitude toward Americans did not seem to be peculiar to Malolos. In visiting other parts of Luzon I encountered the same kind of pro-Americanism on many occasions. It seems to me that the academic community was simply not representative of the common people in this matter.

Another factor in the Malolos research was my being accompanied by my wife and son. I had anticipated that my wife would be most helpful in making contacts and in learning Tagalog. This turned out to be true, but it was not quite that simple. Malolos is in the heart of the Tagalog region of Luzon and is located about 30 miles north of Manila. My wife had been born in Manila of Tagalog parents, but she had been raised in the Bicol area of southern Luzon speaking Tagalog at home and Bicol outside. Now my wife's immediate family (her mother, a married brother, and a married sister) all live in different parts of the Tagalog and Bicol regions south of Manila. They and some relatives in Manila lavished hospitality on us whenever we were able to visit them, but we had no relatives in Bulacan Province. The people of Malolos were very kind and very friendly, and the fact that my wife was a Filipina who spoke fluent Tagalog was certainly an advantage. Still she was identified more as a Bicolana than as a Tagalog. Added to this was her marriage to an American and her residence in the States. None of these characteristics carried any stigma, but they all combined to make her somewhat of an outsider in Malolos.

In learning Tagalog I relied a great deal on my wife. Before leaving for the Philippines she had taped some lessons from a Peace Corps Tagalog learning manual, which proved very helpful. I used these tapes to practice Tagalog before leaving the States and also for the first month or so in Malolos. But my proficiency in Tagalog never approached my proficiency in Ponapean. Tagalog is no more difficult than Ponapean, but there were several important differences in the circumstances of my studying the two languages. Before going to Ponape I had spent four months of intensive study at the University of Hawaii with Don Topping, an outstanding Pacific linguist, and a Ponapean student acting as a language informant. Since I was being supported by an N.I.H. fellowship and research grant, I was able to spend full time studying. In preparing for the Philippine study I had fine language tapes and a good language informant but very little time. Since I was employed full time in the Anthropology Department at Ohio State, studying Tagalog had to be fitted in with a number of time-consuming duties for the department.

The language-learning situation in Malolos was also quite different from that of Lohd Pah. In Lodh Pah I was living with a Ponapean family whose members spoke very little English. The other residents of Lohd Pah spoke even less English. In Malolos I was living with my wife who speaks English as fluently as I do. Almost all the other residents of our barrio also spoke English, and many spoke it quite well. So for them and for me the temptation was always to break into English after I made a few attempts to say something in Tagalog. Finally, after being in Malolos a short time I realized that learning a new language from one's spouse is a lot like learning to drive from one's spouse. It might sound ideal in theory, but in practice it is filled with complications. Spouse and student (or spouse and teacher) are two roles that are quite difficult to combine. So I switched to working with other barrio residents as my language teachers. Eventually I advanced to the stage of being able to hold simple conversations in Tagalog, but I was never able to carry on long, detailed interviews in Tagalog as I had done in Ponapean. I was forced to interview mostly in English and to use an interpreter whenever I interviewed someone who was very weak in English.

Having a child with me in the field was also an interesting experience. To remind our son that his Filipino and American heritage should be a source of pride we had baptized him "Eric Bayani." "Bayani" is Tagalog for "hero." When we arrived in Malolos Eric Bayani was just past two years old. God had been kind to Eric and had blessed him with his mother's good looks and Filipino features. Fortunately the only thing he inherited from me was a light complexion. This combination of physical features is considered quite attractive in the Philippines and Eric became an instant celebrity in Malolos. Both adults and children were constantly touching him, pinching him affectionately, and talking to him. At first he was overwhelmed by all the attention and was quite shy. I think he was simply not accustomed to such an open display of affection from strangers. But he quickly adjusted to the situation especially as he began to understand and to speak Tagalog.

I used to take frequent walks around our barrio, around the town plaza, or around the market place. Almost invariably I took Eric along with me often straddling my shoulders since he would tire from the heat rather quickly. He was frequently the occasion of my conversations with people and his presence was a definite plus in my acceptance by the people. A number of people commented favorably about my fondness for Eric. One evening I was drinking with a friend of mine from our barrio and he said that many of the people felt at ease with me because I was like a Filipino in the way that I treated my son. He said that American men are usually too busy to spend time with their children and don't want to be bothered with them, but Filipino men are affectionate with their children and always have time for them. I don't agree completely with either stereotype presented by my friend, but I think he was right in saying that my having a child with me added to my acceptability among the people of the barrio.

Another consequence of being accompanied by my family in Malolos was that I was far less mobile there than on Ponape. It was possible to attend meetings and to interview people in other barrios of Malolos and even in other towns. But with a family there was no possibility of changing residence frequently as I had done on Ponape. Of course, with only five and a half months in the field, part of which had to be devoted to studying Tagalog, it is doubtful that I would have changed residence often anyway. My point is simply that the presence of a family in the field removed this option.

Summary and Conclusion

The anthropological fieldworker is neither a disembodied spirit nor an unfeeling and uninvolved machine. Every anthropologist is a human being whose personal characteristics and personal circumstances have an effect on the research that he or she does. In this chapter I have tried to contrast some of my personal circumstances during my fieldwork in two areas and to analyze some of the effects of these circumstances on my work. What impresses me most in my reflections is that usually any one factor or characteristic is advantageous in some ways and disadvantageous in others.

Being a priest certainly rules out some areas of study for an anthropologist. A detailed study of local sex practices, for example, would not

have been considered an appropriate activity for a priest among the Ponapeans. Nor do I think that I could have gathered reliable detailed data on
the religious beliefs of the Ponapeans, especially on any non-Christian beliefs. But nothing was considered inappropriate about a priest studying
the traditional and the contemporary political systems in detail. Investi-
gating this subject I was able to take full advantage of the positive image
and the immense good will established by many of the priests among the
Ponapeans.

Because I was single I was also able to take full advantage of the mission
residences and the mission logistics. It was possible to travel around the
island as much as necessary to conduct many interviews in widely scattered areas. This procedure turned out to be both good and bad. By conducting these interviews myself I had more direct control over the data-gathering process than had I used a research assistant to do the interviewing — a
luxury which I simply couldn't afford at the time. I also had direct contact
with people in many sections of each municipality on the island. This contact gave me first-hand knowledge of some important similarities and differences in the political system as it functioned in various parts of the
island. On the other hand it was not possible to gather the intensive data
on a broad range of topics that would have been possible had I spent all
of my time in one locality.

In Malolos I was identified simply as an American anthropologist with
a family and both characteristics influenced my research. The positive
image that many Filipinos have of Americans was a great help. Having a
Filipina wife was also helpful in learning Tagalog, in making contacts, and
in obtaining some kinds of information. But, as I have indicated, there
were complications in each of these areas. Finally, having a child with me
was a definite help in terms of acceptability within the barrio and the
town and in the many informal contacts that he occasioned. But caring for
my family was certainly time-consuming and limited my mobility.

At the conclusion of my Malolos study I was convinced that an anthropologist would be more efficient in doing fieldwork alone than accompanied by a family. In the summer of 1975 I had occasion to test this conviction when I spent two months visiting the six district centers of Micronesia on a pilot study for a later project. I was supported by a research
grant from Ohio State University, but we simply could not afford the
personal expense of my wife and son making the trip. The trip was quite
enjoyable in many ways. In most districts I stayed in Jesuit mission residences and caught up on the news about all my Jesuit friends. I also met
many former students in all of the districts. And I certainly had all the
time I needed to devote to the pilot study. But those two months were

the loneliest of my life, because my wife and son were not there. I still think that an anthropologist is more efficient in conducting fieldwork alone than accompanied by a family, particularly if one's research is a planned, focused study and not a general village ethnography. But I would now say that efficiency should not be the only criterion for planning fieldwork. By taking a family to the field an anthropologist is made hostage to all the limitations and demands of a family member in any society. To my mind this does make the anthropologist less efficient, but it also makes him or her more human. And as long as anthropology involves the study of human beings by other human beings, this is a quality that I would rank above efficiency.

CHAPTER 7

Between Being Near and Distant: Reflections on Initial Approaches and Experiences of an Indian Anthropologist

R. S. KHARE

When an anthropologist decides to study one's own culture, he introduces several important considerations for himself as well as the discipline as a whole. Some of these are conceptual, some procedural, and some directly resulting from the fact that the investigator and the people studied *share* a culture,. Actually, the last feature, being strongest, may be found coloring the other two, making it plausible to examine the case of a "native anthropologist".[1] If we award this label a temporary place in this essay, fully realizing that such a label needs systematic exploration, it offers us a locus for examining a series of issues and experiences which would not only be enriching to the discipline but also presenting a mirror to the anthropologist himself. Our use of the term "native anthropologist" is thus for analytic convenience. It helps us discuss fieldwork under a frame of reference which is wider than the one afforded by the label, "Indian anthropologist." Also, my argument here is that despite the proverbial cultural diversity and complexity of the Indian subcontinent, an Indian anthropologist studying India exemplifies a case of the native anthropologist. Most often, the intensive, prolonged research of an Indian anthropologist (excepting that conducted by the governmental agencies) is carried on in his *own* cultural region. It is conducted under a shared nativity. When this is not so, there is an attempt by him to discover this sharing; it is a part of his mental disposition more than a matter of quantitative incidence. However, equally importantly, this sharing proceeds under an inherent strain of empathy and alienation (see Section II).

A native anthropologist may be actually carrying a reverse manifestation of the same internal strain which pervades anthropology and anthropologists in general. If it challenges him to treat the familiar under an intellectual distance and "objectivity," it also encourages him to discover the unfamiliar within his own society and to handle it under an assumed familiarity. Burdens and strains which these demands bring along are strikingly different from the beginning, and remain so always. The native and the anthropological therefore enter in an interminable dialogue within this anthropologist, whether he consciously handles it or not. Submerging this dimension under the notion of a scientist's objectivity towards what he studies (including one's own culture) does *not* resolve the problem; its consideration is only postponed.

There is, however, a more usual way of looking at what studying one's own society represents in anthropology. It is merely a continuation of what one sooner or later does in one's career as an anthropologist: he begins to look at one's own culture through a series of perspectives which his anthropological knowledge and fieldwork offer him. Thus, insofar as there is such an overlap, his concerns are concerns of any anthropologist. But this approach assumes too much too uncritically. It does not give proper recognition to the significant analytic differences involved in two conscious decisions, when one consciously decides to study one's own culture *first* vis a vis that when it is carried as a secondary implication of the decision to do anthropological work on other cultures. A native anthropologist most centrally represents the issues contained in the first decision, which, as we realize, could be for substantial practical, historical, as well as theoretical reasons. He may also represent a complex interchange between anthropology and sociology, depending on his location.[2]

A native anthropologist is "born" either circumstantially (as is often – but not always – true in a country like India) or through some conscious planning for definite intellectual reasons (as is now exemplified in increasing cases in the U.K., the U.S., and France, who customarily become an "other-culture" anthropologist, returning later in their careers to study their own cultures). However, since a circumstantial entry can be either retained or dropped later on by one's conscious decision to work on another culture, a planned entry for sound intellectual reasons can occur either at the beginning or in middle or at the end of one's career – whether once or repeatedly. In both cases, however, it is crucial that this concern must yield a stable intellectual commitment to such studies. What is started circumstantially could be carried on for increasingly "better" research reasons, and with increasing planning and forethought.

In this essay we will concentrate on the formulation that what a native anthropologist is best conveyed by is what he goes through to be an anthropologist, and how he develops some of his procedures, values and perspectives to conduct his work. But even this formulation may be too large to consider within the space of a single article, unless we concentrate on its first part, expanding on the approaches and experiences of a native anthropologist as he goes about initiating and repeating his fieldwork in his own culture. Such an account will have to proceed under another qualification:

Given the absence of any systematic analysis of the conception of "native anthropologist," we will present a preliminary, mostly suggestive discussion of the "passage" of an Indian anthropologist during his fieldwork — its ups and downs, especially when cast as a human experience shared between an anthropologist as an affected "native" and natives as this anthropologist's guides, informants and discussants in the field.

AN INHERENT STRAIN

When a prospective native anthropologist proceeds on his "journey" to become an anthropologist, the "unknowns" in front of him in his maiden field-work are by no means insignificant. Like other anthropologists, he also spends sleepless nights. However, difficulties may be located in different places, and be significant in different ways, when compared to the case of an anthropologist working on another society. Fieldwork remains an incomparable "initiation rite" for this anthropologist, despite any amount of rigorous training and "tip-giving" by one's teachers within class rooms and outside. For "going to the field" is as much to learn more about oneself under known and unknown (and predictable and unpredictable) circumstances of one's own culture as about those whom one goes to study as "people of the same culture."

A native anthropologist's essential burden in the field, especially in initial phases, is twofold. On one side, and naturally close to him, is his awareness of his nativity, at least as he has till then known (or imagined) it to be; on the other is all that learning about "the anthropological perspective" that goes on within one's class-room, and with those who have been in front of oneself as anthropologists. The second burden is definitely heavier for him than the first, for it includes a systematic socialization into an acceptance (and presumably understanding) of the "tools" and "terminology" of a discipline that must make him think and act in a certain way, called "anthropological". Such an acceptance is initially *passive and imitative*. He finds himself doing whatever he does essentially because other reputable anthropologists have either done it or are still doing it. For example, in the Indian circumstances with which I am familiar, this acquisition for the aspiring candidate becomes a particularly ambivalent burden. It attracts him as an alternative way of seeing and understanding what goes on in his own society but it also "alienates" (see note 2) him as it brings forward its foreign roots, procedures and assumptions, which may tend to miscast and misplace the significance and interrelationships of what this insider has known to be "the fact." How to make sense of one scheme in terms of the other – an essential tension of any anthropological exercise – thus appears before him.

This tension, however, emerges before the novice slowly, and is held by him mostly at the fringes. It is unconsciously carried. What he may be initially conscious about is the fact that he learns anthropology (and learns to be an anthropologist) some of the time, while he is a native the rest of the time. However, as his professional training progresses, he consciously learns "to leave his nativity behind" in order to extend the first into the second; and as he keeps doing so during his "professional life," he may see a dynamics along the four basic configurations of his "native self" vis a vis his, if one may so express it, "anthropological self" – first is the condition where one considers oneself native first and anthropologist second; second, where one is anthropologist first and native second; third, where one is indistinguishably both a native and an anthropologist; and fourth, where one is an anthropologist first and last. (One could of course also formulate to cover that situation where an attempt to inculcate an "anthropological self" fails so utterly that one remains the native first and last, despite anthropological training.) These configurations usually present themselves in two ways: first as if they were sequential stages which one passes through as one "becomes" an anthropologist, and second as ever present intellectual conditions and postures which one keeps resorting to in varying combinations, irrespective of one's length of training in the discipline. Viewed as the second, which probably is subtler and closer to what goes on with a native anthropologist, notice how the third configuration carries an idea of "balance" rather than a gradation. However, this condition might be, strictly speaking, as difficult to achieve and maintain as those where one is either only an anthropologist or a native. Actually, therefore, one may attempt to "resolve" the basic tension by going *through* these configurations in combinations rather than one at a time.

But once this finer (life-long) dynamics of the intellectual tension is recognized, we may return to consider those broader phases of transition that this tension sets up for a native anthropologist's initial journey in the field.

In a cultural area like northern India, a novice initially has at least three types of guides in front of him – those other anthropologists (native and others) who have already worked in the same region (and on the same topic or issue); the people under study; and those all other anthropologists who become general path-finders for the discipline as a whole. (See Marriott (1966) for an example from the same region where the second and third are perceptively juxtaposed.) However, as they guide the novice they produce before him another arrangement of the same tension we have mentioned above. The novice is guided to an "imitative alienation" from one's own culture — to put a laborious "distance" between what one studies and what one considers one's own. The disciplinary dictum is clear: "Think as the anthropologist does, and do in the field as an ethnographer would in order to be initiated." Imitating previous anthropologists, the novice thus produces an intriguing "alienation," a hopefully perspicacious "distance" with the people of his own culture.

But as he does so, it is evident to him that the expectations and assumptions of the people of his own culture, of his own habitual behavior, do not easily allow him to become "distant." Actually, the novice may be tenaciously seen "as one of our own" by the natives, normally disallowing "imitative alienation" to lapse in an estrangement from one's own culture. (However, if the latter is allowed to occur, an anthropologically fertile location, I think, is passed up.) Normally, these two tendencies, one for alienation and the other for remaining close to the nativity, work as mutually restraining forces, offering that tension that an anthropologist finds necessary and creative for his work. However, the same tension can equally easily give way to one tendency over the other, even in the career of a single anthropologist, altering the configurations we have mentioned above.

These observations, we must note, help summarize aspects of an intellectual, rather than a chronological, diary of the native anthropologist, since it accounts for distinguishable shifts and transitions in this anthropologist's *conscious* understanding of what he successively does (and how he tries to accomplish his goals) during his career. He may notice a constant "rethinking" on his behalf, making the significance of many initial steps in one's career alter with time. What one may do initially without much deliberation, merely as "learning" procedures and postures, may later on begin to take on meanings that could have not been discovered before. Similarly, if a native anthropologist learnt by imitation and emulation first, he consciously tries to seek more and more the significance of what he does and why in subsequent stages of his career. Often, the initial phases may be succeeded by (a) that given to conscious critical assessments of the "native self" and the "anthropological self," and (b) that directed towards discovering one's own analytical alternatives.

Running through all of these phases, however, is the same basic tension that helps the native anthropologist place himself on the "fringes" of his own culture in order to examine its "within," whether by itself or under comparison. This tension is *qualitatively different* for a non-Western native anthropologist, most importantly because, as a given historical fact, anthropology is introduced as an "external" intellectual and cultural tradition to which one learns to adapt in thought and action throughout one's life. (The "otherness" that this property brings along should be carefully and perceptively compared with the case of the Western native anthropologist. For if anthropology always helps inculcate a distance with one's own cultural system, the nature of this distance may yet be distinctly different in the two cases, partly because anthropology most often remains a "we/they" emphasizing discipline.) However, *ideally* this difference does not have to exist for this reason, for anthropology *must* after all reflect an unconditionally universal concern of human mind, and accordingly, it does develop from "within," wherever it develops.

AN INITIAL PASSAGE TO FIELD

In the background of the above general characteristics and concerns of the native anthropologist, I shall now present my field experiences for possibly illustrating some further properties of the same tension that an Indian anthropologist must face. In doing so, let us consider fieldwork as a "total" human experience. It means that one can not be a part-time participant — intellectually or otherwise — in anthropological fieldwork; it must be seen as, and be allowed to take over as, an absorbing experience among human beings. If one looks at himself as an anthropologist in this experience it is because he is first of all (and most importantly) a human being participating with other human beings. This fieldwork is a consequence of one's earnest curiosity for learning ways of the human beings, whether close to oneself or distant. One's fieldwork is learning by those series of human experiences where one opts to learn by directly participating in them.

Thus viewed, fieldwork provides occasions for continuous examination of what goes on "out there" as well as "within myself" (i.e. in terms of my shifting perspectives and attitudes towards what is being studied). My illustrations here will be attending the latter. I shall try to present the changing significance of what went on during my "early" vis a vis the "later" phases of fieldwork. The same event, the same people, and the same situations, thus, acquire differing meaning and purpose for me as I move along in my understanding of that field experience. The latter never stops to yield "learning," provided I remember to return to it for more under appropriate junctures of my own inquiry.

I shall present my observations on two simultaneously operating dimensions of my initial fieldwork in northern India (the Lucknow-Rai Bareli region of Uttar Pradesh) during 1958-1963: One relates to the procedures and postures which I, as a native anthropologist, had acquired as I initiated a study of a familiar society and culture, while the other is a reconstruction of the views that the "native" (i.e. one's own people) produced on this novice's attempt "to become an anthropologist." Locations of this initial work were a village (called Gopalpur) near Lucknow (a large city and the capital of the state of Uttar Pradesh), and this city itself. By this choice, therefore, I was dealing with a full range of urban and rural-urban people of different (including the highest and the lowest) caste, economic, and educational backgrounds. If there were "illiterates" I was talking to, there were also highly educated informants to approach. (Later on, I was to discover the value of finely-felt social experiences and observations some of the "illiterates" had unpretentiously carried with them.)

Given the surprising diversity and richness of this universe of my study that was almost too suddenly appearing before a novice (especially from the surroundings that he had thought were all too familiar and known), let us handle only few relevant dimensions here. We will thus first handle few predominant concerns and approaches of the novice to the native, reserving the succeeding pages for the converse relationship. The latter is particularly appropriate when "natives" do not present a passive picture of themselves or withhold their participation in a native anthropologist's fieldwork. Sometimes it amounted to being an "interference" that an anthropologist might have wanted to avoid — carefully but surely.

As I now recall and rethink what went on in the initial phases of my fieldwork in Gopalpur and Lucknow, especially as I was trying to learn myself to do anthropological fieldwork just after being exposed to those published and classroom versions, I was trying to do several things at the same time. Though I could not see it this way at that time, I was constantly trying to imitate, initiate and establish procedures and perspectives to move myself *away from the native* (and away from the nativity that is supposed to interfere in anthropological perspectives on human events) so that I could study him better. Putting this distance in between was then (as now) a complex, several-sided process. If it was not a mere alienation, the latter was in certain ways surely present in it. It was partly a rebellion against the known and the familiar and partly an audacious attempt to minimize the unknown and the unfamiliar by down playing the significance of the question: "How little does one really know about one's own culture?" To admit that one can be surprisingly ignorant about numerous aspects of one's own culture and society is normally rather hard to admit, particularly when learning about cultures may be one's main business.

98   R. S. KHARE

However it might have been with others, my initial forays in the field, I
distinctly recall, were marked by the discovery of my ignorance about my
own culture.

This ignorance is not merely about this or that particular content of
one's own culture but it is more importantly about realizing that the
hidden and the unfamiliar exist in the midst of the familiar, and that to
learn about it involves essentially the same anthropological perspective
(with some definite differences, of course) which is followed in intercultural studies. It is also the realization that "nearness" like "otherness"
is a highly contextual property of social relations, so that those people
who share the same language, the same cultural norms, and the same
generational upbringing within a shared cultural region do not yield "nearness" without an "otherness." Only that the latter comes masked by a
familiarity that, in some ways, is made doubly difficult to penetrate.

Introducing an analytically useful "distance" between the native and
the anthropologist is a common aim, but for securing it there are no definite procedures. Constant improvisations go on for being near yet distant
from one's won people. The native anthropologist introduces a form of
"distance" from the beginning, assuming that he, unknowingly, could be
too close to the "natives." Briefly, therefore, if there is a challenge to
penetrate one type of otherness, there is another one introduced for yield-
ing measures of aloofness towards the "familiar" native. This is the genesis
of an unseen, initially unconsciously encountered, tension in which the
anthropological inquiry thrives.

How does a native anthropologist go about being near yet distant to his
own people is a major question for systematic study. Here I can merely
illustrate it under a range of dynamic relations which appeared before me
during this early (1958-1963) phase of my fieldwork. A spectrum of this
tension was best represented to me by the four vantage points produced
by my four informants: a village leader, a Kanya-Kubja Brahman caste
leader, a Kurmi (lower caste) householder, and "the department." The last
refers to *my* perception and presence of a formal "locus of learning"[3] that
had symbolized to me varied essential procedures and perspectives necessary to "produce" an anthropologist.

Let us handle these four vantage points, beginning with "the department," since it did play, I still think, a dominant role, directly or indirectly, in setting forth a certain image and substance to my approach to
anthropology. Subsequently, we will return to consider the three informants as early "initiators" from the other side.

"THE DEPARTMENT": PHASES OF IMITATION AND INITIATION

As is normally true, the influence exerted by such a training facility as a university department of anthropology on a beginner is enormous and lasting. In this case it became a locus of one's attention for both that it provided and lacked. It offered the class-room spangled precepts and theories, provided glimpses from others of what it meant to be an anthropologist (and supposedly a good one), and exuded an ethos of active commitment to anthropological fieldwork. In doing all this "the department" would of course project itself as a venue for learning and "doing proper anthropology," where one imitated one's favorite teachers at one end, and initiated oneself into international, intercultural complexes of on-going anthropological standards, viewpoints, and "frontiers," on the others. Amidst the insouciance of a beginner, a basic stance of the discipline was thus encountered.

For a novice going to the field to start his career, "the department," when located so nearby and so organized as the above, offers the picture of a standard bearer — the one in terms of which "good" anthropological work should be generated and evaluated. (Obviously, it is more so if there are little or no chances of exposing oneself to more than one department for a comparative evaluation.) The novice may look towards it for guidance when facing an anomalous or difficult field situation, or when what is being given as information by one's informants is not being made sense of. Thus, ranging from practical tips for the field to an analytical frame of reference against which to systematize one's data, "the department" represents an anchor to the beginner in an otherwise unpredictable sea of human behavior, even if the field concerns one's own people, However, too many hopes of this kind from "the department" must remain misplaced and counterproductive, for this center is never a substitute for working out solutions to one's own perceptions, predispositions and field problems.

Particularly in the phase under discussion, "the department," as perceived and handled by me for its influence on my fieldwork, surreptitiously produced a near-yet-distant approach to "the native." If it emphasized the necessity of gaining reliable field data from the people for "doing" anthropology, it did so under an "imitative alienation." The quality of this alienation is hard to describe, for though inspired by that "scientific" aim of introducing a "distance" between the field worker and the native that supposedly makes an anthropological account more thorough and reliable, it is in practice neither simply a scientifically controlled distance nor an outright rebellion against one's own culture.

Yet subtly it is both. The imitative alienation indicated here comes from "soaking" oneself in the major works of anthropologists working on "the native" all over the world (where it is most often the Western anthropologist found handling the non-Western peoples and cultures), and from those Indian anthropologists as teachers, seniors and colleagues who, though Indians, had themselves exemplified versions of this alienation that comes from emulating and assimilating the Western anthropological tradition. However, over time as one proceeds in one's career as an anthropologist, the characterization of this alienation can significantly change (which is not simply always with reference to the native, since it could also be in terms of the ways of anthropology and anthropologists). Emphasizing the constructive phase of this alienation, which is after all helpful, I think, in the anthropological perspective, it is most often turned into an asset for an intensive "study of their own people" by native anthropologists. As is commonly said, it helps discover those "blind spots" that one's cultural familiarity (and close social identification) easily produces and tenaciously endures.

A native anthropologist, more accurately, as was true in my case, swings back and forth between being near and away from his own people on the one hand, and between being attracted to and alienated by anthropological assumptions and procedures, on the other. Inspired by the images of the anthropological standards that I had gathered in my initial phase, I was trying to be, as it were, beside myself – to be successful as a non-native before my own people! Conversely, I was expecting my varied (often urban and educated) informants to be equally tolerant of my imitative alienation from them, for all of it was to be in the spirit of becoming an (though necessarily a native) anthropologist. It was as if I was asking them to see me (at least some of the time) as an aspiring anthropologist so that I could have a right to see them from a distance, and yet not be seen as a true stranger.

By the time, however, I had been able to deliberate about procedures for manipulating and managing my own nativity in the field, presence of the "department" was being left behind. As if the only watchword left was: "you are now on your own, and your *passe-partout* is your own understanding of the human ways and yourself." Thus had also begun to emerge redefinitions of "the field" and "the fieldwork": For it was neither to be a scientifically bounded laboratory nor merely an expression of one's idiosyncratic inventions. It was real enough to be found out there, where people as human beings behaved along their own collective representations – a "laboratory" of ideas and actions and of moving boundaries of the real, the anomalous, and the significant. My faceless natives had soon thereafter begun to have faces *and* intellects, and the anthropologist in me was humbler as he became more and more conscious of his ignorance about himself and about what he would call "the native." One may dulcify the concern caused by this ignorance by hoping that this realization will somehow speed up one's own learning.

Now let us only briefly (given the constraints of space) consider the initial phases of this journey from the other side – the people themselves, especially in terms of those who became my first series of path-opening "informants." (This term is more like an euphemism for some long-shared relationships and their deeper significance to my fieldwork; see, for example, Khare 1975).

"THE INFORMANTS": THREE FACADES, FACES, AND FRAMES OF REFERENCE[4]

Recalling the very first occasions of fieldwork in early 1958 in a village in Uttar Pradesh (e.g. for sketches of this village, see Khare, 1962, 1962a, 1964), I distinctly remember the awkwardness I had felt in facing villagers as interviewees and "objects" of observation, and in consciously tutoring myself that I should be a "proper" interviewer and observer. This awkwardness was not entirely from being ignorant about an Indian village and its inhabitants, for I had had several exposures to such surroundings (though never as a long-time resident in any village). It was rather from assuming and awarding shared images to myself and to others in (almost) a self-conscious manner. But equally importantly, it was an awkwardness that I had socially felt; I do not know, however, if the other side had felt the same way or not. For all the indications that I could get would suggest that these initial informants, particularly those previously acquainted, had treated me "as one of ours." This initial perception is to be logically expected, since one normally attempts to interview first those whom one either knows (however feebly or distantly) or those who are one way or the other "known strangers" (i.e. known to somebody whom I may know either feebly or indirectly). An overt emphasis on tracing such "connections" may be a distinctive quality of the native anthropologist's procedures in the field. One might say that his fieldwork most often begins under a strongly shared notion of nativity, which the people under study, if not the anthropologist, keep in front for good reasons – it is *their only way* of making sense of what is done by this person, who calls himself an anthropologist but who seems like any other "educated *bābū*" of the society.

Clearly, therefore, it is essential to recognize that there are at least two distinct perspectives present in the beginning phases of such a fieldwork. One is as the beginning anthropologist sees it and the other which the people under study form about this anthropologist and subtly communicate it. However, as the subheading of this segment of the essay suggests these perspectives change over time from both sides, and our concern here will be limited mainly to changes which the beginning fieldworker begins to descry from his side. What follows therefore is my perspective of what went on in the field in terms of the three chosen informants and myself. These had represented to me a cluster of anthropological concerns and meanings, and had in the beginning played the roles of a conductor, a guide, a member of dramatis personae, and, figuratively speaking, even an *accoucheur* and an *agent provocateur*.

(1) For example, *a Kayastha village leader*, who facilitated my entry into his own village as he was known (but no relation) to me from before, had represented a familiar face (apparently as he would say) "without a facade." He was my natural link from a city (Lucknow) to a village (Gopalpur) since he maintained houses at both places and was as reliable as a city dweller for villagers as he was for me as a villager. Yet he was an ex-Zamindar (landlord), a representative of the "feudal establishment" of pre-Independent India, and was of higher caste in a predominantly low caste village. He was an active factional leader always ready to play his politics of consensus and compromise (as he would call it, though for lower caste villagers it was all "an old game of his").

His previous acquaintance with me (and my father) soon presented itself as a mixed blessing. If he was a reliable initial conductor, counsel, and guide on the social history of the village (and of the place of his ruling family in it), his perspective of the "other side" (the lower caste groups and their versions of what the village was), as expected, was incomplete, biased, and "behind times." Attempts to distract and detain me into these were also evident, and he thus awarded himself, as I would call it, a "limited face" in relation to my aim of reaching the whole village. But despite this handicap, the leader (with his relatives) was representing to me a vital frame of social reference without which the village could neither be sociologically described nor understood. For his family history was most often also the moulding force for the entire village's social history.

This informant, in general, stood out as a "guide-conductor" in the field. If as a guide he would see me as "a young man in need of guidance and training in societal affairs" ("just as a growing plant is trained"), my efforts (as I now see them) would be to free myself of the "control" that guidance always implies, including him to acquire a conductor's role. However, the fact that he would revert to being a guide was not surprising to me as a native anthropologist, for it is a deeply seated cultural norm that an older person in India follows. What is more important is that an anthropologist be able to diffuse or neutralize such controls through appropriate (socially approved) interpersonal procedures. Moreover, guidance also means opening new avenues of thought for the one who is being guided: it does not always bring controls. Initially as a guide, this informant on his own became more and more of a conductor as the time went on — as he exhausted what he knew and as he learnt about my research needs to know more about more. This was a noticeable change, succeeded by even the third one, where he would not only listen to whatever I might have learnt from other informants but he was receptive to new information, for he was, as he would say, "not a frog in the well" (this metaphor comes from a Sanskrit proverb which is also popularly shared by the educated today). Thus also emerged a more realistic (and dynamic) range of roles that I refer to by calling him a guide-conductor, for the latter ultimately refers to varying constellations of my inquiry, and his guidance. These strains, however, changed with changing interpersonal relations between us.

(2) In comparison, under limited contrast, appeared the case of my second informant, *a Kurmi householder*, who, living in the same village for generations, represented the lower segment of the village. If uneducated and illiterate (though he had in 1958 learnt to scribble his name in Hindi, instead of the "thumb impression," on formal papers), he was mentally alert, socially outgoing, and in speech articulate. In post-Independent India his relationships with the Kayastha leader had changed, "for it was now his turn to come to us seeking our support," according to him. But since he was neither hostile nor cool towards the Kayastha leader, the latter had introduced me to him in a highly casual manner during one of his early evening "rounds of the village" (as the Kayastha leader would put it, for, whenever present in the village, he would make these rounds as a practice; for him it was his way of saying "Rāma, Rāma" (Hello) to the villagers met outside their own houses). As expected, the Kurmi householder received me courteously but with a distance, particularly the one that came with an identification with the Kayastha leader. First of all, I was from the city (*saharuā*) and was known to the Kayastha leader from before. Second, I was prying into everybody's affairs, whether of the high or low caste, in a manner that was not quite the way any other visiting government official or worker (or erstwhile landlords) would do. This difference could not escape the acute mind of this person in the village and he was rather the very first one to open our relationship by asking a barrage of critical questions about my work and intentions. One relevant

exposure he had was of his own son, who was then going to a neighboring high school, and was helpful in explaining, at least in part, "that new way in which now people go out to villages to get educated."

In comparison to the Kayastha guide-conductor, the Kurmi house-holder represented maieutic ways of learning to me. It was an indirect, subtler method of making me learn about lower caste perspectives and life conditions without appearing to exert control over me. It helped me recall Socrates' metaphor of the midwife, where one person helps another "give birth" to new systems of information and understanding. (This metaphor is expected to represent certain psychoanalytic or even mystical religious processes. However, here our reference is simply to symbolically powerful use of critical hints, allusions, and experiences so that an informant, even if unconscious of his role (recall, for example, Socrates' uneducated slave boy asked to prove Pythagoras' theorem, and its entailed problems), projects himself as an *accoucheur* in an anthropologist's learning process.) Thus, though the Kurmi householder could not see himself as a guide or a teacher, given the system of caste precedence in his mind, he could of course create direct or indirect conditions helpful to my "birth" (i.e. acceptance) in lower caste surroundings. True to maieutic practices, he would wait for me to respond to what he was informing (or watching me behave in, say, a lower caste feast) rather than rush to tell me all about what I was expected to know or do or say. Though this vital frame of reference for learning in the field can not be elaborated here, the signif-icant point is that one learns in the field in several different ways, changing procedures from one major informant to the next.

(3) Now let us compare, but only briefly (since he has also been previously discussed elsewhere; see Khare, 1970, 1975), the case of my third informant – *A Kanya-Kubja Brahman* from Lucknow, who was central to my decade-long studies of his caste group. In comparison to the Kayastha and Kurmi informants, whose locality was shared but caste was not, here caste was highest but everything else varied. Dealing with a Kanya-Kubja Brahman, when one is not himself/herself one of them, the Kurmi's encounter is reversed. Since these Brahmans consider themselves highest even within all other cognatic Brahman groups, they exclude "others" quickly and (mostly) unambiguously and rank themselves intricately and exhaustively. Thus, as I did not belong to their caste group, the very first impression I had was that I was strikingly exterior to them. Most of them being city dwellers and educated, the strength of this distance was rather as surprising to me as was the weak impact of my shared nativity on them. However, as expected, the old, the orthodox, and the women would illustrate this distance in a more rigid manner than

would the young and the modern. But since it is the former who know
more about the actual social life and guide the rest, the anthropologist
tends to give them a natural priority.

In comparison to the Kayastha village leader and the Kurmi householder, this Kanya-Kubja Brahman had offered the profiles of an Indian
dialogist. I say Indian because his own view of himself would always be
one of a learned Brahman, a pundit, who was not merely ready to respond
to my questions, but as our contact progressed over the years, he became
involved in structuring (an effort with good intentions but not always
welcome to an anthropologist) situations and dialogues that would help
my aims. If he would tell me some features of his own subgroup or family
in a certain ceremonial circumstance, he would expect me to tell him
whether that is how I also saw it or not. If not, then a dialogue (*samvāda*)
must start on the nature of differences we encountered. His reason for
doing so (sometimes disrupting my pace of work) was simple: This would
make me either learn or think about something which I probably had
missed before. Equally importantly, he would think of me as an inquirer
(*jigyāsu*) whose aim was not only to accept what he is told but also to
check it himself. Thus, as the time passed the Indian cultural paradigm
involved in our relationship began to emerge rather clearly: There were
two inquirers (what if one was senior) in each other's company to learn
about a social group. This made the dialogue not only a necessity but an
instrument of learning.

However, I have always wondered about the effects on my inquiry if
this informant had exclusively insisted on his pundit or guru-like view of
himself and if he had not allowed our dialogues to replace his initial
monologues. It did not take long for us to realize that our relationship was
being nurtured by the dialogue; moreover, the latter made a "sociological
discussion" feasible. As this informant had once remarked in 1965,
"without it (the dialogue) only introspection is left, and that is besides
sociology."

Congruent with his view of himself as a pundit, a learned man, he
would keep his dialogues "alive" by, as he would say, tricking me into
"situations of learning." This meant exposing me to situations of everyday
life, where, for example, marriage negotiations were going on; dowry
disputes were being pursued; and interpersonal family relations were being
mended. For him it was to see if I had understood what our dialogue was
all about; for me it was to be taken towards crucial contexts of observation (and limited participation). However, he would go beyond this
categorization when he attempted to provoke me or others to say or do
something that, in his view, would help remove a mask or two to let me

learn what the reality was like. Metaphorically, he acted as an *agent provocateur*. But this was always without harm to anybody, "and only for the sake of learning."

Summary and Implications

I have attempted to present here two interrelated aspects of my initial approach and exposure to anthropological fieldwork. The first concern is with the identity and burdens of a native anthropologist, though obviously the sketch produced here is preliminary and incomplete. It is in this context that I present the other concern – my passage among three informants, where each represented for me a research concern, a phase of my growing up, and a procedure for and a process of learning.

I describe the informants as I found them (and thought about them), then and later on. It has been (and still remains) a human and humane interchange for me. Conditioned by my own cultural background, I perceived informants as elders, as people belonging to different caste groups, and as persons with a richness of their own experience and judgement. In return, my informants did the same, particularly since their cultural region was the same as mine. This fact of shared nativity inevitably influenced my becoming an anthropologist, as it equally probably would anybody else's in such a circumstance, even as we may grant that anthropologists as persons employ varying capabilities for strategically maximizing "pay offs" from their own cultural backgrounds.

Intellectually rendering the familiar intriguing, the near distant, the miniature magnified, the segments link up to the system as a whole that he never "saw" before, a native anthropologist begins by producing imaginative learning procedures for himself. Later on, these games become a serious part of his intellect, for this is what makes him what he is and wants to be. In a way, he adds such several procedures to his perspective in order to neutralize his native colors – to put a distance between the working of his intellect and his own culture. Equally surely, however, this anthropologist must remain fallible in this exercise, because he is like his subjects, only a human being. But making an attempt to let such filters suitably come on is significant enough for the anthropologist, for this alone allows him to see the human in his increasingly total dimensions; without them, he would return to the solipsist, noncomparative particular – and even the parochial, losing his identity as well as vision.

NOTES

1. My usage of "anthropology" and "anthropologists" uniformly refers to socio-cultural anthropology and anthropologists. It excludes allusion to other branches of the discipline because the implications of "nativity" in them are strikingly different.

    This is the abridged version of an essay written to undertake a discussion of the larger issue reflected in only a few opening remarks here: How is social anthropology of one's own culture possible? If yes, what does it conceptually and methodologically imply? If not, why not? Though not fully reflected here, such a presentation learns as much from informants who think and educate as from Western thinkers (not necessarily only anthropologists) who also think and educate about themselves and their *modes* of thought about "others." The Committee on Small Grants at the University of Virginia helped me during the writing phase of this article.

2. Given the native anthropologist's predominant shaping by anthropological methodology, field techniques, and comparative analytical concerns, he does not consider himself a "sociologist" in the usual sense of the term. In reality, this problem of classification is found tied to academic conventions in different countries having significant number of sociologists and anthropologists. India, for example, in the past twenty five years or so seems to have partially blurred the sharp distinction between Anglo-American style social anthropologists and sociologists. The former have strongly influenced the latter in India. Yet this blurring may be incomplete – welcome to some and unwelcome to others, depending upon their academic ("departmental") location and their "entre-preneurship" in exploiting the "scope" of the two disciplines and their overlap.

    However, underlying these situational definitions lies a deeper difference between the "sociologists" who nurtured an anthropological perspective and those who did not: It is in the comprehension and pursuit of that tension that "alienates" one from one's own culture in an unique manner. This alienation is *not* an estrangement, much less a hostile separation or even a sustained loss of interest in one's own (or others') culture, but it is rather an intellectual re-positioning that allows (hopefully) an anthropologist to distinguish and separate ethnocentric and solipsistic perceptions of his own culture.

    Our usage of the term "alienation" in this article will conform to the above specification, although by context it may also imply several subtler shades.

3. This refers to the Department of Anthropology at Lucknow University *at that time.* Our concern on the one hand evidently is with the dominant enculturating profile of this formal place of learning, and on the other (which is rather more significant for this discussion), with *my own perception and placement of such a center in my scheme of learning* at that time in order to become an anthropological investigator.

4. The difference whether one *starts* by studying one's own people or *returns* to them in a subsequent phase of one's anthropological career, is vitally important in what follows. My case of course falls into the first category, and my perceptions and procedures are therefore guided by this condition. A different set of requirements and sensitivities, for example, would be expected to emerge if one learnt one's "hard-core" anthropology in some one else's culture and returned to study one's own later on.

REFERENCES CITED

Khare, R. S., 1962, *Domestic Sanitation in a North Indian Village: An Anthropolotical Study.* Ph.D. dissertation, University of Lucknow.
1962a, Group Dynamics in a North Indian Village. Human Organization **21**: 201-213.
1964, An Indian Village's Reaction to Chinese Aggression. Asian Survey **4**: 1152-1160.
1970, *The Changing Brahmans: Associations and Elites Among the Kanya-kubjas of North India.* Chicago: University of Chicago Press.
1975, Anthropological Fieldwork: Some Experiences and Observations Among the Kanya-Kubja Brahmans. Journal of the Indian Anthropological Society, **10**: 79-96.
Marriott, Mckim, 1966, "The Feast of Love," In *Krishna: Myths, Rites, and Attitudes.* Milton Singer, ed. Pp. 200-212. Honolulu: East-West Center Press.

CHAPTER 8

"Come Ahead, If You Dare"

VICTOR A. LIGUORI

In September of 1964, prior to my first exposure to those isolated fishermen of the Guinea Marshes, the Owens twins came to me concerned.
Senior sociology majors, they had heard I was going into Guinea. They
quickly filled me in on the pathological killers and thieves I was soon to
encounter: they were relieved to know that at least I did have Virginia
license plates on my car and also that the county tag on the automobile
was that of a locality adjacent to the Guinea Marshes.

From the first I was warned:

"Make sure they see the county tag, so they'll know you're local.
Still, never mention that you are a writer (they shoot writers) and
be sure to leave well before dark (they shoot anyone after dark)."

"Watch out for the several 'bad blood' families, the others are
not so bad."

"You mean you go over there alone? Lock your car when you
ride through there. Those people talk and they probably know
you come there alone. Like poor little animals. Don't use my
name. I want to be able to sleep at night without being afraid."

"Maybe you heard about that preacher over there. He came
back with the congregation and sat in a pew to pray with the
people and somebody came up behind him and slit his throat."

People who tell stories of the Guineamen must enjoy the imagery linked to
church, and throats. Another story had it that:

"One of two brothers in Guinea went to prison for a crime both
had committed. The free brother took up with the jailed brother's
wife while he was imprisoned. One Sunday morning after his
release, the jailed brother 'opened the throat' of his brother, who
was in the pew in front of him."

Even from a waterman on Tangier Island, himself stereotyped as thieving
and immensely antagonistic toward strangers, "You don't mean you're
from Guinea? They *kill* people there!"

Even before my first exposure to the people of the Guinea Marshes,
then, I was repeatedly advised of both their isolation and of the universal-
ity of their alleged pathologies. All in all, I was told, like all others and by
all others, "Be afraid. You would do well not to go into Guinea at all.
Leave them alone. But if you do go, at least, be wise and be afraid."

A Fisherman from the Guinea Marshes. [Photograph by Mark Sutton]

What we have before us conjures up in our imagination an image of the Guinea Marshes as located in some remote, inaccessible place. In fact they are approximately 20 miles from my university, the College of William and Mary in Williamsburg, Virginia. Although insulated until rather recently, the Guinea Marshes are not remote; they comprise the southeastern-most portion of Gloucester County, Virginia and front on the shoal waters of the York River. Mobjack Bay and the lower Chesapeake Bay. In the Guinea Marshes, or more accurately, just off-shore of them, is Big Island, a small island community of fishing families. Big Island and the contiguous Guinea Marshes has been the setting of my field research for the last twelve years. The Island is regionally advertised as the most isolated, bizarre and violent place in the Guinea Marshes.

On the way into the Guinea Marshes, that day of my first exposure, I was told by my companion and guide not to be surprised if I understood very little of what was said by the Guineamen. I took all of that lightly indeed. After all, I had five years of commercial fishery field research behind me; besides, I had been forewarned of dangers before, had heard and had discounted all of the exaggerations about isolation and violence and so on. My liaison was from neighboring Mathews County: his grandmother was known to the matriarch of Big Island, who, for over forty years, produced hand-made sails. An aspiring student of anthropology with an eye for "fair exchange", my guide traded an introduction to the people of Big Island for some segments of my dissertation on commercial fishermen of the Middle Atlantic Coast.

If anything, he understated the problems I was to have unravelling the speech of the Guineamen. Our first stop was a household at the end of a dirt road at the end of a long spit of land quite close to the Big Island I had heard so much about. First, we encountered the father of the household sitting in the yard, making crab pots from what looked to me like chicken wire. I watched, I listened; I understood only what I saw. After a bit we went indoors to sit upon a tired old couch and talk. (They talked.) I watched, and listened, at times to the coin-operated television set which competed well for noise until, after a while, it digested its quarters. No competition for noise from women or children. But from behind the partly closed doors of the room I knew that they listened. I had spent hundreds of hours with commercial fishermen and knew lots about gear and technology and seasonal fluctuations, but not enough of our host's language and speech to answer a simple question like, "Is you marr'?" Bewilderment; pain; but when in doubt, smile. My liaison came to the rescue, laughing a response, "No, he's not married." I thought I knew English, I believed I knew lots of French and Italian and Spanish, but on that day I relied totally upon my companion. Those fishermen spoke some incomprehensible combination of chopped off words and emphatic sounds, invented words, Virginia ruralisms and 17th and 18th Century English provincialisms; all delivered *very* quickly. In the course of that initial exposure and those soon to follow, I heard words like 'scri' sto' (prescription store or a drug store), cod bag (scrotum), dirk, turnkey, lights (lungs; window glass), vo'ce co' (divorce court), paralyzed (damned), and copper (penny), to name a few.

I sincerely believe that total concentration upon their speech would not have helped much on that day of my first exposure in 1964, it is academic, anyway because I *could not concentrate.* I did not know where to begin.

I was staggered by the diversity of speech only 20 miles from my university and the sudden inadequacy of all my prior training and experience with Atlantic Coast commercial fishermen. Then I felt a swell of excitement at prospects for future research of all sorts. Realistically, those prospects looked dim, however. How does one study forgotten English fishermen whom one cannot begin to understand? With an interpreter I wished to leave behind immediately? One does not study independent fishermen of the Chesapeake Bay with an interpreter. My field notes record one particular low in my morale that first day: from one waterman, especially eager to show me his fishing gear, I understood *not one word*. No exaggeration – not one word. No liaison around at that point; no one to console me with the fact that this fisherman has a massive speech impediment. *Later*, his mother did it.

> "Don't study (worry) 'bout him, Vic. *We* don't understand what he says. *He* speaks Eyetalian."

My guide asked our host, an obviously respected highliner[1] in this enclave if someone would take us by boat to Big Island. He said he would ask his boy, but gave no assurance that his son would comply. The "boy," a very solid young man of about seventeen invited us aboard his work skiff. We approached and then passed by the oyster shell landing of the Island. We circled. He ran the outboard engine slowly. We could look, but he would not take us ashore. Finally, we coaxed and begged to no avail. "He's afraid of the dogs", my liaison translated. This very powerful kid *was born here and he's afraid* to go ashore. He told us that he had not set foot on Big Island in 10 years. *I*, however, was not to be denied, not that close to the Big Island, regionally celebrated as the most isolated and the most violent place in the Guinea Marshes. It was *my* turn for drama. Not impressive, physically, by watermen's standards, I told John Hess that I would go first if he would put us ashore. If the dogs attacked, they would attack me first. Reluctantly, he agreed. The dogs came; they did not attack. How directly this episode funnelled my thinking into that pejorative mold: Isolation, Violence, and Fear. There was no one there to provide me with a less dramatic, more factual interpretation of what was happening. Only after months and months did I comprehend that this *particular* young man had *no need* to set foot on Big Island. His work is on the water; *his* people are centralized in the mainland enclave 'cross the creek where we came from. He knew well that being afraid of the dogs was legitimate enough excuse to get him off the hook with most visitors. Put concisely, in the words of his people: "He don't go there." Not because he is afraid, not because his uncles and cousins are killers, or even because their dogs are killers, but *because he don't go there*. This man's reaction could be interpreted in several ways. At first, I made the mistake of stressing fear, staggering fear in such a rugged looking lad. In time, I realized otherwise: it was hot; we were consuming his father's gasoline with no hint of compensation of any description. He had other things to do than tour us up and down the paths, between the tall weeds to the various island households, introducing us, strangers, to people in whom he had little interest at this age in his life.

Many of us embarking upon our first field research experiences take far too seriously the fragility of rapport. When I entered the Guinea Marshes, I had all the university degrees I wanted, so I feared no graduate advisors, but I did fear losing rapport. When I discovered that many colleagues from my university, and others from the nearby Virginia Institute of Marine Science, were astounded that I actually got on, and off of Big Island unhurt, my first day in Guinea, I got the idea that this was a research setting which had to be captured at all costs. For me this meant that I could make no mistake which might jeopardize rapport. I feared moving too quickly, asking alienating questions, revealing the fact that I could not at all understand their language. I was aware that there are severe limits to the amount of time commercial fishermen have to spend educating shore folk on whatever it is they think interests them. I feared being denied access to that isolated, radically different island where even those of school age spoke an archaic English dialect with 17th and 18th Century provincialisms among their preferred word choices, where they spent their spare time in incest and in killing and looting strangers. I was so cautious that I asked not one single question — not one — for an entire year. Instead of inquiring, I watched, I floated, I explained myself when I believed I had to. It would have helped a great deal to know, early on, that it was not the worry or the excessive caution which was important, it was the floating. In retrospect, I see plenty of cause to be excited at that research opportunity, to be careful to proceed cautiously and professionally, *but not to fear losing* rapport, not to fear discussing with my informants my major research goals, lest they blow me away. Actually, I never once feared the death or injury I was advised to fear.

Consider the following in more human terms than that of most newcomers, or polished professionals, to maritime cultural studies: What *if* the Islanders became suspicious at my standing around one entire year? What if they should become angry, uncooperative, hostile? We should be clever enough to know that very few human relationships and communication processes *actually* unfold in dichotomous terms: *either* we are well received or we fail to establish rapport and are sent away. If X, then Y — case dismissed! That's not the way it is: not a matter of *if* they get suspicious, angry, hostile. Some might; some will. Work with that; work from that. But most of the time the watermen and other Guineamen are tolerant, forgiving of staggering insensitivity or ignorance, understanding, and very willing to help the researcher proceed in making his or her living "the way he knows how." Looking back 12 years now, at all those outsiders whom I have brought and those who found their way to Big Island on their own, I think perhaps that the Islanders' most consistent response was to uncritically help strangers, regardless of their intent or the level of their inquiry.

It is a simple point, but also one that is well worth repeating: we enter the field with an immense homogenizing tendency. We look for informants to fill certain categories. We go into a maritime community looking for fishermen. Some of them, we are told, and can see for ourselves, are marginal producers (often small-scale, inshore fishermen). We label them marginal fishermen because they don't seem to produce much and they certainly look like fishermen (some of the time). And here the parenthesis is critical. Perhaps, most of the time, when we as researchers do not see them, they look more like fathers, or waterfowl hunters, or third base-men, or churchgoers, or primarily residents of a community. They develop a great deal of their sense of self from these identities, in addition to personal, not status, considerations like being and expressing in a particu-lar setting with their friends and foes and relatives. Herein also lie impor-tant realities, not just in that *fisherman* label affixed by the researcher. Thus, a more significant comparison between people with marginal commitment to commercial fishing and their full commitment counter-parts might be not between the size of their catches, but rather in all sorts of non-fishery interaction. If we fall into the homogenizing trap, our analyses will most certainly be both inaccurate and dehumanizing. If the researcher is in the Marshes only during the daylight hours, he could well define as Guineamen, males in hipboots and cast-off clothing. At other times, in other places, these descriptive criteria may not apply at all.

MARKETABLE ISOLATION

I repeated my initial presentation of self on my second trip into the Guinea Marshes. I explained that I was a teacher, that I was interested in their ways of fishing, and that I had come to the area from New Jersey, where I spent several years with coastal trawlermen. Immediately I was asked by the highliner, the leader of that particular, insulated enclave, "Is New Jersey North or South of California?" I was amazed and shocked; I began linking ignorance about the relative location of two irrelevant states to the pejorative: stupidity (not very humanistic of me, but the humanism came with time). The fisherman then invited me to join him at his work and I learned quickly that he habitually crossed much of a 7 or 8 mile part of the Chesapeake Bay well before a hint of daylight *without a compass* – in fog without a compass. And so I asked him: "You don't use a compass. I can't help but notice. Do you *have* a compass?"

"You mean a lode-stone? Oh, I had a lode-stone four-five years ago, but the boy lost it."

Through the years, I learned amazement at the depth and accuracy of the man's knowledge of the natural history of the Chesapeake Bay. Today at 67, he is an incredible storehouse of biological and ecological information; he is still the highliner of his enclave.

As serious students of anthropology know well, isolation is marketable. In the years since that first exposure, I have bombarded my students with the premise that a responsible researcher in an "isolated" community must also utilize (and publicize) the concept "contact" along with isolation or insulation. It has much less shock value, but it is critical to understanding reality.

In 1965, a regional television documentary capitalized upon and greatly exaggerated the isolation of the Big Islanders. The program included the following, "fascinating, true story.

About 1945, two Internal Revenue agents went to Big Island and told Mr. _____ that they'd come concerning his failure to pay income tax. Mr. _____ said he'd always paid his taxes; he then showed property tax receipts to prove it. The agents then explained to him that he made a lot of money catching fish and that he was supposed to pay taxes on this. And he admitted that he'd gotten a lot of money catching fish, he didn't know how much. After they continued to press him, he went and from underneath of a bed, pulled out a hundred pound wooden fishbox. 'Everything I've got, 'cept what we've used to buy food and all with is in this box. Take out of it what you think I owe you.' They were amazed to find over $19,000 in the fishbox. They counted the currency out, computed what they figured that he owed them in taxes, took it out and left the remaining amount in the fishbox."

Seem like a nice story? It sold well. One thing though: IT NEVER HAPPENED. I've checked and rechecked and very recently I brought my tape recording of the TV program to the man in question. I played him the quote enclosed above. Here is the truth:

"Never was a Revenue Man that come to the Islet. I've heard of that lie, but I never have heard it on tape before. I *never had a fish box in my house*, neither."

This, then, is not just a manufactured story on isolation, media-produced data geared toward making a TV show more interesting. It hurts. It reflects upon the ignorance, morality, and the standards of living of a real, specific living person who has earned not one of these indictments. Viewed humanistically, the story can be seen to be filled with pejorative building-blocks. Never mind the part about ignorance and the IRS: the fisherman meticulously explained to me exactly how, to whom and how much he paid in income taxes for those big catches of the 1940's. Of course, the explanation was unnecessary, for me, but the man was hurt "by that lie," so he did. But think about this: how many of us shore folk picked up on that more penetrating hurt laid upon the man by stating, publicly, *on television* that *he, named specifically*, kept *inside his home, fishboxes*? When scruitinized, the story clearly is not consistent with, nor even feasible given other behavior characteristic of Guineamen. But the story is interesting; isolation is interesting, quaint, novel, and obviously marketable. Some of us want to be entertained. Others, professional enough to be skeptical, nonetheless swallow the falsehoods easily, because we delight in isolation, and especially in the idea of an isolated *island*. I am not alone in my enthusiasm for 17th and 18th Century English speech in 1982, twenty miles from Williamsburg, Virginia. Many are interested in children who decide for themselves whether or not they will attend school and then decide how many days a week they will try to attend, and if those children could actually be legally exempt from compulsory school attendance because they live on an island. What is crucial here is what those of us doing field research in isolated fishing communities *do next* with our illustrations of isolation. Frequently, inaccuracy is a more convenient course, even at the professional level of research. From the dissertation proposal of a graduate student with "four years of field research in the Guinea Marshes", presently working toward the Ph.D. in a reputable American univeristy.

"They are people who manage without cars or public transportation, are unfamiliar with telephones, consider indoor plumbing an unnecessary luxury, do not read at all . . . "

All five points are untrue. One was never true; others have been untrue for decades; others blatantly disregard the staggering social change of the last five years. Furthermore, they are outright falsifications. Yet this quotations in my possession are far from the worst of what is currently being conveyed about the Guinea Marshes of Virginia in that effort to exploit isolation for specific gain.

THE CONSCIOUS, CREATIVE USE OF THE SUBJECTIVE

Sociology students, prior to their first exposure to field research, carry with them a heavy orientation towards "being objective". They read all sorts of essays on social scientific methods and the sins of bias and becoming over-involved. As a result, they promise those of us responsible for preparing them for field research that

"I will divorce myself of any preliminary bias."

"I will introduce myself as a sociologist and try to explain the purpose of my research and my neutral stance."

"I will not hide my purposes distorting them would make me uncomfortable and on guard. Besides, covert research is dishonest; it also hurts the reputation of sociology.

"I will not take sides or employ subjective interpretations."

This general message permeates undergraduate and graduate students of all descriptions, not just those naive few who regurgitate the quotes they have gained from the literature.

Since 1962 I have been continuously engaged in field research with people for whom fish mean livelihood. When most of my informants are sharing those things they care about most, they do not want a neutral, detached observer. They want somebody on their side at least to the extent that the listener does not convey aloof; detached; beyond; above; without emotion or caring. These characteristics in a researcher are far removed from those familiar qualities of ethnicity in the enclave: trust — communicating with a whole person, knowing that person, where they come from, and certainly where they stand. Really intensive rapport, I submit, awaits some sharing of our subjective selves. Be aware of this prior to your first exposure to field research. Continue to endeavor to maintain objectivity through important, specific techniques, but know also something of the phenomenon of being subjective. Let us consider, *as well*, the intentional, creative use of the subjective, both in ourselves, and in those we encounter in the field.

Most of us going into the field to do research concentrate upon our own *status* identities with almost as much zeal as we locate them in our informants. I have been asked by women students I have brought into the Guinea Marshes, "Should I smoke? What if someone offers me a beer?" They concentrate so heavily on idealized role expectations that they never realize that the Guinea Marshes at this time are a person-oriented place, not status-oriented place, not the status-oriented academic bureaucracy from which they so recently stepped. In the status-first presentation of ourselves we radically narrow the range of human research experience we

The author-neutral, detached, objective. [Photograph by George Goode]

might develop with members of fishing families. Come ahead, if you dare. The Guineamen with whom I work are independent, energetic, inventive, expressive people. Not until an outsider offers some expression of his subjective self do they begin to feel the humanity of that newcomer, and respond to it. For those who are illiterate and catch or clean fish for a living, it is very hard to identify with those of us who intellectualize, who cannot dissolve social distance, who cannot present a more open, and vulnerable expression of themselves.

RECOGNIZING DIMENSIONS OF EXPRESSIVENESS

During that year after my initial exposure, I began to perceive that much of what was denigrated in Guineamen as failure to achieve might be seen otherwise if we understand the importance of *expressive* lifestyles. We ourselves are so steeped in instrumental orientations (The Protestant Work

Ethic and rational, technological efficiency), that we tend to grant lipservice at most, but not equal legitimacy to expressive social interaction. There are dramatic illustrations of expressiveness, such as during the years of World War II when a waterman gave another in need twenty pounds of currency without regard to the denomination of the bills, there are countless undramatic ones. In another paper[2] I argue that the marginal work commitment of some commercial fisherman can be something other than an unintended, residual consequence of their failure to compete respectably with the highliners in their fleet. It involves much specific, conscious, subjective expressiveness.

It is very difficult for me to be formalistically neutral with regard to the language and speech of the Big Islanders. I cannot accept it as the simple pejorative it is painted to be by those who cannot understand them at all; there is nothing very simple about it to me. It is rich in expressiveness. It has more inventiveness, spontaneous, vivid creativity than anything of its kind I have ever encountered. White, middle-class Americans, educated with stenciled speech, like myself, might learn from their norms.[3] A few examples follow.

> I was informed of a group baptism to be conducted very close to Big Island by a local Fundamentalist preacher. An Islander asked me if I cared to attend.
> "Did you hear that _____ is agonna get baptized again?"
> "Again? I thought he was already baptized twice?"
> "Why _____ could come to know every fish in the York River and he could not be Saved!"
> A Sunday. Fourteen people sitting in chairs, on the bed, standing in one room of a two room Island household. A mother concerned that all, kin and guests alike, had enough to eat and drink. Beside me sat a nine-year-old, a huge tumbler in his hand, a milk moustache adorning his lips. Furtively, amidst the banter and human confusion he reached for the refrigerator and more milk. His mother stared, then paralyzed him with the words:
> "Touch that 'frigerator door and I'll blind you in blood."

Apparently, it is an easy process for the inventive expressive speech to become translated into total pejoratives. To me it is clear that almost all of the verbal violence which we hear from Big Islanders is an alternative, not a preface, to physical action. It is a legitimate form of aggression, and not difficult to understand if we consider people in the process of spending their lifetimes together on a very small island.

In 1977, a Richmond, Virginia newspaper woman reported that Big Islanders experienced cold so severe that the "children's hair froze to their pillows." This never happened. What did happen was that one of the Islanders, in that perfectly fluent inventive stream of similies and meta-

phors in which they excel, *was saying it was cold*. It was cold enough for
the salt water around Big Island and throughout the Chesapeake Bay to
freeze solidly; but everyone in Tidewater Virginia knew that about the
Winter of '77, so an Islander exclaimed "it was so cold that the baby's
head froze to the pillow" and the newspaper published it as *fact*. The
expression *should* be understood along with many others created daily by
the Big Islanders:
  - The baby who is "quiet as a clam."
  - The oyster which is "fat as a tick."
  - The shingled roof with "its top so steep that it did split a drop
    of rain."
  - That old, experienced boat builder so skillful that he "could
    caulk a picket fence to keep the tide out."
  - The gunsmith so skillful that "he can drill a hole in the fog."
  - "The wind so strong that it blew the stumps out ' the woods."
  - The rainstorm so violent that "it filled a wire basket."

Because of that reporter's ignorance concerning language and speech, the
mother whose children were described as frozen to their pillows was
shocked at the hurtfulness and angry at this unwarranted insult to her
maternal care. By now I realize that when in the Marshes, speaking with
Guineamen, at times I employ their preferred archaic English provincialisms, my speech is much more volatile than in the university; not only do
I chop off the beginning and ending of words with ease, but also do I
think about my 1963 station wagon as 'flicted, I feel, not just believe,
"paralyzed" is much preferable to "damned." The impact on me of the
expressive speech of Guineamen is evident; from time to time colleagues
gently advise, "You have been on Big Island too long."

At this point in my field experience, I know that I have become so
enthusiastic about inventive-expressive speech that, until recently, I have
all but neglected the liabilities and limitations of the dialect of Guineamen outside of the Marshes. School teachers who cannot understand their
pupils from Guinea assume:
  1. That the children cannot understand standard English (Do
     television actors speak anything else?)
  2. The children have speech impediments, or worse.
  3. That the children are mentally retarded and should be treated
     for that.

Indeed, the speech of the Big Islanders and of many watermen in Guinea
is very, very difficult for most people to understand. Outside of the
Marshes, in unequal status situations, Guineamen pay a severe price for
their diversity of speech. Should I as a researcher ignore this because, after
12 years, *I* can understand them and applaud their independent expressiveness?

SOME PROBLEMS IN THE INTRODUCTION OF OTHERS

Through the years I became intent in sharing some of this virgin anthropological territory with selected students and professors. Recalling some of my own anxieties surrounding first encounters and cognizant of the instant rapport that flows to any stranger introduced into Guinea by me, I introduced, over the years, several people from my university simply as *friends.* It was so easily done, that instant endorsement. It yielded incomparable improvement in their own first exposure. But this was a mistake, I learned eventually. Those I introduced were not simply friends, of course; they all bore other important identities. Few of us who teach really know the personal goals and ambitions of our students or fellow university professors; or their personal propensities to sensationalize their experience rather than to responsibly incorporate a day in Guinea into the rest of their sociological and anthropological training. These variables were as hidden from me as they were from their other informants, the people of Big Island. For example, several years ago, my personal and professional sensitivities were jolted in learning that several of seven under-graduates I had brought into Guinea as part of a Special Topics seminar treated my field setting and MY PEOPLE with the same superficiality that many university students treat selected electives in the crunching last weeks of a spring semester.

Similarly, I have brought in a baker's half-dozen of college professors; it was not until I introduced these professionals from my university did I realize the sharpness of their problem orientations, their passion for rational efficiency and instrumentalism. At times I am amused by the tenacity of their commitment to the rules of formal, abrasive interviewing. They forget that no longer, by definition, are they focal points of knowledge and power. They are in a hurry in a context where most others are not. They are ill-equipped to shed their professional formalism and listen. They are not comfortable listening, and so they ask questions. Often they hurry this too. One huge problem arises when we ask the fishermen fragmented, isolated questions without the slightest hint of our hidden concept orientations, or even why the question is being asked. One young professional with the concept "mobility" in his mind (occupational, geographic, inter-patronus mobility — who might know with certainty?) asked a Big Island adolescent, bat in hand waiting "his knock" (turn at bat)

"Are you going to leave the Island?"
Narrowed eyes, a slight shrug, a glance at me, then:
"Not till I get my knock. After the game is over I might go 'cross the creek and get us some drinks."

A picture of neglect? [Photograph by George Goode]

Sometimes this concludes with our being described as "foolish" and that is all. Sometimes, however, the academicians appear stuffy, puffed up, "stuck up". They will never hear (but perhaps might read) how they are perceived:

> "I tell him things he asks. Then sometimes his mind's off like he don't really care what I'm asayin'. If that's the way he looks at us, then the hell with him."
>
> "He seems to be actin' like he's better than all of us."

To summarize, what suits us well in the classroom makes them feel uncomfortable. We don't know how to listen; how to ask relevant questions (we ask loads of obviously irrelevant ones). If we are unaware of even the importance of ritualized, expressive banter, let alone its substantive con-

Ted's Knock. [Photograph by the author]

tent, our field experience with people in the Guinea Marshes is certain to suffer.

If, and this happens often, we cannot understand what they are saying, but we pretend we do understand (because this is part of our professionalism and we dare not admit weakness) how intelligently do we answer questions ourselves, or go on to another meaningful question? Our candid confession of the fact that we cannot understand will only help. No massive assault upon one's professional ego; no insult to the fishermen. Not surprisingly, some point between approximately 1648 and the present, Guineamen have become well aware that they speak differently. They will gladly repeat or explain themselves if we openly indicate the necessity. These techniques of listening, watching and asking relevant questions are not mastered rapidly; long before I improved to any significant degree, I had earned the nickname "Dummy."

CONFRONTING THE PEJORATIVE TRADITION

The researcher, or the casual visitor to the Guinea Marshes, cannot avoid the pejorative tradition. Even if he has heard nothing of the inhabitants, he perceives signs and symbols of poverty which quickly interlock with images of isolation and deviance. Because all of the stereotypes and characterizations of the behavior of Guineamen are so fundamentally pejorative; and now, because so much of what is published locally and contained in the field notes of journalists and student anthropologists selectively focuses upon negatives; because some aspects of Big Island are pathological and because I feel a self-defined responsibility to unravel ethnic diversity from specific definable pathologies, I cannot avoid confronting pejoratives. Sometimes if we prefer, we can wait for a particular problem orientation (e.g. pollution of or scarcities in, seafood resources) to go away. Sometimes, if we feel more comfortable avoiding a particular variable entirely, (incest, violence; death) we do so. If only a small portion of what is said and understood about a particular group of people is pejorative, perhaps that is a prudent course to chart. For several years I thought seriously about burying my manuscript and reams of data because I might offend the sensitivities of my most cooperative informants. The list of those who celebrate stigma and inaccuracy in order to achieve their own goals is not long, but it is firm. When *so much by so many* celebrates pejoratives and when there are few present who are capable of countering sensationalism with sensitivity, humanism and valid, realiable information, who are aware of the intentional exaggerations and selective inclusions of data from brief, fragmented encounters; who know the enormous tendency to generalize about "people in Guinea", when in fact field work has been concentrated on *just one family*, then those few must deal with this directly. How many of us are there who *know* about those intentionally manufactured marketable inaccuracies to be sold in 1982 as significant truths (when they were never valid generalizations even in 1962)? Sensationalism about Guineamen is certain to expand now that their county is undergoing tremendous growth and more and more potential readers hear about the Marshes. Professionally engaged in serious, long term research and publication, compulsively concerned with my own ethical standards in field methodology, unashamed of my strong humanistic concern for the sensitivities of a small number of fishing people who deserve that, I must confront the pejorative traditions by which they allegedly abide. I began this research with the goal of understanding the nature of small-scale, inshore commercial fishing in the Guinea Marshes of Virginia. The goals have widely expanded so that I might unravel and convey dimensions of ethnic diversity, and disentangle these from the pejoratives and pathologies attributed to Guineamen. Confronting pejorative traditions has become of critical importance to my research, although it is by no means the central theme of what I shall publish in the near future.

Each of the following *verbatim* presentations are from people who should, and do, know otherwise:

"They (the school children) can't even speak English."

"Dirty, always dirty when they come to school . . . Strange, they wrap their feet in newspaper inside their boots." (1973)

"A certain odor clings to the body if one works with fish. Cleanliness is not given the same value in Guinea as it is given in the rest of our society."

A teacher:

"They all should be in Special Education because of all the incest that goes on."

"One teacher says, 'Less learning ability: Too much inbreeding.' "

"They are also well known from their violent fights and for their abundance of guns and distrust of strangers. As a result they are a group to be feared, pitied and avoided.

"Dating and marraige occur among close Guinea kin. This is accepted by those in the community and seems to be the expected pattern. It is very convenient to marry kin people who live close by."

"Nobody will admit that they live in Guinea. They'll all say that they live – down the road a ways."

As a field researcher, I am obviously not opposed to the collection and analysis of the social pathologies of others, except when we leave it at that. The process itself of doing field research among people steeped in the pejorative tradition is likely to articulate still more pathologies (especially marketable ones like sex, violence, breaking the law). And thus we take note of and perhaps tabulate sexual curiosities, verbal and physical violence, patterns of work avoidance and the like. Unfortunately in the case of the Guinea Marshes we find an immense tendency to leave it at that, rather than to press the less spectacular truth: some people drink to excess; a very few, on occasion, take possession of what is not lawfully theirs. Instead of being portrayed as what they in fact are: *problems* for the Guineamen around them, their behavior is portrayed as normative. Such "rogues" represent a tiny minority of the people in the Guinea

Marshes and their behavior should not in any sense be perceived of as characteristic of its residents. Indeed, if this is all we know, we have not learned very much about morality or ethics — about the normative order of the community. Should we simultaneously review the overwhelming majority of watermen and their families who are not at all validly summarized by a couple of marketable concepts? If so, we would find these commercial fishermen quietly and routinely pursuing their independent labor and devoting their energies toward the predictable and unknown demands of the sea. They are not violent, they do not steal.

Rather than to attempt to discount, explore or explain each of topics cited in the above pejorative presentations, I concentrate here upon one topic: illiterary.

"THEY" ARE ILLITERATE

Most of the present inhabitants of Big Island are functionally illiterate by our standards; all but six are illiterate by Big Island standards. The children of the Island recognize scattered written words; but reading, for them, is neither a useful tool nor a comfortable experience. A researcher in the field can simply list illiteracy along with the other pathologies of simple folk. He might even be seduced into believing that reading is neither desired by nor useful for the Big Island adults. Or, the researcher might systematically study the phenomenon of illiterary. If parents and siblings are illiterate, small children do not learn to read and write at home; if they are not required to attend public schools, or if they attend only a few days a year, they do not learn to read in school. If those few who do attend school with some regularity are infrequently taught reading, they do not learn to read. The systematic researcher quickly unravels the fact that every adolescent or adult Big Isalnder desires "to be able to read and write all they want". A researcher might convey to professional educators who care that the failures and impediments surrounding illiteracy are complex, that they have nothing to do with incest or genetic capabilities, that there is no parental opposition to education, only to wasting time and to seeing their children undergo painful humiliation in school. This anthropological researcher might explore the interplay between illiteracy and learning arithmetic on one's own; also, study the interplay between illiteracy and the use of archaic, expressive, and inventive speech, not only because these are interesting, but also because their systematic investigation might just be of great practical significance. Two other important notes on illiteracy in this context. Initially, I assumed that because some Big Islanders were totally illiterate, this clearly extended to those other Guineamen who habitually asked me to read or write in their behalf. In time I learned something about the social functions of illiteracy; in time I learned that nowhere in the Guineaman's Guide to Daily Living is there the norm: watermen should spend part of their time demonstrating to Victor Liguori or any other researcher the precise extent to which they *can* read and write. Secondly, even as this is being written, lots and lots of young adults in the Guinea Marshes are learning to read, reasonably well, on their own, after they have left the constraints of their school experience. This is of fundamental importance, yet it goes totally unreported by some presently engaged in field research in Guinea, because they have a vested interest in maintaining and marketing that myth of isolation and ignorance, of maintaining the shock value of total illiteracy.

The professional maritime anthropologist is well aware of variations in orientations among other outsiders who share his research setting. We know the tendency of journalists to romanticize the nature of island living or working and living in a maritime setting in general. University professionals from non-maritime disciplines as well as ordinary shore folk seem to characterize fishing people in insulated communities as "quaint," interesting curiosities, but not quite legitimate components of the real world. For

A group of Guineamen. [Photograph by the author]

me, among other things, they are the subjects of serious, responsible maritime research: fishing people legitimate in their own choice to live or not to live on an island, to make their livelihood from the water through fishing, crabbing, clamming and oystering, as they choose and as conditions permit them to choose.

A CLOSING NOTE

How will Guineamen react to me when they learn that I have published this chapter on field research into their lives? They will quietly commend me for at last getting it into print.

NOTES

1. That fisherman in a fleet who consistently catches more fish than his peers.
2. Victor Liguori, 1973, "Some Perspectives Upon the Study of Marginal Commitment Among Commercial Fishermen." VIMS Contribution No. 567, Virginia Institute of Marine Science.
3. Each of us with some facility with foreign languages learned relatively late in life knows well that we do not really rapidly expand our ability to think and converse in that foreign language until we feel comfortable enough to dive in there with the foreigners and lose our fear of making errors and thus "making fools of ourselves." Our classroom styles are geared toward masking our weaknesses, not toward making us, and those with whom we speak, comfortable and at ease enough to go rapidly about the relatively easy task of learning language and speech. Language teachers who urge us early on to invent; to emphasize, to practice speech with emotion are typically defined, to be charitable, as "foreign" themselves.

CHAPTER 9

Feds and Locals: Stages of Fieldwork in Applied Anthropology

ALLAN F. BURNS

Ethnographic research in an applied setting is significantly different from traditional fieldwork. While traditional fieldwork derives questions of research focus, method and theory from the discipline of anthropology, applied anthropology exists in what Coleman (1972) calls the "world of action." The world of policy action demands that research be tailored to the political realities of public decisions and competing interest groups. Public policy anthropology is done in the "real time" of everyday life where research information is needed at critical times to help inform policy decisions. If the information is not ready or fieldwork is not complete when budget hearings come up or elections arise, then these political events take place without social science input. As Coleman notes, the academic world is not constrained by such "real time" schedules; at least not to the extent that the world of policy action is. In the academic world, research is informed by the theory and data of the researcher. When the data suggest new lines of inquiry, research designs are changed accordingly.

Research organizations specializing in applied policy studies have developed efficient ways of making sure their work fits the demands of public policy implementation. The organization reported on here,[1] Abt Associates, Inc., is just one of many profit making and non-profit corporations that do social evaluation research, usually under contract with the federal government. Abt Associates has a flexible organizational structure for responding to governmental research needs. The corporation is divided into different "areas" of interest such as education, criminal justice, and environment. These areas have overall managers, but the social scientists who do research easily move between areas to pool their talents in order to respond to the rise and fall of government sponsored evaluation contracts. When the company won a large contract to evaluate a large educational program, many social scientists of the company were drawn from other areas to be assembled into a team to carry out the new project. These areas in the company have no claim to longevity; an area can be formed or dis-

129

banded in response to new trends in federal contract initiatives. Unlike a university, the company does not foster department boundaries or disciplinary loyalty. Instead, it fosters multidisciplinary work and loyalty to particular projects. This multidisciplinary strategy is encouraged by the leisure and social organization of the company as well. As common cafeteria style lunchroom, a day care center, tennis courts, and other company wide recreational services provide many cross-cutting friendship contexts that keep cliques from forming and becoming isolated within the corporation.

Many companies like Abt Associates are perceived as specializing in "quick and dirty" social research, research that is not imbued with a passion that is often associated with anthropological fieldwork. Many academicians assume that a price has to be paid when researchers work under government contracts. Contracts are often thought of as highly structured in contrast to the freedom that grants give to a researcher. This loss of personal control can lead people to view government contract work as ritually polluted and sometimes amoral. Indeed, one colleague wrote that this kind of work is "bargaining with the devil" (Clinton, 1976), while another has described the role of an anthropologist in a corporate research firm as a "go-fer" (Trend, 1980) because they are the data collectors who "go for" trivial information at the behest of company gurus. These perceptions of the contributions of anthropologists to policy research are pessimistic. The speed at which research takes place, or more correctly, the real time constraints of policy studies do not result in data becoming unclean. In fact, many policy studies are not as quick as might be supposed. In the case I will report on here, field research was carried out for three years on a project which lasted for eight years. The idea that policy research is dirty because of the loss of personal control over the issues of inquiry is also misguided. Policy research is often freed from the tyranny of disciplinary fads and paradigms so common in academic research.

In 1972 a large scale program of educational and community change was begun in the Office of Education. The project had as a goal creating change in schools and their communities that would be comprehensive, not piecemeal. The project, known as the Experimental Schools Program, funded seven urban school districts and ten rural school districts for five years. This long term funding arrangement was initiated so that the systems would be given enough time to implement and routinize changes without worrying about yearly contract negotiations with the federal government. The amount of support from the government to the school systems varied between fifteen and twenty percent of the yearly school budgets. In the small town I studied, the Experimental School Program contribution to yearly budgets was almost twenty percent. The ten rural Experimental School projects were managed as a group apart from the urban projects. The Office of Education, and later the National Institute of Education which inherited the program, contracted with Abt Associates for the evaluation of program impact in the ten rural communities. This "Rural" contract, as it was named in the company, was entered into with great enthusiasm. First of all, the contract was funded at a very high level, as one of the cornerstones of the program was that enough money should be allocated for the long term evaluation of the projects so that knowledge gained could be applied to future programs of comprehensive change. Second, the Rural contract offerred Abt Associates the opportunity to do groundbreaking research. The ten school districts provided a sample of close to 15,000 students who could be surveyed and tested to examine the effects of both specific treatment programs and general changes in their lives. The contract also called for fundamental research on the organizational changes that each school system underwent, a topic that had been studied in urban settings, but seldom in rural settings. The contract also focused research attention on the communities themselves. With ten communities as a base, new methods of social indicators analysis could be developed, field tested, and utilized over a five year period. Finally, the contract called for "on-site" documentation of the ten communities and of the school projects. This documentation was to be carried out by fieldworkers trained in ethnographic method and theory. This meant that Abt Associates could hire anthropologists to live in the communities for five years. With ten sites there was a potential for a combined total of fifty years of ethnographic research on American communities.

Doing fieldwork in anthropology is sometimes referred to as a vision quest or a rite of passage (Van Gennep, 1960) with a period of separation from family and academic department, a time of liminality with villagers of the third world, and a reincorporation into the academic culture of the discipline through the completion of a dissertation or monograph. In a recent paper on the clinical features of culture shock, Solon Kimball (1981) notes that the cross-cultural trauma of fieldwork results in a personal transformation or education making professionals out of students. In the remainder of this paper I will describe my own fieldwork as a member of the Project Rural team as it relates to this traditional idea of fieldwork as a rite of passage. I shall go one step further by calling attention to the nature of human variation in applied fieldwork and the competing values of the world of policy action and the world of the academy. Where traditional fieldwork can be seen as a socializing institution in the discipline which makes people into anthropologists, policy field research drives people in the direction of becoming non-academic professionals such as government bureaucrats, policy analysts, and even small town city managers. The values of these two competing worlds make applied anthropological fieldwork difficult. In the case of the project, this conflict took a heavy psychic toll on the researchers, most of whom already had extensive fieldwork experiences prior to the project. By the end of the project one fieldworker had been forced by local residents to flee from the community, one had died, one had built a sailboat and left for the far east, one joined an advertising firm, and a few drifted into academic positions. The promise of a major synthesis of American small town culture was only partially achieved through the publication of a special issue of the journal *Rural Sociology* (Wolcott, 1978).

Four stages of fieldwork on this project can be outlined to illustrate this and other applied anthropology projects. The stages suggest a different kind of ritual process than traditional fieldwork experiences because they combine an anthropological interest in face to face interaction with the demands of public policy studies. The first stage is one of selection, the selection of a researcher and a research site. The second is a stage of initial field impressions, both of the researcher by residents and of the community by ethnographers. The third is a stage of research dilemmas engendered by the politically charged atmosphere of research and the demands of long term field existence. The final stage is one of departure from the project.

SELECTION OF SITE AND RESEARCHER

The rapidity of my entree into Project Rural was a sharp contrast to the earlier field research I had carried out in Mexico. Prior to doing work in the Yucatan of Mexico, I had studied the social science literature of the area for several years, learned Spanish and some Mayan, and had written a research proposal. After this my wife, daughter and I slowly drove down from Seattle, Washington, to Yucatan in a Volkswagan bus loaded down with field equipment and personal luggage. We stayed in the field for eighteen months before we returned home to Seattle.

Project Rural was another story. One day in late July I received a letter from a friend while my family and I were in New Mexico on vacation. The friend suggested that I should call the company as they had been advertising for an anthropologist to work on a long term project. My friend knew one of the fieldworkers on the project and had been told that the team was seeking someone who spoke Spanish. I called the company and talked with the director of the project about my experiences and interests. In that first telephone conversation we discussed a problem that was to become central to the future fieldwork, the problem of how we as field-workers would help the local communities. The project director said that we were to be engaged in summative evaluation, not technical assistance, and that this would preclude giving help to the local project. A few days later I was asked to interview in Cambridge, Massachusets, the head-quarters of Abt Associates. In a period of two days I was intensely inter-viewed by key project staff, company officials, and the president of the company. The interviewers were well planned and scheduled; designed, I assumed at the time, to impress me with the professionalism of the research effort and the efficiency of the company. Questions were put to me in rapid-fire order, my time with each interviewer was carefully calculated, and company employees came and went throughout the two days, often only staying long enough to hear my answer to a single question. At the end of the first day I was asked by the project director to "look over" a few of the project documents so that I could comment on them the next day. One of the documents I was asked to pay particular attention to was on the role of anthropologists as "on-site researchers," the official title of fieldworkers on the project. The document was in the traditional of many fieldwork statements in that it described difficulties researchers have in gaining rapport with natives – in this case local residents of small towns – ways of doing participant observation, and the organization of the Project Rural team. The next morning I was ques-tioned at length about my reaction to the paper. The interview was an ordeal or test to see if I understood the difficulties of doing fieldwork as an anthropologist; in this regard responding to the questions was easy.

A day later when I had returned to New Mexico, the project director called to suggest that I should look up an anthropologist who consulted for the project in Oregon. Since my family and I were on our way back to Seattle, this seemed reasonable. We arrived in Oregon late at night after spending two days on the road driving up from the Southwest. The anthro-pologist greeted me at the door in Spanish to see if I indeed spoke the language, then invited me in to meet one of the fieldworkers who was already working for the company. Ten fieldworkers had already been hired for work in nine of the communities with Experimental Schools projects. I was being considered for the tenth community. In contrast to the very formal interviews in Cambridge, the interview in Oregon was pleasant. Although I was exhausted from the trip, I enjoyed the evening and felt both relieved and happy as I walked out to my car late in the evening. I sat down in the car with a sigh of relief only to be shocked by a large cat that bounded across my arms and jumped out the open window. My cry of surprise luckily was not heard in the house or I might not have been offered the job.

A week later my wife and I were invited to more interviews, this time not only at the company headquarters but also in Washington, D.C., and in the town in Arizona where I was to do research. I learned that the company wanted to be sure that the spouses of the researchers were interested in both the communities and the research as five years was a long time to commit to a project. The interviews in Cambridge were much less formal this time. One day later we flew down to Washington with the project director to meet with officials of the Experimental Schools program. After a few hours of meetings we left and flew to Arizona to meet with local school administrators.

The town in Arizona was one of the last to be selected by the program to participate as an Experimental Schools project. It was now the first week in August, just a week and a half since I had learned of the job and the project. We met with a few of the local school administrators and then left. I was offered the job as an "on-site researcher" at that point and was asked if I could begin fieldwork as soon as possible. School was to begin in mid-August and it would be appropriate for me to begin documenting the changes as the school year began. The whole process of my being selected to do research from the initial telephone call to moving down to the town took three weeks.

This first stage of site and researcher selection is clearly different from that of much academic based fieldwork. The site of research was preselected. I had extensive experience in Mexico prior to taking the job and had wanted to work in the Southwest, but I did not have the opportunity to do the kind of background preparation that is possible in other ethnographic research. Rather than choosing a village to work in, the town selected itself as a research site by winning a national competition for Experimental Schools funds. Inherent in their selection was a requirement that an ethnographer live in the community to do evaluation. The rapidity of my selection as a member of the Project Rural team was also different from traditional fieldwork. I was selected as a fieldworker through a corporate interview structure, a structure that emphasized the competing interest groups of the company, the federal agency in Washington, and the local community.

The most important aspect of the first stage was that the field site was to become our only home. Unlike other ethnographic studies, there was nowhere else that we could return to when we wanted to leave the field. We moved in, bought a house, and became tax paying residents of the town.

INITIAL FIELD IMPRESSIONS

When the Project Rural director from Abt Associates and I came to the town and were introduced to the superintendent of schools, we were shocked by his initial reaction to our visit. He was barely civil in his greeting, and then turned quickly and said, "Let me tell you two something. We don't want our children here being used as guinea pigs for any experiments!" This antagonism was something that neither my superior nor myself expected. The project director asked me to speak to this issue. I did, assuring the superintendent that the purpose I and the company had in the town was to document the course of the local project, not carry out experiments on children. I told him that my role would be that of a historian who described how the project was accepted into the community. Although the superintendent seemed to approve of this, I was haunted for months with the memory of that first meeting. What kind of experiment did he think we were contemplating? Why was he so angry? Why had we been subjected to his anger?

The answers to these questions came slowly over the next few months as I came to know the superintendent and his own involvement with the project. He also was new to the community, having been hired in July specifically to manage to prestigious Experimental Schools project. One of the reasons for his hostility was that he did not know at the time whether I was an official from Washington or an independent evaluator. He wanted to be sure that if Washington officials were listening, they would hear that he was firmly in charge and would not be subject to the whims of a distant bureaucracy. Another reason for his initial anger was that he had been subjected to a harsh and humbling experience by one of the senior project officials in Washington a few weeks before we arrived in town. He later told me that he had nearly resigned during his visit because of the way he was treated by officials there. One official in particular grilled him about the details of the local project and the local factions that had developed as the town competed for project funds. He told me that when we arrived in town he had assumed we were part of the Washington agency that had humiliated him and wanted to give the agency a "taste of their own medicine." Finally, the statements of the superintendent could be understood in the context of project vocabulary. The total program was known as Experimental Schools, even though no natural experiments were ever contemplated. There was no randomization of project sites or of treatments for bettering school performance. Instead the ten communities were selected to participate in the program because of the persuasiveness of a letter they had written in response to a call for competition to all school districts in the country. While the term "experimental" had historical meaning for the Washington officials, it had little meaning in the small towns that received funding for the local projects. The superintendent's statements about an experiment pointed to the differing meanings that the term had in the two contexts.

When we moved to the town the next week and began research, the superintendent went out of his way to help me establish my status in the community. He took me on a grand tour of the town and talked of his own academic background as we drove around in his official vehicle. He was still in a doctoral program in educational administration, he said, but doubted if he would finish it because he felt more at home working as a superintendent than writing a thesis. He knew about anthropology because a graduate student in educational anthropology at a nearby university was studying him as an example of a successful Chicano culture broker. The student had followed him around for several months as an observer. "That's what I'd like to do," the superintendent told me, "be an anthropologist and follow people around." His candid talk in the car was in sharp contrast to our first meeting.

On that first day of fieldwork he took me to meet the city manager, the police chief, the mayor, and other prominent people in the town. I declined his offer of office space in the schools as I did not want to define my research as only limited to the schools. He then asked the chief of police to let me use an office in the police department. I graciously refused, not wanting to be confused with the local government operations. Later we met the local newspaper editor who owned several offices on the main street of the town. One was vacant and I was able to rent it as my field headquarters in the town. Later in the day I was introduced to another school official who was leaving to work as a hospital administrator in Phoenix. He asked me to go down to a local bar with him where we met several other people. We rented his house after he left until we found one to buy.

In one swift day we had arrived and become incorporated into the community. We were still staying at a motel at the edge of town, eating our meals at tourist cafes and driving a rental car, but we had quickly been given a place in the social network of the town elite through the superintendent.

Residents of the community knew what anthropologists were and were not surprised that I had come to do research in the town. Some thought that I should be on an Indian reservation, not in a small town, while others thought I was really a sociologist who had accidentally become an anthropologist. One school teacher asked if I was going to write a book like *Middletown* (Lynd and Lynd, 1929) in which I would describe the social classes of the community.

The initial impressions of fieldwork in this applied setting underscored the existence of goal-oriented social behavior in public policy contexts. The superintendent was not simply interested in a researcher coming to the town as much as he was in "sending a message" back to Washington. Later, his grand tour of the town could be interpreted as his way of portraying himself as a bona fide resident in the eyes of other local people by acting as my guide. Another aspect of applied fieldwork apparent in this stage was the fact that the people with whom I was working were literate and knowledgeable about the utility of research. Over the course of the three years we lived in the community many of them became critics of my written reports, others used information I developed to write historical pamphlets on the community. The fact that local community residents had need of my research information became one of the many problems I faced in the three years of fieldwork. Although the Washington agency assumed that the local community was merely a passive recipient of federal funds and that I was responsible to the agency, local residents made up an active pressure group who constantly asked for my help.

DILEMMAS OF RESEARCH

My family and I were originally scheduled to live in the town for five years, the duration of the federal project in the community. As it turned out, fieldwork was ended after three years. We found that just as it is possible to spend too little time in the field doing research, there is also a danger of spending too much time there. The decision to stop fieldwork was not ours alone. The funding agency in Washington had new projects that were being developed and the Experimental Schools Project proved to be a reminder of a policy made many years ago. The group of educator-bureaucrats who had generated the original program had by now all left the agency and new officials saw the project as a survival of a bygone era. Likewise, the local school system in Arizona grew tired of the program. By the end of the third year the new superintendent began to refer to the project as the "Rural Schools Problem." Like his counterparts in Washington, D.C., he too had inherited the local project from a predecessor, someone who he said must have "walked on water" because of the admiration and esteem he had engendered in the school staff. The new superintendent complained that the project had become a millstone around his neck because of the constant requirements for reports and the perceived pressure he felt from Washington to keep the bilingual education portion of the project alive.

The dilemmas of this stage of research were centered around the competing interest groups within the community as well as the company that employed me and the federal agency. Within the community my family and I faced the problem of being professional participant observers, a role that all anthropologists take on in the field. There was no neat progression during our stay in the town between detached observers through community participants and finally to ethnographic writers. From the first day we arrived we felt the conflicting strains of being incorporated into the community and detached at the same time. We were immediately taken into the social life of the community because the town was a crossroads or boom town which grew by welcoming outsiders to add to the resource base (Burns, 1978). Like other professionals who came into the town, we were the subject of a front page newspaper article a few months after we arrived. The town had a strong social cleavage between the Mexican American residents and the Anglos, and much of our research took us into close relationships with both groups. We became active members of the local Chicano social and political organization, even to the point of holding office and serving on the board of directors.

The dilemma of being an ethnographer in a community like this one was that there was little escape from these day to day interactions. Before long I was being considered for several permanent jobs in the community including school counsellor and city manager. Although I dissuaded those who went out of their way top find a permanent place for us in the town, our ambiguous status of home-owning, full time residents working for an out-of-town firm led people to try to help us settle down. The only escape from the press of local commitments was the frequent meetings held for the project staff at the company headquarters in Cambridge and in Washington, D.C. The equivalent of "going home" from the field became the trips to the world of professional policy makers. In this sense the structure of fieldwork in the project inadvertently socialized us toward an identification with the world of public policy, not the world of the academy. The alternative to identifying with the company and the Washington bureaucracy was to identify with the local community, a strategy which some of the on-site researchers followed.

There were personal strains which resulted from this long period of field research as well. After three years of fieldwork my enthusiasm for attending community meetings and interviewing residents wore thin. The sociolinguistic patterns of speech in the community was also upsetting. One line, quick retorts and witticisms in response to complex issues were the expected ways of speaking, especially among school teachers and administrators. After three years of this abridged pattern of discussion I began to wonder if I would ever be able to think and talk in units longer than one phrase. The lack of a home outside of the field site was also upsetting at a personal level. My family and I often wondered what would happen to us at the end of the project. Wacaster and Firestone (1978), two colleagues on the project, have suggested that long term, continuous fieldwork can result in a fatalism and fatigue that takes its toll on data collection.

Two events during fieldwork illustrate the dilemmas of ethnography in this applied setting. In both events out of town people became convinced that I was doing more than ethnographic research in the community. One case was a humorous manipulation of my role by school administrators; the other was a serious misunderstanding between Washington officials and myself.

The first event occurred early in the fieldwork when two members of a consulting firm came to the community to sell a testing and evaluation package to the local school district. This in itself was ironic as the company I worked for, Abt Associates, did the same thing at a national level. When the representatives of the firm came to the meeting room in the school, the superintendent introduced me by my academic title as "Dr. Burns." I was dressed as a school administrator with a sport coat and a tie, and the superintendent smiled as he told the consultants that I was interested in evaluation programs. The consultants had an evaluation package that consisted of many short, weekly reading tests to be given to students rather than the traditional pre- and post-tests given in the school to measure reading achievement changes. They argued that the weekly tests were "process" evaluations, a new and important improvement in educational testing theory. Perhaps I appeared puzzled or unconvinced of the utility of the new package. At any rate, the consultants directed their sales pitch at me throughout the evening, and used me as an example of a "typical administrator" who probably did not know what achievement tests measured. They asked me that question, to which I replied that achievement tests should measure reading ability. "No!" one of them replied, "achievement tests only measure what is on achievement tests!"

The meeting went on like this for two hours at which time the consultants thanked us for our attention and left. The administrators then broke into laughter and said that I must look like a school principal, not an anthropologist. The superintendent had succeeded in manipulating my place in the event as a kind of practical joke. The other administrators had been able to privately enjoy what might have been a boring meeting by misguiding the consultants about my place in the school system.

A second instance of guilt by association was more insidious. Late during the first year of research my name began appearing on the memos that were circulated in the schools. These memos served to schedule meetings, report on school activities, and document local project business. Many of the memos were regularly sent to Washington as proof that the local project was being implemented. As a courtesy to my work as an ethnographer, the secretaries put my name on all school memos. Some of the Washington officials interpreted these memos as evidence that I was actively involved in running the local project, not just observing it. The superintendent went one step further by mentioning my name to Washington officials when they called so that they would think that I was doing my job well and would give me a good job evaluation. The officials interpreted all of this as evidence that I was too involved in the everyday life of the project. The issue came to a climax one day when the local project called Washington to negotiate a contract change. He then went on to announce the people in the room before beginning the actual negotiations. The event was a critical one in the life of the project (Burns, 1980), as it represented a shift from a colleagial relationship between the local project and Washington to an adversary relationship. During the call I did not speak, but the Washington official evidently decided I had gone beyond fieldwork to action. He called my superior at Abt Associates who later called me and discussed my role as ethnographer of the community. I was asked to lower my visibility, especially where Washington was involved. The issue died down soon after this crisis. I asked that my name not be put on memos. The secretaries in the different school offices complied by penciling my name on memos that they sent to me. The local administrators of the school system had indeed asked me on many occasions to take a more active part in the project and in the schools. They knew that I had information about the project and the community that would help the program be more successful. In addition, they knew that as an anthropologist I had a very wise and diverse social network in the community. These aspects of my work were tempting to them as they tried to implement the project. They saw me as a representative of an interest group — the research company — that could be tapped for resources and help just as the other groups in the schools and community could be used. Although my professional contract with the company and the Washington agency forbade technical assistance, the local school administrators tested this policy to see how strict it was. I was both a part of the project and an observer of it. This proved to be the source of the many dilemmas of fieldwork.

DEPARTURE FROM THE FIELD

The act of leaving the small Arizona town and the company was an over-whelming experience. I chose not to continue working for the company for two reasons. First of all I believed at the time that the relationship between the company and the many Washington agencies it did business with was too close. I felt that contracts were being pursued without regard for their merit. Secondly, my family and I did not want to relocate in Boston. We had become westerners. I had been socialized through the project in two directions, in the direction of becoming an applied social analyst and in the direction of becoming a local resident. The attachment to the town as "home" was as great as that to social research. Most of the other social scientists in the company found such attachments unusual and perhaps a little quaint as they had no difficulty in leaving their jobs at night to go home. My family and I decided that because of ambiguity of the pull of the professional world of public policy and the local world of the small town we would escape by leaving both systems. With this in mind we planned our departure from the field and the company to take place exactly three years after we had officially begun the fieldwork. When we left I wrote the following notes in a field journal:

> Saturday morning came and we pulled out on the Interstate. I remember having a kind of hollow feeling similar to that I had when we first drove into town three years ago. I recalled the first months of doing fieldwork and the frustrations I felt as I fought every day and every night with the dilemma of doing a study of the people in this town. I recalled the notes, the memos and the letters I wrote in an attempt to delineate the subjective from the objective and how I hoped that my mind might be quieted if I externalized the battle through writing. It wasn't. Near the end of our stay I came to the realization that the bargain I had struck in the name of doing ethnography took as much out of me as I had received.

Since the end of the project, few of the ten fieldworkers have kept in touch with one another. Once in a while I have been contacted by a few of my old colleagues. One is now working for a research company doing crime prevention research; another told me that he is spending his time writing a novel about an ethnographer who turns into a psychopathic criminal.

Applied anthropological research in the setting of public policy is an area where fieldwork is necessary but yet professionally dangerous. The four stages I have outlined here are steps in the socialization process of researchers, but the socialization can be in two directions at once.

NOTES

1. The research which forms the basis for this report was carried out under a contract between Abt Associates, Inc., and the National Institute of Education, contract #OEC-0-72-5245. I am grateful to the Institute and Abt Associates for the opportunity to do the work and for their encouragement. The views expressed in this paper are my own and not those of either of these agencies. I would also like to thank the people of Willcox, Arizona for their help and Robert Lawless, who encouraged me to describe my experiences for this volume.

REFERENCES CITED

Burns, Allan F., 1980, Crisis Management and Siege: Local Strategies and Federal Programs for Educational Change. Contemporary Education 60: 135-139.
1978, Cargo Culture in a Western Town: A Cultural Approach to Episodic Change. Rural Sociology 42: 164-177.
Clinton, Charles A., 1976, On Bargaining with the Devil: Contract Tehnography and Accountability in Fieldwork. Council on Anthropology and Education Newsletter 8: 25-28.
Coleman, James, 1972, *Policy Research in the Social Sciences.* Morristown, New Jersey: General Learning.
Kimball, Solon T. 1981, *Culture Shock.* Paper presented by the Distinguished Teacher/Scholar of the Year, University of Florida.
Lynd, Robert and Lynd, Helen, 1929, *Middletown.* New York: Harcourt, Brace.
Trend, Michael G., 1980, The Antropologist as Go-fer. *Practicing Anthropology* 313-365.
van Gennep, Arnold, 1960, *The Rites of Passage.* Chicago: University of Chicago Press.
Wacaster, C. T., and Firestone, William, 1978, The Promise and Problems of Long-Term Continuous Fieldwork. Human Organization 37: 269-275.
Wolcott, Harry, 1978, Small Town America in Ethnographic Perspective. Special issue of Rural Sociology 42: 2.

CHAPTER 10

Initial Encounter, Choice, and Change in Field Research

MARIO D. ZAMORA

Anthropologists have studied nearly every facet of human culture and society and virtually every region of the world. They have done research on vanishing tribes as well as the contemporary industrial societies. Despite all these admirable achievements in research and publication, we still have not gone far enough in the study of anthropologists themselves and the changes in their outlook, attitudes, and behavior. While it is true that several biographies, autobiographies, *festscrifts*, and obituaries have already been published, nevertheless, there has not been a strong trend toward the investigation of anthropologists' personal experiences in research or their intellectual growth and transformation, especially that of the Third World anthropologists. The records of anthropologists as themselves should enrich our knowledge of the human being. The anthropology of the anthropologists should be encouraged and pursued vigorously in our discipline.[2]

Two significant concepts tie together my discussion: (1) professional turning; and (2) professional enculturation. The idea of professional turning derived from David Mandelbaum's concept of turning in life history aids in understanding why a person changes his course of study and turns to anthropology. Turning in life history is defined as the major transition that a person undergoes. This transition is accomplished when a person takes on "a new set of roles (cultural), enters into fresh relations with a new set of people (social) and acquires a new self concept (psycho-social)" (Mandelbaum, 1973: 177-204). The concept of professional turning refers to a major shift or transition in interest, career, or profession due to one or several factors or forces.

The concept of professional enculturation derived from Melville Herskovits' principle of enculturation enhances the knowledge of the process of entering anthropology. The idea of enculturation can be defined as "the process of internalizing the norms, values, and expectations of a society or ethnic group" (Simpson, 1973). Professional enculturation can therefore be explained as the gradual learning and internalizing of the norms, values, and expectations of a discipline such as anthropology. All anthropolgoists whether they have turned from another discipline to anthropology or have entered into anthropology directly undergo the process of professional enculturation. This method entails obtaining degrees, doing field research, reviewing books, publishing, collaborating with colleagues in anthropology and other related sciences, and either teaching in colleges and universities or being employed by agencies and companies that utilize anthropology (Zamora, 1980).

The main purpose of this paper is to describe briefly my professional turning and my professional enculturation. Specifically, I raise the questions, to what extent do the initial field research experiences affect my career choice and identity? In the final part of this chapter I consider the wider implications of these changing experiences and views by asking a series of questions, particularly focused on levels of relationship and ethics. I divide this discussion into three related and operationally-defined stages: (1) pre-scientific stage; (2) stage of intellectual trance; and (3) stage of scientific transformation. My changing attitudes and outlook will be assessed under the three categories.

When I had only a vague idea about anthropology as a scientific and humanistic discipline, my ideas, outlook, and attitudes towards anthropology as a professional career were ambiguous. My images of anthropology and anthropologists were the usual stereotypes about the archaeologists and physical anthropologists: that archaeologists merely dig for the buried treasures or that physical anthropologists measure skulls and bones.

I used to read now and then of American anthropologists doing research in the mountain provinces of the Philippines. I never understood why American anthropologists – especially the ones going to the mountains of northern Luzon – spent their time and energy in far flung "primitive" communities. During this period of my life I could only think of one living image of an anthropologist who was publicized from time to time in popular magazines: the late H. Otley Beyer, a leading light in Philippine anthropology (Zamora, ed., 1967b). I never knew about the Beyer-dominated Department of Anthropology of the University of the Philippines and the Museum and Institute of Ethnology and Archaeology of the same university, two institutions I later on headed. I never heard of Fred Eggan, Harold Conklin, E. Arsenio Manuel, and Marcelo Tangco among others, who have been prominent figures in Philippine anthropology. I was not aware of the Philippine program then underway at the University of Chicago under the dynamic leadership of Fred Eggan.

During my undergraduate studies at the University of the Philippines I took a course on race relations under John E. de Young, currently with the Trust Territory of the Pacific in Agana, Guam, another one on folklore of Southeast Asia and Oceania under E. Arsenio Manuel, and a required subject on cultural anthropology taught by Marcelo Tangco, considered the first Filipino career anthropologist in the Philippines (Zamora, 1965b). I read briefly about Franz Boas, Robert H. Lowie, Alfred Kroeber, A. R. Radcliffe Brown, and Bronislaw Malinowski, but still they were not inspiring figures to me as they are now. Despite, however, this initial introduction to some aspects of anthropology as a career, my interest in this branch of knowledge was not fully cultivated. Not even the best performance of instructors at that time could alter my negative feeling and attitude toward the anthropological enterprise. I thought that I was merely fulfilling the basic requirements for graduation for a bachelor's degree in sociology.

In addition, I felt the irrelevance of this seemingly esoteric and exotic profession in my future life, and for the country. I felt the professors doing research and writing books were wasting their time and talent; the volumes they tried to publish would never be read; they would just be consigned to the dilapidated shelves in the University library. I likewise entertained the idea that the foreign professor was hired by the University of the Philippines not to further the ends of genuine scholarship but to protect the interests of anthropologists and the institution he came from. My knowledge of the research process was understandably limited and vague. My attitude toward some institutions the American scholar then represented was one of skepticism. In many ways, I was very naive and uninformed about anthropological research personnel and institutions.

In retrospect, all these thoughts are vivid in my mind as I recall the struggle within me about the aims and the possibilities of anthropology as a future profession and as a course in the University of Philippines. I confess I finished my bachelor of arts degree still in a state of trance about the scope and significance of anthropology for the Republic of the Philippines.

In early 1956 it was announced in a university bulletin that a foreign anthropologist would be a visiting professor for a year in the anthropology department. He was scheduled to teach a course on economic anthropology and another one on research methods. At first I thought this foreign anthropologist was another one of the arm-chair scholars in sociology.

I was advised to enroll in this course, which involved not only class but also field research. I never knew about the importance of field work before. The foreign professor distributed a syllabus which included trips to a nearby village and a cooperative research project on barrio government and community development. The seminar, consisting of six students, emphasized library research and field work.[3]

For the first time, I was introduced to field research in a rural community. At the initial stage I regarded this field practice merely as course requirements to get good grades, but gradually as time passed I began to get interested in the research problem, the methods, and the results of the labor of six students. The class sessions were lively and stimulating intellectually. The field trips on weekends and sometimes on weekdays were interesting and exciting. The professor was very congenial and helpful, but strict with the students.

One of the difficulties faced during the course of field work was language. The professor and at least two students did not speak Tagalog. I served once in a while as an interpreter for the non-Tagalog students and the professor. Having come from another ethnic group (Pampangan), I could not effectively translate and interpret, despite the many years of my study and practice of Tagalog. One of the significant problems I encountered was in the translation of concepts to village informants from English to Tagalog, and vice-versa. For example, how does one render meaningfully the concept of "development" or "community development" to illiterate informants? One way to do this was to offer as many concrete examples as one can give, but this oftentimes leads to further confusion on the part of the informants. I felt inadequate in my translations and was extremely dissatisfied at that point with what I believed then to be my ineffective role as an interpreter.

The professor taught us not only library research but the interview. He also instructed us on how to establish rapport with informants, and a number of pointers generally found in manuals of field research. He even hosted key informants in his cottage in the campus for talks before our seminar. One of our informants was the late Senator Tomas Cabili, a principal figure behind the measure to establish village democracy in the Philippines. Cabili discussed with us the history and background of Republic Act 1408 (law on barrio government). Another key informant was Dr. Y. C. James Yen, the founder of the International Rural Reconstruction Movement and the Philippine Rural Reconstruction Movement in the Philippines. He spoke about these organizations in general and barrio government in particular. All these fruitful class and field experiences in research added to a better appreciation of cultural anthropology as a discipline.[4]

During this stage, my attitude toward anthropology had changed from a negative to a positive one. It gradually dawned on me that anthropology had some meaning and significance in my life and in the lives of the members of the community we were studying. I likewise began to acquire a better impression of and offer added respect for the foreign professor and for his serious and methodical efforts to impart anthropological knowledge to us. I also realized that our informants were not merely passive and unfeeling sources of information but were also human beings participating in an exciting research endeavor. My professional encultura-tion was enriched with the successive field research endeavors.

My positive response to anthropology and the social sciences was reinforced with my one year study and research at Delhi University in India and my field work in a Punjab village (Zamora, 1959, 1965a). Later, I had the opportunity to undertake further doctoral studies in the United States in cultural anthropology, Asian studies, and rural sociology culminating in what I tentatively call the stage of scientific transformation (Zamora, 1963).

My professional turning was further reinforced with my involvement in field research projects in the Philippines and India before my Ph.D. studies at Cornell University in 1959. In 1956-57 I was included in a team research project entitled "A Study of the Functional Literacy Program of the Bureau of Public Schools and the Presidential Assistance on Com-munity Development" sponsored by the community development research council of the University of the Philippines, a research unit still active in 1981. The team was composed of Dr. Buenaventura M. Villanueva, then Community Development Research Council executive secretary and currently a senior level officer of the public administration division, United Nations Secretariat in New York; Professor Vicente Encarnacion, currently engaged in business; Dr. Norberto Timbol, an educator and also a businessman; Manuel Dia, a sociologist and currently the dean of the University of the Philippines' Asian Labor Education Center; Jesus Calleja, a sociologist and presently teaching in a private university in Manila, and myself.[5]

We prepared a detailed questionnaire which was also properly pre-tested. The research took us to several sample provinces, municipalities, and villages. We travelled by plane, bus, jeepneys, or by foot in rain or sun. The division schools, teachers, and municipal officials in all the sample units facilitated our entry into the communities and made the task easier. We either conducted interviews as a team or sometimes split into two or three teams to cover more areas and to interview more informants. It took us several months to complete the nation-wide survey. When finished, our report was classified confidential and was never officially published by the community development research council or by the office of the presi-dential assistant on community development.

This macro-research taught me several lessons in field work I will never forget. I realized the advantages and disadvantages of macro-survey research. The research made me see the importance of cooperation, harmony, loyalty, and teamwork. At the same time, I saw the value of honest disagreements among colleagues. It was such a great opportunity and privilege to work with five serious, hardworking, intelligent, and congenial human beings of different levels of education, background, and disciplines. We worked very hard on our research but we also enjoyed the whole research process. I will never forget the fiesta-like receptions accorded us in the island of Opon, Cebu, the many breakfasts, lunches, and dinners with the hospitable village people across the land, and the long walks along mountains and plains to reach our informants.

As I look back twenty years, when I had a vague idea of what anthropology was and what it could do, I feel I have come a long way in self-discovery. My attitudes and outlook toward anthropology have become more affirmative than before. Anthropology to me now is no longer the esoteric and useless discipline I once thought it to be. Having read part of the literature, exposed myself to some of the theoretical, methodological, and practical developments in the field, and having been guided by one eminent Cornell anthropologist, I feel that anthropology, when properly understood and used by third world scholars and laymen, can have new meaning, purpose, and direction for the so-called developing societies like the Philippines.

Among my current attitudes about some issues in the profession are the following: Foreign anthropological colleagues are partners in the scientific pursuit to investigate culture and society and help alleviate human misery. Informants should be respected as human beings and should never be treated as tools to manipulate for data-gathering; anthropologists should make serious and sustained measures to understand their informants in their own language whenever possible and within the context of the informants' cultural values. While research in anthropology is considered indispensable, nonetheless the informants' rights, confidences, and integrity should not be ignored; we should not spy on them for dubious ends with dehumanizing means; we should not debase ourselves and our discipline by becoming unwitting tools of unscientific/non-scientific entities.

We should strive to make our relations with colleagues, especially those coming from the third world, not only pleasant and fruitful but also just and fair. We should not attempt to dominate the indigenous anthropologists and anthropology.

As fellows of the world-wide fraternity of anthropologists, we should see to it that the genuine anthropologists are given the protection and assistance vital to their ceaseless quest to study the human being and society, in the Third World; on the other hand, the spurious anthropologists, those who masquerade and misrepresent the discipline for all sorts of ends and means, should never be allowed to ply their questionable trade among the trusting peoples of this region. To a great degree, I believe, it is our obligation to safeguard legitimate entities that are truly committed to advance our profession, regardless of creed or color, against institutions and persons who take advantage of the indigenous societies' trust and their inadequate resources and personnel.

This professional enculturation, from the pre-scientific years many years ago to the present, has in fact given me a better and perhaps realistic grasp of some of the dilemmas in our anthropological discipline. My experiences and professional growth lead me to raise more questions about some of our recurrent problems, especially those having to do with human relationships; for example, the relations between local and foreign anthropologists, between anthropologists and their informants, and between anthropologists and government. These topics, of course, have been extensively explored in major journals like *Current Anthropology, Human Organization*, and *Journal of Asian Studies*, but I feel that the issues need wider discussion among foreign and local anthropologists in the light of the academic decolonization processes going on in Asia, Africa, and Latin America.

Before I raise questions on the three levels of relationship and ethics, I wish to include in this discussion a brief perspective of colonial relationships in the third world, especially between American and Philippine anthropologists.

The rapid growth and development of anthropology in the Western world, can be attributed to the vast and varied researches conducted on the colonized peoples. As I stated on another occasion, "British anthropology for example was built firmly on field research in colonized Africa; American anthropology solely rested on the long years of research conducted by American anthropologists on American Indian tribes in North America and later on in Asia, Latin America and Africa" (Zamora, 1971-72). In the list of American pioneers in the study of Filipino culture and society were H. Otley Beyer, R. F. Barton, Felix Keesing, Fred Eggan, Robert Fox, Harold Conklin, Frank Lynch, Donn V. Hart, Charles Kaut, Willis Sibley, Daniel Scheans, and Wilhelm Solheim, among others.

In the course of Philippine anthropological history major figures emerged, two of the leading ones being H. Otley Beyer and Fred Eggan. These two American anthropologists were the dominant innovators in research and training for several decades in the Philippines.

The colonial academic situation was altered to a fair degree with the emergence of a corps of Filipino foreign-trained scholars. Many "native" anthropologists were trained in Philippine and foreign universities; E. Arsenio Manuel, F. Landa Jocano, and David Baradas from the University of Chicago, Mario D. Zamora, Albert Bacdayan, and Wilfredo Arce from Cornell University, Marcelino Maceda from the University of Freiburg, Timoteo Oracion from the University of San Carlos, Zeus Salazar from the Sorbonne, and a younger group of aggressive scholars from the Department of Anthropology of the University of the Philippines. Filipino women Ph.D.'s in anthropology were Patricia Afable, Enya Flores-Meiser, and Crispina Sapaula McDonald, among others.

In addition to their teaching commitments and administrative responsibilities these native anthropologists have been active in research, teaching, and administration. There has been considerable discussion also about rethinking Philippine anthropology by some of them, especially F. Landa Jocano on the study of Filipino values and Fred Evangelista on Beyer's views on Philippine archaeology. On the whole, however, Philippine-American anthropological relations have been cordial, harmonious, and productive (Zamora, 1977).

With this perspective it is appropriate at this juncture to raise the following questions: Should foreign anthropologists train local people? If so, to what extent and degree? To what length should the local people assist the foreigners as research aides? How much time should foreign anthropologists devote in the country to make their knowledge of the culture and society more informed and more thorough? To what extent should they consult native scholars in their search for knowledge in theory and research technique? To what degree should − if at all − foreign anthropologists express their views or criticisms on local scholars and scholarships? To what extent should indigenous scholars criticize foreign anthropologists? Let me turn now to the second type of relations; anthropologist − informant relations.

The relations between anthropologists and informants are very sensitive and significant. The success or failure of any research project will depend on the rapport and goodwill generated; the validity and reliability of research findings will likewise depend on the quality of anthropologist-informant interactions. The following questions may now be repeated here (Zamora, 1974).

How does the anthropologist go about obtaining valid and reliable data from the informant? What techniques or approaches should be devised to gain the goodwill, respect, and cooperation of the informant? Should anthropologists reveal themselves, their research objectives, and design fully and honestly to the informants? Should informants refuse to cooperate in the name of safeguarding their privacy? Can the anthropologist force the informant to reveal information on the ground of advancing knowledge and even for reasons of national security? Should informants have the right to censor the anthropologist's data and findings? What are the fundamental barriers to cross-cultural research and intra-ethnic research?

Finally, the relations between the anthropologist and government have been generally ambiguous and even moot. One of the primary reasons for this situation is the vague delineation of the anthropologist's responsibility in administration. The following questions are pertinent: What is the precise status of anthropological consultants in the government? What kind of advice do they offer? To what length is the anthropologist responsible for the consequences of decisions by government officials made as a result of their advice? To what degree is the government accountable for unpopular or adverse decisions?

It is my view that anthropologists from the Third World should articulate their thoughts on their own intellectual growth and transformation, discuss the products of their research efforts, air their opinions on controversial issues such as ethics in applied social science, and even raise fundamental questions that will have a bearing on the future and that of mankind.

NOTES

1. This chapter is a revised version of a paper presented at the annual meeting of the American Anthropological Association in New Orleans, Louisiana, 28 November-2 December 1973. The major portion of this paper is drawn directly from Zamora (1974) with substantive revisions. I want to thank Mr. Ashwenee H. Sharma for his editorial and computer assistance in the preparation of this paper.
2. The limitations of this paper include the following: (1) The exposition is highly subjective and is based mainly on past observation and participation in Philippine society as well as on current thinking on professional problems; (2) it is designed to provoke further considerations of the present topic, particularly on the part of colleagues from the third world; (3) this paper is, in many ways, speculative since I raise perhaps more questions than attempt to answer them satisfactorily; and finally (4) limitations of time and space prevent me from expanding on several areas.
3. Among my classmates in the seminar were: Professor Mary Hollnsteiner, currently a senior advisor at the UNICEF, United Nations, New York; Professor Prospero R. Covar, now professor of anthropology in the Department of Anthropology, University of the Philippines and Associate Dean (for Social

Sciences); Natividad V. Garcia, Admissions Director, School of Law, Catholic University of America in Washington, D.C.; Aleli Alvarez, Sociologist; and Adelaida Alcantara, Sociologist.

4. As a result of this seminar, I was able to do further research on village governments in the Philippines and to publish (Zamora, et al., 1959 and Zamora, 1967). Another outcome of this seminar was the publication of Hollnsteiner's famous *Dynamics of Power in a Philippine Municipality*, Community Development Research Council, University of the Philippines. Professor Hollnsteiner continued the research and broadened the scope of inquiry, starting with this research village. I accompanied her many times to the village and the municipality of her fieldwork.

5. I tried to obtain a copy of this study in July-August 1981 while in the Philippines but I did not succeed. Many of the facts presented in this brief section are based on recall and on past participant observation.

REFERENCES CITED

Mandelbaum, David G., 1973, The Study of Life History: Gandhi. Current Anthropology 14: 177-206.

Simpson, George E., 1973, *Melville J. Herskovits*. New York: Columbia University press.

Zamora, Mario D., et al., 1959, *An Annotated Bibliography on Barrio Councils*. Manila: National Media Production.

Zamora Mario D., 1959, *An Indian Village Council in Community Development*. M.A. Thesis, University of Philippines.

1963, *The Panchayat: A Study of the Changing Village Council with Special Reference to Senapur, Uttar Pradesh, India*. Ph.D. dissertation, Cornell University.

1965a, A Filipino in an Indian Village: Problems in Field Research. *Asian Studies* 145-152.

1965b, Marcelo Tangco: First Filipino Career Anthropologist. U.P. Research Digest 5 (1): 55-56.

1967, Political History, Autonomy, and Change: The Case of the Barrio Charter. *Asian Studies* 79-100.

1971-72, Ethical Anthropology: Review and Reflection in Philippine Society. Think 6 (4): 2-9.

1974, The Informant-Interpreter as Anthropologist: Trance and Transformation. Indian Anthropologist 4: 1-10.

1977, Cultural Anthropology in the Philippines, 1900-1983: Perspective, Problems and Prospects. In *Changing Identities in Modern Southeast Asia*. David J. Banks, ed. Pp. 311-339. The Hague: Mouton.

1980, Professional Enculturation and Turning in Life History. Eastern Anthropologist 33: 255-262.

Zamora, Mario D., ed., 1967, *Studies in Philippine Anthropology (In Honor of H. Otley Beyer)*. Quezon City: Alemar-Phoenix.

CHAPTER 11

Filipinos Were My Teachers

PATRICIA SNYDER WEIBUST

As the tides are inextricably called to the shore, comingle only too briefly and then recede, depositing their gifts upon the sands and sweeping up treasures for Neptune, so anthroplogists are enigmatically drawn to the lands of diverse cultures where they too comingle and when they depart they leave behind their influence during a transforming moment in their lives and carry off with them priceless learnings to be shared with colleagues. While the analogy between tidal activity and anthropological fieldwork is far from perfect, it is more than simply a poetic introduction for there are similarities in the rhythm of flood and ebb as two worlds interact.

This chapter is an attempt to convey something about the human aspects in the flow of fieldwork which have been stowed away since 1970 when I spent a year conducting a casestudy in a town on Negros Island. It is to be hoped that they will be of interest and assistance to others, but it must be admitted that of all the knowledges carried home with me, these less academic pearls and rubies are of inestimable value and it is with feelings of excitement and poignancy that I approach the luxury of unwrapping and sorting them for the first time.

LOW WATER

Amassing together the forces necessary to embark upon a fieldstudy is a crucial period since the setting of initial parameters cannot so easily be done or redone when one is already in the field and gross mistakes can jeopardize the whole project. This low water phase encompasses two principal activities: formulation of a research problem; and making arrangements for entrance into the fieldsite.

In my case, there was some difficulty in settling upon a subject for research. As a doctoral candidate at Syracuse University, I was enrolled in a program to examine relationships between schools and development, but after considerable study of so many scholarly treatments of modernization

I came to the disturbing conclusion that the theory of development is based upon an unfounded assumption that the quality of life varies directly with the amount of energy a socio-cultural system is able to utilize. While this may be true up to a point, at the upper end of the development continuum there is a level which should be labelled "overdeveloped", when increased consumption of energy is actually dysfunctional to human wellbeing. Symptoms of overdevelopment are evident in current concerns with pollution, overpopulation, shortages of food, water and fossil fuels. Although I felt under obligation to do so, it seemed the height of folly to follow the popular research trend of assessing how well the schools in a developing nation were promoting the cause of modernization when I could not honestly think that this was necessarily a yardstick of progress. Although academically credible, such a study serves to further endorse the validity of this theory.

I was very curious to probe into what might be considered to be a more fundamental problem: how the process of socio-cultural change operates in schools and which elements are undergoing transformation in a particular locale. A literature review uncovered Coser's theoretical works on social conflict which are buttressed by numerous other theorists and field researchers. Conflict theory asserts that there are two types of conflict: one serves as an arena for reaffirmation of values and norms, and thereby maintains the system; the other contains value conflicts and has the potential for triggering change. Conflicts in the various subsystems, such as education, can be studied to find out which norms and values are being continued and which ones are under question. This appeared to be a viable framework for the study. In retrospect, it was probably a wise choice, for this type of investigation is so demanding that it would be most debilitating to be burdened with a problem which did not reflect total personal commitment.

It was also necessary to hone in on a good fieldsite. I had majored in Asian studies because of my own interest in that area of the world. India was dismissed as a possibility because their problem of overpopulation dwarfs all other concerns. Japan is too highly industrialized, China was closed to outsiders and mainland Southeast Asia was embroiled in a war. The Philippines was chosen over Indonesia because of the language problem in the latter and due to the influence of Professor Donn V. Hart, one of my advisors, who encouraged me to execute this study in Casco *poblacion* where he had researched several other topics.[1]

The literature on social conflict in the Philippines is limited to "think pieces" and descriptive bits and snatches in casestudies but nothing substantive enough to serve as a basis for hypotheses about the content of conflict. And so, the study was conceived within the framework of conflict theory, set in Casco and designed inductively to describe and conceptualize all of the regular social relationships in their two schools and what happened during conflicts. Due to the research proclivities of my advisors, there was no objection to the methodology but subsequently it has been astounding to discover the numbers of university professors who do not even understand inductive approaches to research.

As far as techniques are concerned, I took an anthropological research course. Particularly useful were the experiences of others with ascribed roles, indirect interviewing and various combinations of participation and observation. The course would have offered a more thorough preparation if we had had the opportunity to conduct a mini fieldstudy.

A major concern when anticipating a field expedition, especially if it is to be halfway around the world, is finances. Fortunately I had another year left under an NDEA fellowship. The subsistence allowance which was rather spartan in Syracuse, was quite generous for living in Casco. Transportation expenses were allocated out of assigned tuition monies, which actually saved the government a considerable amount of money.

Another matter to be taken care of is to contact those whose support can facilitate the study. Professor Hart launched into a "pro-Snyder" letter writing campaign. He dispatched introductions to numerous people who had befriended him in Manila, Dumaguete City (the provincial capital) and Casco. Coring, his former research assistant in Casco, replied that he would be happy to act as my counsellor and would locate a home where I could stay with a family of teachers. I followed up on Professor Hart's efforts by corresponding with all of these people myself and made a reservation for two weeks at a missionary guest house in Manila. A fellow Filipino anthropology student, who was returning home to Manila, volunteered to meet me when I arrived.

The next step was transportation. Although it may be a sign of weakness or highly undesirable for an anthropologist, I must confess to an uncomfortable fear of flying. However, for some reason, I feel snug and secure on board a ship and was thankful that it was possible to secure passage over on a Norwegian freighter. Filipino regulations required a paid-up return ticket, so an open airlines reservation was made.

Last minute mundane preparations included disposal of apartment furniture, buying Travellers checks collecting copies of my credentials, family farewells, obtaining a visa and updated passport, and packing. I fought the urge to bring a surfeit of things and limited luggage to two medium-sized suitcases (which I could carry myself if need be); one with heavy cotton clothing, and the other with a small typewriter, books and a camera.

THE FLOOD BEGINS

The flooding phase of a fieldstudy subsumes a number of variables. From my notes, it appears that time, the speed of immersion, is an influential factor. Early contacts with informants, and the common as well as unique aspects of culture shock emerge as important elements. Ascribed roles are notably visible in these early days. And questions arise about the conduct of one's personal life. Unless the investigator is thoroughly conversant in the local language, this can present a challenge. Lastly, reactions to humor can test the degree of acculturation one feels she has achieved.

I would typify my approach to Casco as a leisurely one. The Norwegian cargo ship I boarded in New York took almost three weeks, via the Panama Canal, Los Angeles and San Francisco, before docking in Manila. This was a period of detachment, complete relaxation and freedom. Suspension in time and space during this cultural hiatus allowed a psychological rest, a fallow if you will, which readied me for the tremendous spurt in personal growth which characterized the whole fieldwork experience.

The first rude shock in this mild state of euphoria came when we were awakened at dawn to negotiate customs while still anchored out in the bay. I discovered a fraudulent customs agent going through my suitcases and attempting to appropriate a tape recorder which a passenger had presented to me. For the next two weeks the missionary guest house was my home in Manila where I confronted an international variety of transients, played tourist and most importantly, established an operational base by meeting with educators, anthropologists and politicians who had access to relevant information. Concentration upon these familiar tasks served as a soothing relief from the array of bewilderments which were encountered. The intense heat, the black market money exchange, transportation, communication, an anti-American demonstration and an earthquake of medium intensity all conspired to test the mettle of a relatively naive foreigner. Nothing in my university training offered any guidance whatsoever in dealing with these anomalies; one simply had to rely upon common sense and I think that my enjoyment of Manila was a result of meeting these challenges as well as gratitude for the overwhelming hospitality which was extended.

The next step in immersion was to spend another two weeks in Dumaguete City, engaged in activities similar to those in Manila. There were, however, three important distinctions as I moved closer to the fieldsite. First, the hierarchy of officials were those in direct authority over Casconian personnel and were therefore people whose goodwill was vital and to whom the study had to be explained. Thanks to Professor Hart's advice, I was forewarned to approach those who held the real power and had the respect of others in the systems. I was uncertain about how to describe the study. Research has shown that Filipinos try to provide the "correct answers" and they tend to regard conflict in a negative way. In the hope of presenting the least possible threat and increasing validity. I disclosed only that my study required a complete acquaintance with the schools in Casco, stressing that no evaluation would be attempted. Second, was the presence of two groups who were of tangential professional concern, but to whom a foreign anthropologist was of social interest. There were a few American missionaries stationed at a university, who maintained an astonishing distance between themselves and Filipino culture. And there was a rather amorphous collection of young foreigners and upper class Filipinos who generated some highly exuberant parties. I could intuit danger in too close an association with either group because of the implacable wall among social classes. The third difference from Manila was in regard to physical amenities. Telephones, water and electricity were much less reliable. Air conditioners were scarce. Transportation consisted of pedicabs (motorcycles with springless sidecars big enough for two Filipinos or one American) and *tartenellas* (horse-drawn carts, the horse being of uncertain vintage).

Coring orchestrated a delightful introductory visit to Casco during All Soul's weekend. These two days were a blur of brilliant intensity which registered certain indelible impressions of the people and their culture. The power structure was elucidated quite clearly by the order in which we met with the mayor, the priest, the judge, the two principals and many of the teachers. Personal characteristics stood out starkly by contrasts. I was very embarrassed to be such an object of curiosity, especially at the cockfight where a drunk comedian from a *barrio* attracted quite a crowd by teasing me about wealthy Americans, along with some earthy humor. I sampled *tuba*, the local buri palm wine, and a day or two later was admitted to the university hospital for a week to treat the resulting diarrhea. Since national elections were immanent, the governor made a speech at a political rally in town and the weekend ended by my accepting a ride back to the city with him, seated next to his bodyguard who casually rested a small machine gun on his knee. It was unsettling, to say the least, to someone who had never before even seen a gun.

The final move to Casco was accomplished without incident. Coring made provision for me to room and board with a family in which the mother, father and two daughters were teachers, and whose home was situated conveniently across the street from the schools. He had negotiated a reasonable monthly rate of twenty-five dollars. I very quickly came to appreciate just how wonderful it was to have Coring's counsel. He was the municipal tax collector, very well regarded in the community and was involved in both schools as a parent and as a P.T.A. officer. I acquainted him thoroughly with the study and throughout, he was unerringly able to suggest the most knowledgeable people to interview and the most central activities to attend. He was already well versed in fieldwork methods from his association with Professor Hart. I paid him the equivalent of his salary, about twenty-five dollars a month, to work with me during evenings and weekends. He graciously offered his services without compensation but was certainly able to put the money to good use educating his ten children. A number of secondary informants were relied upon, beginning with elderly citizens and later, as my judgment improved, a host of others, of course principally including educators.

Although I anticipated culture shock and believe that it was minimized by the gradualness of immersion, for several weeks there was a tremendous sense of helplessness. I really didn't know how to accomplish the simplest of life's activities: brushing teeth, buying a Coke, visiting a teacher, taking a bath, mailing a letter, treating sunburn, playing with children, attending school, talking with students, etc. I could not fully understand what was going on around me and particularly could not sort out the usual from the unique. One of the more insidious dimensions of culture shock was in the relationship to one's environment. Coming from New England where we are surrounded by solid building walls and cradled in forested hills, I was uneasy living in unscreened buildings and participating in so many out-of-doors events.

I had thought that Casconians would expect me to act as a young, single, female American researcher which should bode well for gathering data since they were already accustomed to Professor Hart and many of their teachers were young, single and female. What was surprising was the immediate assignment of an additional Peace Corps role. Two Peace Corps men had been assigned to Casconian schools a few years ago and I had to contend with the expectation that I too wanted to be thought of as a "helper". They expressed eagerness for me to begin teaching at once so that they could observe and imitate my methods. It was a dilemma as the last thing I intended to do was to interfere in the social relationships of the schools yet it was essential to actually participate in the teaching process. I knew full well that they were only trying to afford me a feeling of being useful because they perceived that this is what I wanted. I opted for guest teaching appearances on the English language and on American culture in a number of classes and requested that they grant me a little time to

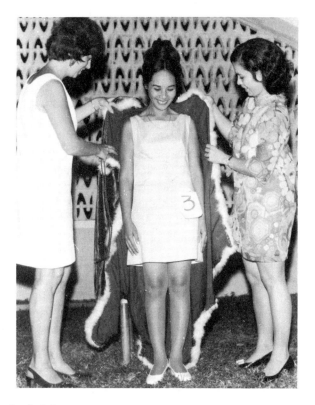

On the left, I am helping to regally robe the fiesta queen in Casco.

become familiarized with the schools before assuming a regular teaching assignment, hoping that in time I could become more unobstrusive. This strategy worked very well.

School activities soon settled into a routine but for a much longer duration my personal life was discombobulated. I was torn between "being myself" and a desire to "step into the shoes" of Filipinos and emulate their behavior. The problem was that young, single Filipinas were not supposed to smoke, drink, gamble, attend cockfights, engage in out-of-doors sports like swimming, or openly date on a casual basis. These strictures imposed a series of enigmas for me. While I am sure that Casconians did not expect an American to exemplify their model of an ideal Filipina, there was still an undefined threshold of propriety.

As far as romance was concerned, I was fortunate to experience the gamut from traditional to modern. On my first night in town, I was honored with a very proper serenade. Everyone thought it strange that I made no mention of it the next day until they discovered that I had slept through the whole thing! The bachelor teacher who had co-ordinated the serenade, along with a friend or two, trailed after me at a distance for several days and I asked Coring what response was appropriate. He advised me to ignore them. Later in the year, a friend of my landlady's son invited me to a formal university dance. This was accomplished with customary formality, the invitation being extended months in advance and with my landlady's permission. About a month ahead of time, he came to the house one afternoon to discuss the date and I was chatting with him on the patio when my landlady bustled out and abruptly ordered me to go into the house to eat my dinner. The evening meal is never served before 7, yet I had to sit down all by myself to a table laden with food. No-one ever explained this sequence of events but I can surmise that it was designed to objectify my lack of interest in the young man, which is the ultimate in proper behavior for a Filipina.

One funny incident occurred when the postmaster, a married man with eight children who was renown for drinking binges when his wife was away, settled into a long bout at our *sari-sari* (general) store, which was attached to the house. When I returned from school, he flattered me with lavish compliments and by late evening, when he was thoroughly inebriated, we could hear him shouting to the universe of his great love for me and desire to marry and accompany me to the United States. My landlady bolted the main door that night, but the following day while I was sitting outside waiting for the bus to the city, he returned to the pursuit and decided that his eighteen year old son in high school would be a better match for me. Coring complained to the mayor and he chastized the postmaster for embarrassing the town. For weeks afterwards the postmaster would carefully avoid walking anywhere near our house and was unmercifully teased by the townspeople.

At the more modern end of the spectrum, I met several very wealthy Filipinos who attended parties in the city. Their approach to romance was much more assured and bold, particularly when it involved a foreigner who was not "under the wing" of a correspondingly high status family. They rarely came to see me while I was in Casco where I was surrounded by "my people" but joined in common social events in Dumaguete City and occasionally we had a movie date. I very quickly learned that even among these supposed liberals, they still believed that when a man and woman are alone together, he could not resist the opportunity for sexual adventure and she could not say "No".

A most ludicrous example of this happened while a group of us were camping out for the weekend on a beach, snorkeling and scuba diving on an incredibly beautiful coral reef. At night the men decided to go on a bat hunt and this eager beaver researcher tagged along – after all, I had never participated in a bat hunt. Somehow, I'll never know how, I found myself in the middle of a coconut grove with slippery husks underfoot, wearing only sandals to protect my feet. This is a favorite home for cobras which have been known to fatally strike out at intruders. I was alone in the absolute darkness with a complete stranger who carried his rifle and a flashlight to shine up into the tops of the trees where the glint of the light reflecting in a bat's eyes, pinpoints the target for a good shot. I was absolutely terrified of stepping near a cobra and this man actually sat down and launched into an impassioned plea for me to fly off on an informal honeymoon in Japan! For lack of anything better to do, I dissolved into giggles and when I had gained control of myself, counter-attacked with a lecture on marital fidelity and how a trip to Japan with his wife would revive their great love for each other.

As far as the other personal aspects of life which were conundrums, most expectations were much clearer than with romance. I continued to smoke, my one big vice, as I could not envisage changing this habit amidst so many other stresses. Drinking of alcoholic beverages was quite optional as far as I was concerned, so I refrained from doing so. It was interesting that the mayor who was well acquainted with Americans, offered me American liquor at fiestas even though I always refused. I noticed that Coring bragged upon a number of occasions that I did not even drink beer. Gambling and cockfights were equally optional. Just for fun I did learn how to play the popular Filipino poker, *piat-piat*, and went to one or two *barrio* cockfights but these little touches posed no problems.

Water sports were a more serious issue because of the heat and my own love for swimming and fishing. I could not pass up the opportunities for a daily dip with such a lovely river and ocean frontage in close proximity. Many times, I joined with some teachers in an outing but the married ones were too busy with family responsibilities and the single ones, who had more free time, had not been socialized into this form of recreation, so I frequently swam in the river alone during the late afternoon. Although this violated Casconians' sense of the necessity for companionship, I think it did not seriously damage my reputation.

The only Filipina who was close to my age, unmarried and an accomplished swimmer, was the Adult Education Supervisor. We hiked for days together making the rounds of almost all of the *barrio* schools in the municipality. Unfortunately, this woman was reputed to be an *osikan* (which loosely translates as a witch) who owned a *sigbin* (a spirit which appears as a kangaroo and can transport its owner anywhere in the world, as well as play tricks on other people). While she was an intelligent and sparkling associate and we could have expanded our educational commonalities into a wider friendship, I decided against it because she was definitely a marginal in the eyes of the townpeople.

I think that my one major failure was that I did not become fluent in the Cebuano dialect. During the first few weeks I followed a programmed text with Coring each evening. It was very good but I needed the time for interviews and for typing up notes. I continued to pick up a little casually, but most everything in the schools was conducted in English and people liked to practice their English when talking with me. While I feel that I had access to all of the information required for the study, there were times when friends were relaxing around their homes speaking in Cebuano and I would not understand much of what was said. If I were to do it over again, I would allot an extra month to learning the language before beginning any research because once entangled in the field there are too many other imperatives.

Periodically I was caught up short in the realization that I was still very much of an outsider because I did not appreciate the same sense of humor. There were three types of joking, all of which did not seem very funny to me. Early on I was exposed to varieties of sexual humor. Several foods had sexual connotations: bananas (of all sizes and shapes), fried eggs, sausages and rice cakes were particularly alluded to as being analogous to sexual organs. The game being played was that if a single female understood the jokes, she was not a virgin, and if she did not comprehend, at least she would be disconcerted. Animals, especially dogs, which Americans treat as family members, were eaten and it was considered great sport to fling rocks at them. Lastly, was the treatment of marginals. Homosexuals, crazy and retarded people were jeered at and occasionally, rocks were even cast at them. While I never could wholeheartedly enter into these jests, I did manage to approach a more neutral expectation.

HIGH WATER

The high water phase of fieldwork is the reward for weeks, or months, of hard work, doubts and adjustments. It is the time when the researcher can finally relax, secure in the knowledge that she is accepted as a student of the culture. Probably as a result of that sense of surety, empathy with those around her grows. The careful groundwork laid in the flooding stage has set into motion a flow of data which now submerges her and the Sirens cajole with a dazzling array of unrelated subjects. Outsiders of radically different social class can interrupt the research but, at this point, are no longer a worrisome threat to rapport as would have been the case earlier. A rather unusual research technique emerges. By not asking questions and, in fact, by expressing reluctance to meddle in sensitive matters, informants become eager to discuss matters which they had been evasive about previously. High water turns to the ebb just as one is becoming apprehensive because the "work" of research is too satisfying.

I can well remember the moment when, after months of uncertainty during which I was constantly concerned about whether I was doing everything right, all of a sudden I relaxed. I don't know how else to describe the feeling. Without warning, one day I began to feel at ease and comfortable to be finally accepted in the ideal role, that of a student who could implicitly trust Filipinos to be my teachers. And they were magnificent teachers, according to some philosophies, for they inundated me with answers to the research questions, provided solutions to queries which arose along the way and most importantly, revealed new puzzles to solve.

There were four explicit incidents which contributed to this sense of admission as a beginning student in the school of Filipino culture. One afternoon there was a stormy faculty meeting at the elementary school. Afterwards, the teacher who had instigated the conflict revealed that she had considered aborting this outbreak of hostility because I was there but then decided to go ahead since she thought that I would understand and should learn about all their life, not just the pleasantries. On the way to a *barrio* fiesta, a lawyer, whose wife had initially refused to have me board with them because she was afraid I would want American food and comforts, apologized and said that they were mistaken as I seemed to appreciate things in the Filipino way. My landlady's daughter confided that I was not at all like the Peace Corps they knew for I did not evaluate critically by comparison to America. And lastly, I had been confused because the mayor and I were operating on a different time wave. I would arrive late to our meetings and he was always there on time or even early. Finally, when I felt I knew him well enough, I asked him what was going on. In deference to me, he had been following "American time" whereas I, in my attempts to copy local practices, had been using "Filipino time".

As a sense of harmony with life in Casco grew, my focus changed from concentration upon myself and my research to solicitude for those around me. I was especially bothered by the hardship imposed upon poor families by their fulfillment of the expected total hospitality routine. Yet it was clear that people took great pride in this accomplishment. There did seem to be a way to at least minimize their burden. If I acted as a guest, sitting in the living room admiring pictures and diplomas, they treated me accordingly. However, if I lent a hand in the kitchen or played with their children, this alleviated some of the formality. However, their deep-seated system of reciprocity became part of my life, too, and even to this day I am contributing to what I feel is really a lifelong debt for there is no way I could ever adequately repay all of those who made life so good for me there.

Strangely enough, after so much effort in the flooding phase, during high water the data literally poured in with very little exertion on my part. Teachers enthusiastically buttonholed me to expound upon the latest eruptions at school and the protagonists involved were quite willing to discuss their viewpoints. I scheduled special meetings with teachers to solicit their cooperation in gathering basic demographic data and to explore the nature of their interactions with parents. I began to teach English daily in sixth grade and in the fourth year at the high school. Since I had observed Casconian teachers for such a long while, I could slip into their role with reasonable ease and had a joyous time with the youngsters. But there were one or two occasions when I reacted without thinking, according to the dictates of my own culture. I remember one such occurrence when a high school boy was copying his seatmate's essay. I had a burning impulse to march over and tear up their papers, but I checked myself. When I told Coring about it, he paled for an insult of this magnitude could have far reaching consequences.

While it may sound ridiculous, there was a problem at this point in resisting the temptation to be sidetracked by numerous opportunities which opened up to investigate irrelevant but fascinating topics. Once one becomes somewhat familiar with a culture, its monolithic facade can be penetrated. There are so many interesting subcultures in the Philippines, both on Negros and other islands. I did visit a few, but only for tantalizing glimpses. More immediately distracting were those curiosities which were present in or near Casco: people who were renown for their healing powers, childbirth customs, voodoo practices, courtship and marriage realities, the new mobility of middle class government employees, etc.

While I think it was correct in the flooding phase to ascertain a threat to rapport with Casconians in too intimate ties with the upper class, the potential reality of this hazard was made evident in the spring when one of the wealthiest and most powerful of the hacienderos from the north of the island, paid me an exploratory flirtatious visit. He just walked in unannounced one morning. I did not recognize him and spent a half hour or so bantering with his amorous innuendos. My landlady, who was at school, went into a tailspin for days when she heard that such an important man had been a guest to her home without being subjected to a lavish reception. There were other sporadic visits by American and Filipino friends which sometimes interrupted my work. Luckily they were not too frequent. At this later stage when my reputation was well established, a few happenings of this type were not damaging. Still, my hosts were amazed when I refused an invitation to a party given by this wealthy clique so that I could accompany my landlady on a trip to her cousins' home in a northern city.

One of the things that surprised me most during my research was the process of revealing sensitive information. It seemed that once I was more or less accepted, this kind of data was shared without my asking questions. And, in fact, the more reluctant I appeared to be to pry into these matters, the more insistent people became to divulge them. I am referring here to two specific categories of information in Casco. The first is sexual practices. Despite what the literature conveys, not all Filipinas are virgins at marriage. There are "shotgun weddings" as well as a practice in some *barrios* of essentially selling a girl's virginity in order to insure her becoming the fiesta queen. The other area is spirit beliefs. People were very very hesitant to talk about them because they thought that a Westerner would think them to be foolish. Yet, as with sexual behavior, the more I protested that this might be a delicate matter which they would not care to discuss, the more ardently they pressed the data upon me. And Casconians have a rich spiritual inheritance.

Toward the end of high water I was disturbed because I was finding my fieldwork too much fun. Having settled in happily, with the collection of data progressing nicely, established friends in Casco and Dumaguete City, plenty of outlets for at least dabbling into interesting sidelights and great freedom for adventures in snorkeling, exploring caves, riding motorcycles, etc., I was nagged by the possibility that something must be wrong because all seemed to be going well.

THE EBB BEGINS

And on this high note, the ebb begins. Psychological and physical withdrawal commence. As with the flood, the time factor is a consideration. Each researcher must decide what gifts are to be deposited upon the sands the most pervasive one, of course, being human ties. And even as one leaves after considerable immersion in a culture, there may still be surprises in store.

As the school year ended in Casco, everyone scattered for their vacation activities and I moved in to babysit with a missionary's home, dachshund and Siamese cat, in the capital where I reviewed my notes for a month or so to look for gaps and filled in on the workings of the Division Office. In response to my plea that I would be lonesome, Casconian friends arrived in droves which afforded me opportunities to return some of their hospitality and to learn more in casual conversations.

I was conscious of an obligation to leave some tangible gifts and discussed possibilities with the teachers. We selected a wall clock for the elementary school and my typewriter for the high school. I planned to send presents to my close personal friends since they preferred goods from the United States. I also did some shopping for souvenirs to bring home and tried to take a brief vacation to Moro territory in the south but delays in processing my luggage through customs required me to stay put.

After farewell parties, it was time to depart for Manila and my last vivid memory is the shock I felt when my landlady's daughter asked me if all Americans thought Filipinos had tails! During World War II the American troops had made up a song called, "The Monkeys Have No Tails in Zamboanga." Apparently the "monkeys" referred to the Filipinos living in this city on Mindanao. I am still dumbfounded to think that the cruel ethnocentrism expressed in this historic song is being visited upon such an outstandingly lovely and well-educated Filipina.

As I left from the Dumaguete airport, within sight of the wreckage of a plane which had crashed the day before, there was a sense of unreality. Even now as I solidify the whole process I do not understand why there was no sadness at all in leaving, yet a very strong pull to return. A freighter journey around Africa completed the ebb and the gradualness of this departure, as with the entrance, perhaps minimized reverse culture shock which was nevertheless apparent when I felt strangely out of place waiting for a cup of coffee in a Virginia restaurant, being searched for drugs by customs agents in New York and speeding home through the greenery of New England.

LOW WATER

And so we reach low water again, where one is called upon to disseminate the knowledge acquired of foreign shores. Always there are ties to that shore, the extent and continuing nature of which have to be determined. There is a pragmatic technique of extending field research by mail, as well as deeper moral commitments based upon personal involvement. Serendipitious effects of the research can lead one to tangential leaps in intellectual growth.

Within a few days of my re-entry, I was teaching at the University of Connecticut and faced with the monumental task of sharing what I had learned with others. The "publish or perish" world is indeed a very real culture scene. Aside from uncovering the implicit as well as explicit rules to this game, it is difficult to adequately represent the fieldsite, disheartening to be confined at times to quickie synopses and disturbing to encounter misunderstandings. There are professional imperatives which impel one, unless the circumstances are unusual, to become a generalist. Economic stringencies drastically limit the numbers of specialists a university or college can support. Yet, after the intense in-depth study of a field research, I felt a compulsion to learn more about some rather isolated questions and was scornful of the more superficial treatments of knowledge which are widely rewarded.

Without conscious intent on my part, in continuing to correspond with friends, the line between the personal and the professional was blurred and I found myself really doing fieldwork by mail. As puzzlements appeared while I was analysing the data, I would write about the uncertainty and many times received clarification. A few years after I left, martial law was declared in the Philippines, and my friends wrote about their own experiences with this political change and even sent me current books and articles. Our correspondence is on a deeper personal level also. The exchange of family news, advice, pictures, presents and loving concern will probably continue indefinitely.

As a result of my experiences as a field researcher in the Philippines, several years after my return I became engrossed in a project to study ethnic groups in Connecticut and to prepare curricula for the public schools. Lost at sea and merged within its depths for these interim years, I had forgotten the excitement, the quickening, as once more I was carried to mingle with a foreign shore. The phases were the same and again I found that reluctance to pry during high water produced some spectacular discoveries. The feeling of startling aliveness as I discovered new dimensions of myself by becoming the student of another world was the same too, yet ever fresh.

A further consequence of the Filipino study has been a compelling quest to find an alternative to the development theory of cultural evolution which would account for the quality of life which I experienced in Casco. The only alternative which I discovered was synergy, a theory propounded by Ruth Benedict and Abraham Maslow. Much work needs to be done to distill and refine their thinking, but they have laid a foundation which has attracted me into exploration of a relatively untrammeled path of theorizing and perhaps future research.

NOTES

1. Casco is the fictitious name of a *poblacion* located on the southern coast of Negros Island.

CHAPTER 12

The Observer Observed:
Changing Identities of Ethnographers
in a Northeastern Thai Village

CHARLES F. KEYES[1]

Early in 1963 my wife, Jane, and I began anthropological field research in a village in northeastern Thailand. In our initial encounters with villagers of Ban Nọng Tụn we were seen as alien *farang* or "Westerners" about whom villagers had only vague ideas. After we began to appear in the village regularly and particularly after we moved into the village, we found that villagers began to change their ideas about our social identities. I had rather expected, on the basis of reports written by other anthropologists working in other societies, that at some point we would become "accepted" into village society and be given social identities – most probably based on fictive kinship ties – which would establish us in the community for the rest of our stay. We did establish quasi-kin relationships with the family with which we lived and with the kinsmen of this family. Such relationships notwithstanding, our social identities did not become unalterably fixed during the course of the 15 months we lived and worked in Ban Nọng Tụn. On the contrary, we found that villagers altered their perceptions of us as social persons both as a consequence of their observing our actions and more particularly, as a consequence of their reflection on certain events in which both villagers and we were participants. Moreover, our social identities in the eyes of villagers continued to undergo further transformations even after we left the village because we returned to visit Ban Nọng Tụn during subsequent field work in Thailand in 1967-1968 and 1972-1974.

It is my thesis that the changing nature of our social identities as Western ethnographers in a northeastern Thai village sprang not from our peculiar nature as undefinable aliens but from the cultural premises which the villagers employed in determining all social identities, their own included. What our presence did was to bring these premises into play perhaps more frequently than might otherwise have been the case. The "anthropologist effect" which has so often been assumed to be the source of distortion in the ethnographic endeavor was, in our case least, a stimulus for leading villagers to reassert their own cultural assumptions. Villagers were not forced to transcend their own world view in order to construct identities for us.

That this was so was not immediately apparent to us for at the beginning of our field work we were all too conscious of being aliens. As anthropologists we had been prepared to try to transcend our own cultural premises in order to gain access to another tradition on its own terms. Yet because we really knew, at least in the beginning stages, very little about the culture of the people we were living and working among, we tended to interpret the situations in which we engaged with villagers in terms of the "objective" concepts of social sciences which we had learned. If our contacts with the villagers had not been so intensive, or if we had not lived in the villager for a long period of time but had rather only visited the village to administer questionnaires, and then withdrawn to settings with Thai and other Westerners in which our "objective" understandings would have been reinforced, then I doubt that we would ever have comprehended the premises which the villagers used to construct an interpretation of our as well as their own identities.

BECOMING A VILLAGER IN BAN NỌNG TỤN[2]

In late November 1962, after having spent 3½ months in Bangkok, we moved to the small provincial capital of Mahasarakham situated in the center of the northeastern region of Thailand. We rented a house in the town, and with the assistance of local officials, started looking for a village which would be suited to my research interests in the relationship of a northeastern Thai village to the large society in which the village is situated.

One of the officials, Khun Wichian, a community development officer for a "commune" (*tambon*; a collectivity of approximately 10-15 villages) in Mụang District, Mahasarakham was particularly helpful, With his assistance I found a village which seemed to suit my research needs. On December 28, 1962, Khun Wichian took me on his motorcycle to the community of Ban Nọng Tụn and I made the first contact with the villagers with whom Jane and I would become so well acquainted. I was extremely fortunate in being introduced in Ban Nọng Tụn by Khun Wichian for I soon came to realize that he was a man of exceptional qualities. In a letter dated January 27, 1963, I wrote the following:

One of the greatest assets both to my work and to my feeling welcome in Mahasarakham is due to . . . [Khun Wichian]. Mr. [Wichian] is the community development officer for the commune . . . in which I am working . . . I have been quite impressed with his sensitivity to the things which are most important to making his job a success. And he takes his job most seriously, not for thought of advancement but because he is interested. Being a native of the Northeast, he is welcomed in the villages and seems to understand them far better than Thai from the Central Plains . . . who have a hard time adjusting to the Northeast. Because I am working in a village in "his" commune, he was assigned by the District Officer to help me all he could. . . . He has served as interpreter, as liaison with villagers, as my preceptor in good Thai etiquette (as when dealing with [Buddhist monks] . . .), and as a friend. All this he has done without any sign of being put upon and without demanding from me that which he thinks I might be able to give (this is certainly contrary to some of the local people in town who want me to do everything from getting them into an American university to teaching them English).

Khun Wichian continued to be our mentor and mediator for the first few months of our work and thereafter remained our closest friend outside the village.

Ban Nọng Tụn ("the village of the pond where one is easily startled") is located about 15 kilometers from the city of Mahasarakham and about three kilometers down a side road from a major highway. In 1963, somewhat over 700 people in 119 households lived in the village which was divided into four (and for some purposes six) "neighborhoods" (*khum*). The whole village was located on a high ground and surrounded by rice fields.

I recorded my initial impressions of the village in a letter, dated January 11, 1963, to another anthropologist who was working in another northeastern Thai village:

I am quite pleased with the village, as it seems to be quite traditional, not too developed, yet close enough to the town. . . . I have had two trips to the village so far and will go there again this afternoon. . . . The headman has seemed cordial enough . . . , although he is quite reserved and seems very nervous with me. . . . The other villagers seem tolerant enough of me, but there certainly hasn't been a great opening of arms and taking me into their bosom as seemed to be the case with you. They are all still a little uncertain about what I am after and what effect I will have on the village. But, . . . I have only been in the village on two occasions and I shouldn't expect to be wholly accepted as yet.

I knew that the "total acceptance" which I had specified in my letter could come about only by Jane and I becoming regular participants in village activities. From early January on I began to commute to the village, sometimes in the company of Wichian or Jane, sometimes on my own. I quickly came to realize that most of my conversations with villagers seemed to be carried out with younger men. Although I was reasonably fluent in Central Thai, the local language, a dialect of Lao, was quite different. Many of the young men in the village spoke at least some Thai which they had acquired while living and working in Bangkok for several months to several years.[3] The older men (beyond the age of 40), were not comfortable speaking Central Thai and almost no woman spoke anything but the local language. I always sought contact with the headman, a man in his mid 40s, during my first trips to the village. Yet, although he could speak central Thai as a consequence of his having to interact with officials, my relations with him were initially quite formal as he tended to structure our encounters according to the patterns he employed when dealing with government officials.

Within a short time, whenever we came to the village, we found ourselves seeking out one or two people. The first was the headmaster of the village school who by virtue of being a teacher was completely fluent in Thai. His wife, also a teacher in the school, was the only local woman who was able to converse easily in Thai. Unfortunately, the headmaster and his wife were not Ban Nong Tun villagers, neither having been born there nor being current residents. Both commuted to the village from the tambon center and stayed in the village only during school hours.

The other person with whom we found that we could communicate was a young man who had recently opened a village shop and a generator-powered rice mill. Khun Ngao had spent six years working in Bangkok during which time he had saved enough money to buy the mill and to build a simple shop in Ban Nong Tun. On coming to the village from Bangkok, he had married a daughter of the family whose land he had rented for his enterprises. Kuan Ngao was to become, we would soon find, a key mediator in our efforts to enter into the social world of Ban Nong Tun.

Not only did we find that Khun Ngao was able and even interested in talking with us but that his shop cum rice mill was an excellent place for us to meet other villagers since people came there throughout the day either to buy things at the shop, to have their rice milled, or to wait for one of the local truck-buses which stopped there. It was eminently reasonable, therefore, that we should arrange to live with Khun Ngao when we moved into Ban Nong Tun. He agreed to divide his shop in half, built a backroom for us and another for himself and his wife, and to install an attached privy and bathing area. Although the decision to undertake the rennovations and construction was made in early February, it was not

Residence of the author and his wife in the village of Ban Nǫng Tụn, 1963-1964.
The left side of the building is the village shop and residence of Khun Ngao and his
wife, Khun Nuan. (1964)

until early April that the house was ready for us to move in.

In the interim period I began field work in earnest with a sample survey
of households designed to familiarise myself with the nature of household
composition in the village. Jane and I also began to gather systematic notes
on various village craft processes — notably cloth making and blacksmith-
ing — and on food preparation. These activities helped to establish that
we were quite serious about learning about village life. Nonetheless, we
remained outsiders, *farang* ('Westerners') who made visits to the village,
asked a lot of questions in a language (Central Thai) that was only partially
comprehensible to the majority of villagers and then retreated back to
town. For our part, the village was still only a source of data, and not a
social context in which we had any place.

During the first three days of February 1963, Ban Nǫng Tụn held a
major *wat* (temple-monastery) festival. Although the village always
sponsored an annual festival centered around the recitation of the 'Great
Life" sermon, i.e., the Buddhist story which tells of the life of Prince
Vessantara, who was believed to have been the Lord Buddha in his last life
before he was incarnated as the Buddha, this year's fête was more elaborate
than usual. The festival was also held to honor a ranking monk, the

brother of the headman, who had just recently passed a higher level of examination in the sacred Buddhist literature written in Pali. In addition, the occasion of the annual ritual was also used to raise money to be used towards the construction of a new village school. To attract large numbers of people from surrounding villages, the festival organizers — local villagers belonging to the *wat* committee together with the school teachers — arranged for a variety of entertainments: boxing, folk dancing (*ramwong*), folk opera (*mǫlammu*), fireworks, performances by skilled players on the *khaen*, a polyphonic reed-pipe instrument, and movies.

The *wat* festival was the first occasion on which Jane and I had any interaction with Buddhist monks in a conspicuously public way. The village *wat* had, at that time, only one resident monk, a young man who had, as is the local custom, taken holy orders for only a temporary period. Although we had called on this young monk, his youth had not marked him as a key person for my researches. At the festival, however, not only was a ranking monk to be honored, but all of the other senior monks in the vicinity had been invited to participate in the ritual. During the course of the festival, we engaged, with Khun Wichian's and Khun Ngao's guidance, in showing customary respect towards these monks. We also openly expressed, on many occasions during the period, our great interest in Buddhism and in Buddhist customs. As villagers became aware of our actions, they begin to see us as having committed ourselves to their Buddhist-derived ethos.

Many of the people attracted to the festival from neighboring villages were quite curious about our presence. We overheard some people from Ban Nǫng Tụn saying that we had come to study local customs in *their* village (*ban hao*), obviously indicating that they had been specially set off by our interest. Later on we were quite often to hear Nǫng Tụn-ers referring to the fact that we had honored them by choosing to work and live in their village. This claim provoked a few days after the festival one of the very rare outbursts of hostility towards Jane or me which occurred during the whole of our stay in Thailand. A village teacher from a neighboring village stopped us on the road one evening and in an obviously drunken voice demanded why we had attended the Ban Nǫng Tụn fair and given money to the Ban Nǫng Tụn school when we had not come to the festival in his village and given money to his school. Fortunately, his friends were quite embarrassed by his manner and succeeded in getting him to leave us alone. (He himself apologized later.) While the incident was rather disturbing, it established the fact that we had begun to develop an identity associated with Ban Nǫng Tụn.

On the last day of the festival, we publicly presented the commune headman (*kamnan*) with a sum of money to be used for the school-construction fund. We had indicated to Khun Wichian that we wished to make a donation and had consulted him about how much he felt would be appropriate. The amount we settled upon was more than would be given by any single family in the village, but was not at such a level as to indicate that we were vastly more wealthy than any villager. Not only did we receive public attention for the gift in the village, but Khun Wichian also brought our action to the attention of the provincial governor who had a certificate drawn up acknowledging our contribution towards community development. In retrospect, I think that this contribution represented the first step towards the eventual establishment of ourselves as patrons for the village. But we were not to be cast in this role fully until after we had left the village and then returned to it in another guise. At the time, our donation demonstrated only that we had a particular interest in the welfare of the village of Ban Nong Tun.

Both Jane and I were self-conscious observors of the events of the festival, attempting to record in our notes those aspects of the festival which we felt should be captured for our ethnographic account. We were also aware that our actions were being observed, although at the time we did not think of these observations as involving more than a passing curiosity about two *farang* ("Westerners") strangers. In fact, in addition to its overt ritual functions the festival also had become a rite of initiation for us. Subsequently, villagers would interpret our actions with reference to a knowledge that we had acted in accord with the local ethos, had demonstrated a particular attachment to Ban Nong Tun, and had offered material support for Ban Nong Tun institutions.

Our incorporation into the village became more concrete when, in early April, we finally moved into the expanded village shop which Ngao and Nuan, his wife, had prepared for us. We had consulted with the headman about an appropriate time on which to take up residence and he, in turn, had taken us to an old man who was skilled in astrological and other magical practices. Phonjai ("Grand Father") Siha had determined that Friday (*wan suk*, the day of the planet Venus; the name has homoymic connotations of well-being), the 12th day of the waxing of the moon of the fifth lunar month (i.e., Friday, April 5, 1963) at nine in the morning would be an auspicious time. We moved into Ban Nong Tun as near to that time as we could.

By sharing a residence with Khun Ngao and Khun Nuan, has wife, we acquired kinship-type relationships with them and with Nuan's family who lived next door. According to village custom, one's kinship ties are always conditioned by one's choice of residence. With Ngao and Nuan we became like siblings or siblings-in-law and on occasion I would refer to or call Ngao *phi*, "elder sibling".[4] Mae ("Mother") Hom, Nuan's widowed mother became our most patient, gentle and affectionate guide to village ways. Villagers came to think of us, in some instances, as part of Khun Ngao's household or as part of the extended family which had Mae Hom as its head. We, too, came to feel that Ngao, Nuan, his wife, Mae Hom, and Mae Hom's other children were like relatives acquired according to the normal pattern of post-marital uxorilocal residence as followed in the village.

Our kinship place in the village was also confirmed by one old village man who had been puzzled by the fact that two *farang* should choose to come to live in Nong Tụn. He had been further puzzled when we told him that we had been born in separate societies, Jane in England and I in America. Several months after we had begun to work in the village, he told us that obviously we had been husband and wife in Nong Tụn in a previous existence and had, therefore, been destined to meet and marry, even though we had been born far apart, and, further, that we had been destined to return to the village.

Having established ourselves in the village by virtue of residence and concomitant quasi-kinship connections, we began to participate, insofar as we could, in the normal village activities. Our efforts were welcomed in all spheres. We both joined in rice cultivation work and participated in all rituals. Indeed, my interest in rituals became so well known that, on occasion, monks or lay ritual officiants would wait until I had arrived before beginning or they would even stop in the middle of a ritual to explain to me what had taken place. Jane was instructed in cloth-making, joined other women in collecting insects, aquatic life, and various wild plants and in preparing food for feasts, and was present at births. I was invited to join men in fishing, to assist in making illicit rice wine and rice whiskey, to watch the slaughter of animals and the castration of pigs, and to be present when (illegal) gambling took place.

While villagers came to accept that we had a place in the village through our connections with the families of Ngao, Nuan and Mae Hom, and while our participation in village activities confirmed our village status, villagers remained aware of the fact that we were also *farang* and that we operated not only at the village level but also in other spheres lying beyond the village. The villagers formed a concept of our social identity that took into account our involvement in the other social worlds.

Jane harvesting rice in Ban Nọng Tụn. (1963)

The author harvesting rice under the guidance of Khun Ngao and a village girl. (1963)

Jane being shown how to make rice noodles by Mae Hom. (1963)

FARANG AS A SOCIAL IDENTITY

Prior to our coming to the village, villagers had only vague ideas about the characteristics of *farang*, white Westerners, since they encountered *farang* rarely, if at all. Once we had settled in the village, however, an interpretation of *farang*-ness became essential for them.

We quickly found that the most salient characteristic which villagers ascribed to *farang* was that of being wealthy. All evidence which villagers had available to them confirmed their conviction that *farang* were uniformly rich. Many young men who had been to Bangkok had been struck by the costly clothes worn by *farang* whom they saw there. Even the local *farang* — missionaries, Peace Corps Volunteers, and occasional travellers — were observe to drive motorcycles or jeeps (a term also applied to Land Rovers), to own refrigerators, radios, and watches, or to display other of the outward signs which villagers viewed as marks of wealth. The American-made movies which the majority of villagers had seen, usually in conjunction with a travelling medicine show or a temple fair, had also shown America — the *farang* country *par excellence* — as a vastly wealthy society.

While we could not deny the evidence of the wealth of *farang* which villagers had observed, we tried to live simply to demonstrate that we were not wealthy *farang*. This meant, for example, that when we used Thai canned meat for making curries, as we sometimes did since we could not depend on buying meat in the village and, without any refrigerator, we could not store fresh food bought in the town market for more than a few days, we would dispose of the empty tins inconspicuously in town. Even then, what we discarded from our meals often caused comment. Since there were no orange trees in Ban Nọng Tụn, villagers rarely ate oranges. It was noted with some interest that given the amount of orange peels in the garbage which we put into the pig swill that we must eat oranges quite often (which, in fact, we did). We never brought a radio to the village, but even then, two cameras, a typewriter, and long-burning kerosene lantern all elicited comments regarding our obvious wealth. The most telling fact of all, mentioned a number of times by Khun Ngao and others, was that we must be wealthy since we had been able to afford the costly fare from America to Thailand. We tried to explain that we had been given money by a foundation in order to come to Thailand to carry out research, but our explanations required an understanding of a social world of which villagers had no knowledge. Still, our mode of life in the village did suggest that there were at least differences in the relative wealth of *farang*, and that while we were still rich *farang*, our resources were not of conspicuously vast proportions.

We came to understand that villagers place great value on generosity (*cai kuang*) and considered that the wealthy person who used his wealth only for his own benefit was greedy (*khi niao*), a quality which has the status of a "sin" in Buddhist terms. We were, therefore, expected to share whatever resources we had. When it became known that we had a supply of medicines, those with afflictions sought us out. They recognized that we did not have the medical expertise of the local herbal doctor, or the "injection doctor" who gave shots of penicillin-procaine for almost any ailment, or the nurse in the nearby health center, or the trained nurses and doctors in town. Thus, they did not ask us to treat what they considered to be serious afflictions. But we were expected to dispense asprin, cough medicine, soothing creams (the most popular being mentholatum), and so on. We learned to be careful about making known what we had available lest we should be asked to use up our limited supply of antibiotics and several other medicines which we had brought for our own use. I was somewhat surprised to find villagers asking not only for the tobacco which I used for my pipe, but also to smoke the pipe itself. I thus bought myself a second pipe which I kept available for communal use and also tried to keep cigarettes on supply to offer instead of my pipe. Almost every item which we had in our house, with the exception of our cameras and typewriter, was borrowed at one time or another. One old man, discovering that we drank tea for breakfast (a beverage which was not consumed by anyone else in the village, being too expensive) made it a practice to come to our house early every morning (usually before 6 a.m.) to ask to join us for a cup of tea. There were several villagers who made a regular practice of asking to "borrow" money. Had we ever showed ourselves to be reluctant to comply with these requests, we would opened ourselves to the accusation of being *khi niao*.

While many if not most villagers thought of *farang* as being wealthy, they had, prior to our arrival, little idea about what other attributes a *farang* might have. By observing us in our interactions with other *farang* who came to the village, villagers began to construct a more detailed picture of *farang*-ness, albeit a picture constructed in their own cultural terms. We were visited twice by another graduate student in Anthropology and his presence helped to make our status as students of local customs seem less anomalous to villagers. Another visitor who made a marked impression on villagers was a brother of a friend of ours who had hitchiked around the world and who arrived in Ban Nọng Tụn on a government liquor-distribution truck. His shaggy appearance together with his stories of his adventures gave villagers an image of a different type of *farang*, a type which they would later learn from the radio and other sources to call *hippi*. But even this visit was not nearly so dramatic nor so significant as two other visits to the village by other *farang*, one by a group of American soldiers, and the other by my parents, my sister, and an aunt.

In late May 1963 a group of American soldiers from the Quartermaster Corps established itself in a camp near the town of Mahasarakham. The group caused quite a stir among the villagers for at the camp they saw large vehicles, immense refrigerators, gas storage tanks, and what were then, to their eyes, strange creatures in unfamiliar uniforms. Although within a few years American military personnel were to become a conspicuous part of the scene in northeastern Thailand, in 1963 the build-up of American forces in Thailand had barely begun. By early June some two thousand American troops arrived in the vicinity of Mahasarakham to participate in "Exercise Thanarat" (Thanarat being the surname of Sarit Thanarat, then the Prime Minister of Thailand) sponsored by the Southeast Asia Treaty Organization. For several days, villagers from districts around Mahasarakham literally deserted their communities to watch 600 men parachute with their equipment into an area near Rọi-et (a town some 45 kilometers from Mahasarakham and about 35 kilometers (from Ban Nọng Tụn), to observe mock warfare taking place along the nearby Chi River, and to stare at the tanks, canons, jeeps in camouflage, and GIs waving as they rolled past.

Why the soldiers had come to the area was a complete mystery to most villagers. That such was the case was a surprise to one American lieutenant who told me: "We sent trucks with PA systems to explain about the coming of the troops and why they are here." However, these trucks had travelled only along the major highways, and villagers in most communities had heard only rumors about the exercise. A few thought that the soldiers had come to fight in Laos. Most, however, were quizzical and I was asked over and over again who the soldiers had come to fight. When I tried to explain that they were participating in an "exercise" (*sǫmrop*), only the part of the word which means to fight or to do battle (*rop*) was understood. Thus, the question of whom was the object of military attention remained an open one as long as the troops were in the area.

In conjunction with the exercise, the American Army instituted a Civic Action program to provide people in the areas in which the troops were operating with certain goods and services. The program entailed the distribution of 55 large tanks for storing rain water to rural schools, village temple-monasteries, and rural health centers, provision of some health care services to those who came to field medical centers, and donation of packets of school supplies (notebooks, pencils, a ruler and an eraser) to some thousands of village school children. The communities in the province selected for the program were chosen by SEATO officers (both Thai and American) without any consultation with local officials. These activities had but momentary significance to villagers in the vicinity of Ban Nǫng Tụn, however, for they were soon vastly overshadowed by a much large civic action project instituted in a village about six kilometers away from Ban Nǫng Tụn.

In the wake of the exercise, which ended on June 19, 1963, the 593rd Engineering Company (Construction) from Fort Sill, Oklahoma arrived to carry out several projects in the area. Again, these projects had been determined upon without reference to local officials. They had been planned, we were told, in order to leave a lasting legacy from the troops which had been present in the area. The two major projects included the building of a new school in the chosen village and the construction of an earthen dam nearby.

In a perverse way, the building of the school could not have given villagers any better picture of one aspect of American character − the propensity to do things on a grandiose, Cecil B. DeMille, scale. The school was designed to accomodate 800 students in 20 rooms, replacing a one-room school which had previously enrolled about 100 students. The cost of the materials alone, I was told by the commanding officer, was $25,000; in addition, the building involved two weeks labor by 180 American soldiers flown in with their equipment directly from the U.S. after the exercise was over. Another 20 Americans worked on the dam and an additional 20 Filipino soldiers were attached to the unit to build desks and chairs. The huge expenditure of money and labor in constructing the new school contrasted sharply with those involved in building a local school under Thai Ministry of Education specifications. The cost of building materials for such a school for 200 students would have been about $1,500; labor would have been recruited locally and have cost little. Because a larger school was constructed, it was decided, by military officers, not local education officials, that the pupils would come from seven different villages in the area. When construction of the school was completed, a dedication ceremony was held and was attended by officers from Bangkok and the U.S. Photographs of the project were published in the Bangkok newspapers and, presumably, were sent to Congressmen and Senators in the U.S. so that they could see the concrete results of the money they had allocated. By 1967 when I returned to Ban Nọng Tụn, the American-built school was serving only a single village and enrolment had dropped once again to slightly over 100 students.

During the exercise and especially during the two week period when the Civic Action contingent was stationed nearby, villagers from Ban Nọng Tụn had the opportunity to observe the behavior of a very large number of *farang*. These observations were hindered, however, by the fact that only one of the Americans (and none of the Filipinos) could speak any Thai.[5] Again, the presumption that *farang* were all wealthy was strongly confirmed. Villagers were startled by the amount of meat, canned goods, soda pop, and other expensive food items consumed by the soldiers. Enough tobacco was given away to villagers to keep several villagers supplied for weeks to come, and the discarded C-ration tins quickly found their way into nearly every house for several kilometers around. In addition to their obvious wealth, the soldiers were also observed to have some peculiar habits which villagers quizzed us about. One day we were asked if anybody drank water in America. It turned out that no soldier had been observed to drink water (obviously having been told not to), but drank only liquids (usually soda pop) from tins or bottles. A number of villagers also commented on how loud the soldiers talked and on how easily a number of them lost their tempers (a fight between two soldiers one night having provided a fascinating sideshow for hundreds of villagers).

Villagers also assumed that since we were *farang* we must have some relationship to the American soldiers. It was hard to persuade them that we had no kinsmen among the soldiers. Even after we established this fact, villagers still expected that we could use being a *farang* to gain special favors from the soldiers. Several villager elders, including the headman, kept asking me to make specific requests of the soldiers — to build a new school in Ban Nọng Tụn, to grade the road from the village to the main highway, to provide a water storage tank, and so on. Finally, I consented to contact the commander of the contingent and to ask if he could do anything for the village. The headman and a couple of other villagers went with me to the camp to talk to the commander. While, as I expected, none of the specific requests which villagers had made could be filled, the commander, whom I found to be quite sensitive to contrasts being created between the village in which the school was being built and other villages in the vicinity, did offer to have new desks and tables built for the Ban Nọng Tụn school. About a week later, rather roughly built desks and tables were brought to the village and a small ceremony of presentation was made. In the eyes of the villagers, I had proven, albeit to a very limited extent, that I was capable of being a patron who could provide the village with some tangible benefits.

For Jane's and my part, we found the presence of the American troops, from the first arrival of the group from the Quartermaster Corps until the final departure of the Civic Action Engineering contingent, to be highly disturbing. In a letter to another anthropologist who was working in Thailand at the time, I vented some of my unhappiness about the state of affairs:

> Some anthropologists get amoebic dysentery; some are encamped among hostile natives; some have to live in harsh climatic conditions; but we have to have the American army breathing down our necks. But it is what the soldiers are doing that really gets my ire up. Someone decided that as "repayment" to the people of Thailand for trampling down their rice stalks and putting tanks in the middle of paddy fields and for generally disturbing a rather peaceable community, that a school building in *one* needy village would be a nice idea.

I went on to note that Khun Wichian, the Community Development officer with whom I had been working closely, had observed that "The Americans have made it bit difficult for us to promote the CD ideal of encouraging villagers to help themselves." We did not realize at the time that what we had thought was a temporary, if nonetheless upsetting, intrusion of American soldiers into the lives of rural peoples in Thailand was to become within only a few years a massive fact of life for villagers in neighboring Vietnam and a conspicuous fact for villagers in parts (including much of the Northeast) of Thailand. Being *farang* was to come to be interpreted as not only implying inordinate wealth but also as implicating a seemingly capricious power which could be used either to construct inappropriate edifices or to destroy a village. Fortunately for us, this aspect of *farang*-ness was never ascribed to us by villagers in Ban Nọng Tụn, and save for the incidents which I have described, villagers there had no further traffic with American troops.

At the end of December 1963, my parents, my sister, and an aunt travelled to Thailand to visit us. We had been somewhat apprehensive about this visit for fear that knowing how much such a trip would cost, that villagers would revise upwards their estimates regarding our relatives wealth. However, the visit of my family to the village had a very positive implication for the way in which villagers viewed us.

On the day my family visited Ban Nọng Tụn the central event was a huge feast. The meal included a delicious form of black glutinous rice which had just been harvested, fish caught earlier in the morning, a variety of local dishes which Jane, Khun Nuan, the wife of the family with whom we lived, and Mae Hom had made, and rice wine which Khun Ngao had made. The sharing of food between my family and the family in the village with whom we lived established a bond which has remained to this day with both sides keeping up contact through us. Although my family's visit was very brief, it was sufficient to establish a connection between some villagers and my kinsmen which was not greatly dissimilar to the connection forged between families in different villages who were connected through marriage and the associated wedding rites which also involved the common consumption of food. Our *farang*-ness was no longer so alien.

Although our *farang*-ness had been a given fact prior to our entry into Ban Nọng Tụn, it was only when we became actors in the village context that the nature of our *farang*-ness emerged in the eyes of villagers. By the end of nearly a year in the village, a year climaxed by the visit of my family, it could no longer be assumed that all *farang*, by definition, were rank outsiders. By being *farang*, we were not, thereby, precluded from being actors in the social world of the villagers. Still, we remained *farang* in certain ways. Based on their observations prior to our arrival in the village, on observations which they made of other *farang*, including those with whom we interacted, and on observations of our behavior, villagers continued to attribute to all *farang*, ourselves included, a quality of relatively great wealth. Insofar as we acted in village terms, we were expected to use our wealth in accordance with the value villagers placed on generosity. In addition, being *farang* was also seen by villagers and giving them access to those who commanded certain resources. As the incident in which we were asked by villagers to request benefits from the American Civic Action contingent shows, we were expected to use this access in order to act as patrons for the village. Finally, being *farang* clearly indicated that our action could never be confined to the village social world; we would at some point return to a *farang* world, perhaps never again to return to the world of the village. Even before that happened, we were seen to make periodic trips away from the village, drawn by commitments which were not always fully fathomable by the villagers.

LEAVING THE VILLAGE AND POST-FIELD WORK IDENTITY

Villagers were sensitive to the fact that we did not remain continuously in the village throughout the period of our field work. At times we would retreat to a house which we had the use of in the nearby town of Maha-sarakham. Here we could find time to write up our field notes, write letters, replenish supplies and do other necessary things which we did not have time nor opportunity to do while in the village. More rarely we made trips to Bangkok and to other parts of Thailand. Our trips to Thailand were occasionally rather prolonged when they involved having to deal with visa problems or attending to other matters connected with our research. These extended absences tended to have a rather unsettling effect on our relations with villagers. The first time we returned to the village after having been gone for ten days we were told by several people, including Khun Ngao and the headman, that they had thought that we had returned to America. Similar comments were also made whenever we were gone for any long period. Our trips away symbolized to villagers our attachment to a world, a *farang* world, to which they knew we would eventually return.

This attachment, as both villagers and we ourselves knew, would at some point lead us to bring our residence in Ban Nọng Tụn to an end. We set our departure for early April 1964. Before leaving, we had to dispose of a small number of goods which we did not plan to take with us, the most important being our small motorcycle. We sold the motorcycle to Khan Ngao and gave the rest of our goods to him and to others with whom we had been close in the village. A few people, we heard indirectly, were disappointed by what they got or did not get. For our part, we felt overwhelmed by the generosity of villagers who gave us gifts of silk and cotton cloth, hand made pillows, and even a sack of the local glutinous rice.

Our movement between two worlds was the subject of ritual concern during the last day we spent in the village. The first consideration was to select an auspicious departure date. In fact, the day we settled on was not that which had been recommended by the village astrologer, but one we had insisted on because this day fitted in with our commitments in Bangkok. When we were later robbed in Bangkok, one villager wrote to us that this happened because we left the village on an inauspicious date. Given that nothing more serious happened on our travels back to the States, a more basic aura of moral security must have been provided by the other ritual activities we engaged in prior to departure, including the securing of our "vital essence" or "soul (*khuan*) and the ritual chanting of "auspicious" sutras (*suat monkhon*) by monks. On the afternoon of the last day, a crowd of villagers, led by a ritual specialists, "tied our wrists" (*phuk khaen*) with cotton thread, thus ensuring that our "vital essence" would remain with us during the shock of the major change residence which we were about to undergo. This ritual "securing of the vital essence" (*su khuan*) is essential in northeastern Thai (and in Lao) practice on all occasions when one undergoes a major change in lifeways. In the evening, a number of senior monks whom we had invited from the town and neighboring villages performed the auspicious chanting for our benefit. Following the chanting, a folk opera performance (*mɔlam mu*) was staged at our expense in the grounds of the *wat*. We saw this performance as a small gift which we could make to the villagers as a way of thinking them for their hospitality and cooperation.

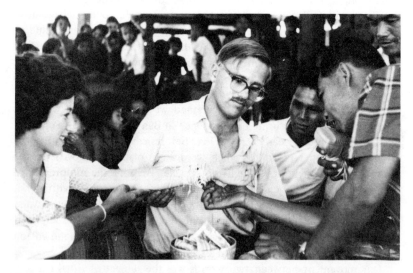

The author and Jane at the ritual "soul-securing" (*sekhuan*) performed just prior to departure from Ban Nɔng Tụn at the end of field work. Khun Wichian is tying Jane's wrist. (1964)

Khun Ngao tying the author's wrist to "secure" his soul at the ritual marking leave-taking from Ban Nọng Tụn. (1964)

The following morning, after we had offered food to the monks, we got into a rented truck with about 20 villagers and went off to the railhead in a town some 90 kilometers away. Villagers stayed with us until we boarded the train, and then they took the truck we had rented back to Ban Nọng Tụn. When we left on that train, both villagers and we believed that we might never have the opportunity to participate again in the same social world. Yet, paradoxically, while we had left the village, our final actions, in the rituals, had served to reaffirm our public commitment to acting in accord with the ethos of the community. Our leaving of the village had reinforced our ties to the village.

In fact, our departure in April 1964 did not mark the end of our involvement in the social lives of Ban Nọng Tụn villagers. Between 1964 and 1967 we kept contact with the village through irregular correspondence with Khun Ngao, the headman of the village, and Khun Wichian. We also sent occasional gifts and photographs to villagers and several of our friends made visits to Ban Nọng Tụn. While our contacts were sporadic, they did serve to affirm our continued interest in and concern for the people among whom we had lived. Then, in mid-1967, funding for a project in northern Thailand made it possible for us to return to Thailand. Even before we went to northern Thailand to begin the project, we made a visit back to

Ban Nọng Tụn. During this trip, we not only renewed personal relationships with villagers and introduced our infant son Nicholas to them, but we also committed ourselves to an action which was to give us a new identity in the eyes of many villagers. We arranged to sponsor the ritual of *thọt kathin*, a ritual at which robes and gifts are offered to the *wat* and the monks at the end of Buddhist lent (which, in 1967, came in November).

In early November 1967 we returned to Ban Nọng Tụn to carry out our ritual commitments. We bought the gifts and food to offer to the monks and to give to guests; we rented equipment to provide electricity and sound in the village for the occasion; we hired a folk opera troupe; and we provided money to be used towards the construction of a new residence for monks. The occasion was not ours alone, however; many others from Ban Nọng Tụn, from neighboring villages, from the town of Mahasarakham (including the mayor, other officials, and teachers), and even from amongst our friends in other parts in Thailand joined in the "making of merit" which a *thọt kathin* involves. In part because we mobilized significant personal resources and in part because we attracted a large number of donors and participations for the *thọt kathin* in Ban Nọng Tụn, we became publicly identified as patrons of the village.

Our altered identity and recognized linguistically by some villagers. Whereas before we had been called by rather informal titles or by our personal names, now we were addressed by many with the status-elevating title of *acan* (Skt. *acarya*), "teacher", or, in my case, as *dọktọ* (English, doctor). This latter title provided recognition of the Ph.D. I had earned, in so small part, because of the dissertation I had written about Ban Nọng Tụn.

For our part, we assumed the role of patron with some self-consciousness, recognizing that it was the only identity which would permit us to show our gratitude for the social acceptance, the active cooperation, and the acts of generosity which villagers had shown toward us. We have continued our role of patron subsequently. Since 1968 we have provided an annual scholarship for pupils from the village who seek to pursue their studies beyond the fourth grade, the uppermost grade in the local school. We have also contracted to buy craft items made by villagers on a number of occasions, in particular in conjunction with collections made for the Burke Memorial Washington State Museum and the American Museum of Natural History.

While to many villagers, particularly the younger ones who had little contact with us during our original stay in 1963-1964, we have become rather remote patrons, we have continued to have much closer relations with the family with whom we lived during our field work. Ngao's house, since 1967 a much larger and more solid building than the one we knew in 1963-1964, has continued to be our home when we visit Ban Nọng Tụn. And when we do stay with Ngao, we do not merely reminisce about "old times" but attempt to fill each other in on the events which have happened since last we met.

The changes have included the birth of a number of children to the two families, two boys in our case and four girls and a boy to Ngao and Nuan, Ngao, we have found, has prospered, having opened a large rice mill and built a larger shop in 1967 and developed a trade in local products which necessitated his buying a truck in 1972. Yet, his prosperity has been marred by troubles and even by tragedy. He suffered a major robbery in 1968 and had to traffic with a number of corrupt officials before he could succeed in seeing the leader of the gang of thieves sentenced to prison. In 1973 Mae Hom, one of her sons, and four other villagers were killed when Ngao's truck (which he was not driving) overturned while taking a group of villagers to a wedding. We ourselves were as shattered by the news of this accident as we would be by the news of a similar calamity befalling any of our own real relatives.

Ngao has attempted to confront the changes in his life not only by managing his affairs as wisely as he can, but also, in recognition of the uncertainty of his own fate, by sponsoring rituals involving both the blessing of his home by Buddhist monks and the securing of the souls of the members of his household. It is indicative, I believe, of the close relationships we have with Ngao and his family that on two occasions, once in 1968 and again in 1973, we have jointly sponsored such rituals.

The bonds formed with Ngao and his family transcend the barriers which are inherent in any social identities, whatever their cultural basis. With others in Ban Nọng Tụn our relationships have been less intense and, consequently, we are viewed more in terms of the cultural glosses placed upon actions than in terms of an emotional significance which cannot be reduced to words. Writing as I do after a four year break in any direct contact with villagers, I am aware that our social identities for most Bang Nọng Tụn villagers may be becoming a part of the history of the village rather than a factor in their on-going social life. On the other hand, circumstances permitting, it might be possible to add yet another chapter to the story I have told here, albeit one which would be conditioned by the chapters which have previously taken place.

CONCLUSIONS

At the outset of this paper, I suggested that the social identities which my wife and I acquired while engaged in field work in Ban Nọng Tụn were not ones which we imposed with reference to what we believed to be our significant attributes but were ones which made sense to villagers in their own cultural terms. To the extent to which ethnographers come to understand their own identities in the field, they also succeed in gaining insights into the culture of the people they are working amongst. The process of recognizing the social basis for one's participant identity is often not easy and may produce an identity crisis as severe as any recognized by psychologists. In our case, such a crisis, despite occasional irritations at the invasion of our privacy, never reached acute proportions. Indeed, it is difficult to say when we came to appreciate that we had accepted village-defined identities for ourselves. However, by the middle of 1963 almost all references to our relations with villagers stop appearing in both my field notes and in our letters to friends and relatives; I had come to take these relations for granted.

Our incorporation into Thai village society was greatly eased, I believe, by the fact that in Thai cultural terms who one is by virtue of one's birth is less important than what one makes oneself through one's actions after birth. This cultural premise, although I cannot develop the argument in this context, is predicated upon the Theravada Buddhist theory of Karma as it has been interpreted by villagers. One's birth (northeastern Thai, *sat*; Central Thai, *chat*; from Sanskrit *jati*) status is by no means totally irrelevant. In our case, the fact that we were *farang* by birth was a conditioning factor to be taken into account by villagers in their efforts to determine our identity. For at least one man, however, this fact could be strongly discounted by postulating that we must have been villagers in a previous incarnation (*sat kọn*). Even for the majority of villagers for whom our being *farang* was significant, what being a *farang* meant could only be ascertained by observing what *farang* do. Since we attempted to act in ways which downplayed the differences between *farang* and Thai, villagers tended to construe our *farang*-ness with reference only to those most conspicuous attributes which knowledge of other *farang*, including of those whom they also saw in the local context, strongly confirmed. In particular, it was generally assumed that *farang* are more wealthy than Thai, and we were not considered as exceptions. In addition, by virtue of being *farang*, villagers recognized, and we could hardly deny it, that we would not remain premanently as actors within Thai society.

Even being *farang*, we could still act like kinsmen vis-à-vis the family of Ngao, Nuan, and Mae Hom and thereby become, and still remain, kinsmen of that family. In this we were no different than a number of villagers who had been "adopted" by other families. Moreover, just as "adopted" kinsmen often retained ties to their natal families without seeming contradiction, so, too, could we be seen as having strong ties to my natal family when my parents, sister and an aunt visited the village without compromising our kinship ties with Ngao, Nuan, Mae Hom and their family.

By acting as villagers in participating in rituals, contributing to the support of local monks, and joining in many normal village activities, we also were considered as villagers. Again, we were no different in this regard from the significant number of villagers who had been born in other communities and who had settled in Ban Nọng Tụn after marriage. However, unlike most of them, we eventually left the village and have not, even on subsequent visits to the village, resumed acting in the ways we did during our first period of field work. We have, thus, ceased to be villagers. Yet, even here we are not dissimilar to some others who have lived in Ban Nọng Tụn and have subsequently left the village. Not only have many males born in the village left after marriage to settle in another village, but there are others who have migrated away permanently to other rural parts of the country or to a town or to Bangkok. Many of those who have left continue to provide support for those in the village, remitting money to parents, providing room and board for village students who continue their education in towns, and making public donations to the village *wat*. Our becoming patrons through the sponsorship of a *thọt kathin* ritual and through subsequent gifts and other benefits extended to the village are clearly recognizable acts in village cultural terms.

In contrast to our actions, the lavish expense for a new school built by the American Civic Action team, although thought by the sponsors to be an act of patronage, was totally incomprehensible in villagers' terms. The Americans who decided on what would be an appropriate civic action to undertake in a village in northeastern Thailand without having any idea of what was significant or in proportion in terms of that village is not dissimilar to the anthropologist who imposes a theoretical framework on ethnographic data without taking into account what is the meaningful basis for action in the community in which the data has been collected. Field work entails the reworking of any and all *a priori* theories with reference to the cultural premises underlying the actual practice of ongoing social life. Such reworking is not merely at an abstract level, but it is intimately connected with what constitutes the social person of the ethnographer himself. Knowing what one becomes by being the observer who is observed in the context of one's own acts can also reveal what are the cultural premises which inform the actions of those one observes.

EPILOGUE

After writing this paper in 1978, I once again had the opportunity to return to Ban Nọng Tụn. In 1979 I made a short visit to the village to arrange for a new stint of field research which I then carried out in the summer of 1980. I was welcomed by Khun Ngao, Khun Nuan, and their children and rejoined them as a relative-of-sorts in their home during my six-week stay. I found that my relationship with Ngao created some problems for me in dealing with a few villagers as the community had become factionalized with Ngao a prominent member of one faction. Factional disputes also colored the patronage role that Jane and I continued to play through the provision of scholarship monies for village children each year; several men let me know that they resented the fact that I channeled the money through Ngao. Still most villagers of both factions seemed pleased that I maintained a continuing interest in them over such a long period of time.

Given the short duration of my field trip in 1980 I tended to spend most of my time with villagers whom I had known well in 1963-1964 (although I did do a survey that entailed interviewing someone from every household). I regretted particularly that I was not able to spend more time talking with young adults, i.e., those who had been children when Jane and I were living in the village. I would have liked to have discovered whether or not their images of us were the same as or different to those of their elders. Since these young adults came of age during a period when *farang* influences were much greater, even in the village, than they had been during their parents' youth, and since they did not interact with us intensively during our first stay, they may well have formed rather different pictures of us as *farang*.

Ban Nọng Tụn villagers no longer draw exclusively on their observations of Jane and myself in constructing interpretations of *farang*-ness. During the decade between mid-1960 and mid-1970, the American bases in the Northeast provided employment for many northeasterners including several from Ban Nọng Tụn. Several other Nọng Tụn-ers, like other villagers from the region, found employment with Americans in Vientiane, Laos, prior to the American withdrawal from that country. One couple in Ban Nọng Tụn had spent twelve years working for American families in Laos and had contemplated passing themselves off as Lao refugees in order to migrate to America. While they did not do so, the woman who had been the youngest school teacher in Ban Nọng Tụn in 1964 did migrate with her husband, who had worked at an American base in Thailand, and her children to Los Angeles in the early 1970s. In 1980 several villagers talked to me about people from other villages in the vicinity who had also gone to live in America. In the past few years an increasing number of *farang* have visited Ban Nọng Tụn, having heard about the village directly from Jane and me or having read something that I have written. Villagers, and especially Khun Ngao to whose house the *farang* visitors typically make their way, thus have had the opportunity to observe the behavior of *farang* at close quarters in much the same way as they had observed Jane's and my behavior. These contacts, together with those of some villagers with Americans on the bases in Laos, have provided windows that did not exist in 1963-1964 that permit views into a wider world in which *farang* play such a conspicuous role.

The new glosses that villagers give to *farang*-ness is a function not only of observations of more *farang* behavior. *Farang*-ness has also taken on new meanings in village culture as a consequence of the pervasive influence America has had on Thailand in the past two decades. This influence is evident in dress styles, in songs popular in the village, in the news heard on the radio, in television programming (television came to Ban Nọng Tụn in 1980 following the electrification of the village), and, probably most importantly, in the school curriculum. These new cultural influences have expanded the horizons of the worldview of many, perhaps most, younger — those under about the age of forty — villagers. This emergent worldview, and the interpretation that those who adopt it give to the actions of the two *farang* ethnographers who lived in Ban Nọng Tụn in 1963-1964 and who have returned from time to time since, has already become a focus of my next phase of research.

NOTES

1. I am very indebted to my wife Jane not only for being my copartner in the ethnographic undertaking discussed below but also for providing me with her invaluable critical comments on the paper.
2. My field work in Thailand in 1962-1964 was supported by fellowships from the Foreign Area Training Fellowship Program.
3. In a survey which I carried out in 1963, I found that 48.5% of all men over the age of twenty had spent significant periods of time living in Bangkok although only one woman (0.7%) had done so. Of the men who had lived in Bangkok, 87.5% were below the age of 40. In 1980 I found that while the percentage of

men over the age of twenty who had worked in Bangkok had apparently complete data may not have been collected) dropped to 38.7%, the percentage of women with similar work experience had increased to 16.7%.
4. Northeastern Thai, like Thai, kin terms for siblings are not differentiated by sex.
5. Villagers were puzzled that the Filipinos could not speak Thai. After all, as one villager said, "they look like Thai."

About the Contributors

David J. Banks received his Ph.D. from the University of Chicago. He is currently Associate Professor of Anthropology at the State University of New York at Buffalo and has done fieldwork in Malaysia in 1967-1968, 1971, 1974, and 1978-79. His book *Malay Kinship in Crisis* is forthcoming.

Allan F. Burns is Associate Professor of Anthropology at the University of Florida. He has done research on contemporary Yucatec Mayan linguistics and folklore and has worked for a private research company as an educational anthropologist. His most recent book is on Mayan narrative — *An Epoch of Miracles* — and his recent work has included the creation of a children's radio program and evaluation of bilingual education programs in Miami.

Currently working on sojourning orientation, marginality, and remigration among recent Tagalog migrants to the U.S.A., *Enya P. Flores-Meiser* is with Ball State University. She received her Ph.D from Catholic University of America and has done fieldwork in Brazil and the Philippines.

Daniel T. Hughes received his Ph.D. from Catholic University of America. Currently Professor and Chair of the Department of Anthropology at Ohio State University, he has both taught and done fieldwork in Micronesia and the Philippines. His fieldwork focuses on traditional and contemporary social and political systems.

Charles F. Keyes is currently with the Department of Anthropology at the University of Washington. He did his Ph.D. work at Cornell University and his fieldwork in Thailand and other parts of Southeast Asia. He is the author of several articles published in U.S. and Thai journals. Among his book is *The Golden Peninsula.*

With a Ph.D. from Lucknow University, *R. S. Khare* is currently Professor of Anthropology at the Unversity of Virginia. He has done several years of fieldwork in India, the latest being in 1978-1980 on the Lucknow Chamars, focusing on food and nutrition among the untouchable women, children, and the aged.

Robert Lawless is Associate Professor of Anthropology at the University of Florida. Holding a Ph.D. from the New School for Social Research, he has done fieldwork in the Philippines and New York City. His most recent book is *The Concept of Culture: An Introduction to the Social Sciences.*

Victor Liguori is Associate Professor of Sociology and Associate Scientist of the Institute of Marine Science at the College of William and Mary. Holding a Ph.D. in anthropology and sociology from Princeton University, he is primarily a maritime anthropologist specializing in commercial fishing communities and fishery technological subsystems.

Professor of Anthropology at the College of William and Mary, *Vinson H. Sutlive, Jr.* completed his Ph.D. at the University of Pittsburgh and has spent 11 years in Sarawak. He publishes in both Iban and English, is editor of the *Borneo Research Bulletin*, and is coeditor of *Studies in Third World Societies.*

Charles Wagley received his Ph.D. from Columbia University and is currently Graduate Research Professor of Anthropology at the University of Florida. A past president of the American Anthropology Association, he has done pioneering fieldwork in Guatemala and Brazil. His most recent book is *Welcome of Tears: The Tapirape Indians of Central Brazil.*

Patricia Synder Weibust received her Ph.D. from Syracuse University after completing fieldwork focusing on schools in a Filipino town. She is currently working as an educational anthropologist in the School of Education at the University of Connecticut. She recently completed a work on Italian-Americans in Connecticut and is doing further fieldwork in a small rural Norwegian community.

Mario D. Zamora is Professor of Anthropology at the College of William and Mary. With a Ph.D. from Cornell, he was Chair of the Department of Anthropology at the University of the Philippines from 1963 to 1969 and then Dean of the University of the Philippines at Baguio City until 1973. He has done fieldwork in India and the Philippines and is coeditor of *Studies in Third World Societies.*